THE HARD WAY AROUND

The Spray *in Australian waters*

The Passages of

THE HARD WAY AROUND

Joshua Slocum

GEOFFREY WOLFF

ALFRED A. KNOPF NEW YORK 2010

THIS IS A BORZOI BOOK
PUBLISHED BY ALFRED A. KNOPF

www.aaknopf.com

Knopf, Borzoi Books, and the colophon are registered
trademarks of Random House, Inc.

Library of Congress Cataloging-in-Publication Data
Wolff, Geoffrey, [date]
The hard way around : the passages of Joshua Slocum /
by Geoffrey Wolff.—1st ed.
p.   cm.
"A Borzoi book"—T.p. verso.
ISBN 978-1-4000-4342-2
1. Slocum, Johsua, b. 1844.   2. Sailors—United States—Biography.
3. Ship captains—United States—Biography.   4. Voyages around the
world—History.   5. Single-handed sailing—History.   6. Liberdade (Ship)
7. Destroyer (Ship)   8. Spray (Sloop)   I. Title.

VK140.S6W65 2010   910.4′1092—dc22   [B]   2010018344

Manufactured in the United States of America

First Edition

FOR TOBY—BROTHER, STORY-ENABLER, FACT-CHECKER
"IN BUCKRAM?"

Yes, the world's a ship on its passage out.

—"The Pulpit," *Moby-Dick*

CONTENTS

PART ONE *Sailing into the World*

PROLOGUE	The Tales He Could Have Told	3
ONE	Unafraid of a Capful of Wind	7
TWO	Coming Aboard Through the Hawse-Hole	13
THREE	Master Slocum	33
FOUR	Love Stories	47
FIVE	Enterprises	61
SIX	*Northern Light*	77
SEVEN	Mutiny	87
EIGHT	Stranding	113

PART TWO *Sailing Around It*

NINE	Salvage	131
TEN	*Destroyer* and Poverty Point	141
ELEVEN	The Great Adventure	157
TWELVE	What Came After	191
	Acknowledgments	215
	Bibliography of Sources Cited	217

Joshua Slocum

The Washington *at Cook Inlet*

ONE

Sailing into the World

Shipwreck at Tierra del Fuego

The Tales He Could Have Told

JOSHUA SLOCUM'S *Sailing Alone Around the World* (1900), his account of his audacious achievement as the first to complete a solo circumnavigation, is a tour de force of descriptive and narrative power. His two previous accounts of his voyages—*The Voyage of the "Liberdade"* (1890) and *The Voyage of the "Destroyer"* (1893)—are less remarkable only for the huge shadow cast by his masterwork. To know what he achieved is to understand why the National Geographic Society, learning about Charles Lindbergh's solo transatlantic flight in 1927, elevated Lucky Lindy to a small pantheon that included such notable voyagers as Dr. David Livingstone, Sir Galahad, and Joshua Slocum. To read Slocum is to understand why George Plimpton, in a charming personal essay about the most intriguing men and women known to history, wrote that Slocum would be one of the few he'd bring back from the grave to share a dinner and conversation. And what Plimpton knew of him didn't include the books that he'd been too busy to write.

Slocum might have made a grand adventure story of daring, catastrophe, and self-salvage from the facts of his honeymoon voyage as master of the *Washington*. Following his wedding in Sydney, Australia, to Virginia—the American daughter of a gold prospector—the couple sailed to Cook Inlet a couple of years after the United States bought Alaska from the Russians. Seward's Icebox (aka Seward's Folly) teemed with salmon that Slocum and his crew meant to catch, and did, but the *Washington* was driven aground and destroyed during a gale. Slocum rescued his crew and their haul by building small boats from the wreckage, then daring to make the difficult passage to Kodiak Island and thence to Seattle and San Francisco, where the fish were sold at a pretty price.

And it would be a thrilling study of enterprise and exotic geography to read Slocum's account of his adventures with the *Pato*, a small packet that he and his family came by in Subic Bay as recompense for the year they spent on a crocodile-infested beach, searching the branches above for boa constrictors and shaking centipedes and scorpions from their boots. Slocum had been hired to build a steamship hull, but instead of his promised payment he was given the *Pato*, without a deck or cabin. Never mind: he built what he needed to float his family and to trade in the Pacific, and soon they sailed the schooner from Manila to Hong Kong and the Okhotsk Sea to fish for cod. Four days before the fishing began, Virginia gave birth to twin girls, but she then stood undaunted at the *Pato*'s rail with her infant son, Victor, hand-lining the huge fish aboard. It was a great catch, and once the *Pato* was so loaded she barely floated, Slocum sailed to Portland, where he sold the fish door-to-door. The twins died. The *Pato* next sailed for Honolulu, where his boat was shown off in an informal race against the fastest packet in Hawaiian waters, and won, whereupon Slocum sold her for a small fortune in gold pieces.

And it should be wished that Slocum had written the serial tragedy of his voyages with his family aboard the *Northern Light,* the apogee of his merchant-shipping career. At Hong Kong in 1881, aged thirty-seven, he became one-third owner and master of "this magnificent ship, my best command," as he uncharacteristically boasted. The medium clipper *Northern Light,* built eight years before and after the age of clipper ships had passed, had a length of 233 feet, a beam of 44, and three decks. It was not only huge, spreading acres of canvas, but also built to demand attention: "I had a right to be proud of her," Slocum wrote, "for at that time she was the finest ship afloat."

Students of tragedy will recognize these words as a foreshadowing prologue, the pride that cometh before the proverbial sad headline. Slocum's hubris at first seemed justified as the *Northern Light* sailed to Manila, Liverpool, and New York, where her progress up the East River was blocked by the Brooklyn Bridge. She had to have her topmasts dismantled to pass under this monumental connection in the web of land routes and steam-powered conveyances that were rushing together to end Slocum's calling.

Having refurbished his ship, Slocum began his voyage to the Pacific with a crew that makes of "motley" an encomium. They got as far as New London, Connecticut, before the *Northern Light* exhibited a character flaw, the failure of her rudder. The crew mutinied. The Coast Guard intervened, but not before a mutineer stabbed the first mate to death.

Slocum wrote about none of this, nor about forging ahead with the same awful crew, seeing the prophetic Great Comet of 1882, and passing near Krakatoa after its initial eruptions in May 1883 and before its final cataclysm in August but in time to sail into a sea of boiling pumice. He did commit to paper his rescue of Gilbert Island missionaries adrift for more than forty days in an open boat, and his transport of these grateful castaways to Yokohama, where he attempted unsuccessfully to have members of his restive crew removed. He sailed on for the Cape of Good Hope, where the ship's rudderhead—the same mechanism that had brought such dismay near New London—twisted off. Huge seas then opened other weaknesses of hull structure, and only furious pumping kept the ship afloat, till the pumps' slowing discharge was noticed, a trickling brown syrup as thick as molasses, which in fact was what they were pumping—a gummy slurry of the hold's cargo of sugar and seawater.

In newspaper interviews and court depositions, Slocum did record what befell him next. He reached a lucky haven in Port Elizabeth, where the *Northern Light* was patched up and he hired as a mate an ex-convict, Henry Slater, who was traveling under forged papers. Sailing for New York, the crew again mutinied, and Slater was put in irons and confined to the hold on a diet of bread and water for fifty-three days. Upon arrival, Slater was freed and Slocum arrested, charged with excessive and unjust punishment of his prisoner. The trial was theatrical, with reversals of fortune and conflicting testimony, and the *New York Times* editorial page, rushing to misjudgment, vilified Slocum as a barbarian unfit to command a ship. He was fined and lost his ownership of the *Northern Light,* which was worth less in any case than repairs to her hull and rigging would cost. She was dismasted, sold as a coal barge, and tugged port to port by a steamboat, sooty as the dust clouds from Krakatoa.

It's no wonder Slocum didn't wish to tell this sad tale, which nevertheless deserves telling. What he did write was more than enough to secure his standing as a great writer, navigator, and adventurer, our American Sinbad. The historian Bruce Catton wrote of him in 1959 that it was fitting to "mention Slocum on the same page with Columbus, because all true voyages of discovery are basically alike." And what makes a voyage "true"? Above all, it must be inward, "concerned first of all with something in himself, if it be nothing more than the conviction that if he searches long enough he can make the world give him something he has not yet had."*

*Bruce Catton, "Mariner's Quest," *American Heritage* (April 1959).

Brier Island Bootery

Unafraid of a Capful of Wind

In the fair land of Nova Scotia, a maritime province, there is a ridge called North Mountain, overlooking the Bay of Fundy on one side and the fertile Annapolis valley on the other. On the northern slope of the range grows the hardy spruce-tree, well adapted for ship-timbers, of which many vessels of all classes have been built. The people of this coast, hardy, robust, and strong, are disposed to compete in the world's commerce, and it is nothing against the master mariner if the birthplace mentioned on his certificate be Nova Scotia. I was born in a cold spot, on coldest North Mountain, on a cold February 20, though I am a citizen of the United States—a naturalized Yankee, if it may be said that Nova Scotians are not Yankees in the truest sense of the word. On both sides my family were sailors; and if any Slocum should be found not seafaring, he will show at least an inclination to whittle models of boats and contemplate voyages. My father was the sort of man who, if wrecked on a desolate island, would find his way home, if he had a jack-knife and could find a tree. He was a good judge of a boat, but the old clay farm which some calamity made his was an anchor to him. He was not afraid of a capful of wind, and he never took a back seat at a camp-meeting or a good, old-fashioned revival.

—JOSHUA SLOCUM

THUS BEGINS *Sailing Alone Around the World,* and who could stow more tightly the essentials of his origins? Insistently laconic and instinctively musical, Joshua Slocum's sly prose exposes the writer's history and circumstances even as it casually hides emotional turbulence. His narrative art, in harmony with his temperament, profits from a wholesome tension between candor and reticence. It is not incidental that the greatest memoirs—*The Education of Henry Adams,* say, or Nabokov's *Speak, Memory*—share this friction between warring impulses. The wary but exuberant course of Slocum's exposition (from the subtle boast of "nothing against the master mariner if the birthplace mentioned" into the flat declarative sentence that follows, "I was born in a cold spot") effortlessly slips character into the skin of style. Slocum kept faith in the surface integrity of such available data as time, latitude and longitude, wind strength, wave height, and the mathematically measurable relation between celestial objects. This confidence was never undermined but always complicated by his acceptance of the consequence of the unseen—shoals, submerged hazards, confused seas, tidal rips—and the latent power of the unsaid.

Foremost among the missing from Slocum's capsule account of his earliest history is his mother, whom he adored and who died in 1860 when he was sixteen, causing him to run off to sea and stay there. Fine features, notably alert eyes, and an aura of tenderness and encouragement commend the little that is known of Sarah Jane Southern, who was eighteen when she married John Slocombe (the family name before Joshua hitched a reef in its spelling). She was remembered by a family member as delicate and frail, with too many babies coming too frequently; Joshua was the fourth of her eleven children, born between 1834 and 1860. Her father was the keeper of the Southwest Point Light on Brier Island, at Westport, the treacherous Atlantic Ocean entrance to the Bay of Fundy, and it was to Westport that the family moved when John Slocombe's fruitless labors to plow a living from that wind-blasted clay farm finally became an anchor that he cut loose.

This was no casual figure of speech, inasmuch as Joshua himself failed—less with resentment than with resignation—at farming on Martha's Vineyard after his solo circumnavigation, thereby spitting up the anchor he had tried to swallow. He knew how to farm: his father had put him behind the harrow when he was six, steering a gray horse that was blind in one eye. "Advanced in usefulness," as his own son would remark, the child could shoe a horse before he could read. He just didn't want to shoe a horse, no more at age sixty than at six. His happy memories of the North Mountain farm, if seldom voiced, were ungrudging. Slocum fondly remembered being able on clear days to see from this altitude as far as New Brunswick, with a spectacular view of the Bay of Fundy two and a half miles distant. An enterprising reporter, David T. Hugo, traveled during the 1960s from Martha's Vineyard to Slocum's childhood farm with a view to interviewing someone who might have known the legendary mariner, and was put in touch with Charles

Barteaux, at that time ninety-three. With Barteaux at his side, Hugo marveled at the view. "Yes, but you can't eat it," responded his guide. Overhearing the exchange, the current owner of the farm, plowing his field, said he'd gladly trade the view for better soil.*

Nostalgia had an uphill climb in such a place. It was a rare eruption of ecstatic recollection that in 1902 caused Slocum to invoke with such pleasure a homestead not much superior to a pioneer's rough cabin. He told a magazine interviewer of the huge fireplace that provided heat. "And what good things to eat came from those old fireplaces—oh! Those barley cakes and those buckwheat flapjacks—oh!" Thus his only tribute—forty-two years after her death—to his mother.

His father—six feet tall and two hundred pounds—was severe, embittered, self-righteous, and self-pitying. He was brutal, too, without tolerance for the inclinations of others. A deacon of the Brier Island Methodist Church, this evangelist's zeal did much to animate Slocum's contempt for cocksure missionaries and blustering preachments of all kinds.

More immediately, his father's retreat to Westport ended Slocum's formal schooling in the third grade. The one-room school at Mount Hanley, almost contiguous with the Slocombe farm, is now a museum. It was a happy place to have studied, run by a superintendent locally celebrated for his innovation. But now the child, ten, commenced (at his father's command) full-time Dickensian labor. John Slocombe, like many coastal farmers, had spent winter months cobbling shoes, tedious piecework. Not exactly a blacking factory, his boot shop, a converted fish shack perched on a wharf, was if anything worse than the shoe-polish warehouse where Dickens was sent to work writing and affixing labels at the age of twelve. Situated harborside, the better to torment young Slocum with a tempting view of coastal cargo carriers and fishing smacks, the sweatshop fabricated knee-high cowhide boots for local fishermen. Slocum worked ten hours a day, paid only room and board. He soaked stinking hides in stinking vats. "Pickling" this was called, the skins drenched in an odious mixture that frequently included urine, offal, brains, chrome, and noxious acids. This stew softened the hides, but before the leather could be stretched over lasts it needed "scudding," the removal with a dull blade of bits of hair and flesh. It was then the boy's

*David T. Hugo, "Nova Scotia to Martha's Vineyard: Notes on Captain Joshua Slocum," *The Dukes County Intelligencer* (August 1969).

duty to stitch the boot, each stitch individually knotted with waxed thread. He would then fasten the boot's thick soles with hand-whittled wooden pegs driven one by one—many, many—into awl bores by his cobbler's hammer as he sat bent-backed, squinting and pounding.

Young Slocum became handy with an awl, and with a jackknife. An unacknowledged catastrophe is hidden in the charming reference above to his father's ingenuity, that he could make it home from a desolate island if given only a knife and a tree. With something like his own cast-away's incentive to escape, at twelve or so the boy stole time from his sweatshop grind to whittle and construct a ship model, an elaborate likeness of a finely rigged clipper. The Slocombe house near the boot shop had a cellar, and there he built the model on the sly and there his father caught him at it. Victor, the eldest of Joshua's four children who survived infancy, describes this appalling scene in his 1950 biography of his father,* who was "putting the finishing touches on [the] ship model which had taken many furtive moments to make." John Slocombe thrashed the boy for his devil's work, for wasting time on useless fancies, mere vice, vanity. "John was of the old-fashioned Methodist type . . . a powerful exhorter of the sinful, as though there was any temptation on Brier Island to worry about." He raged at his son, tearing the delicate ship from his hands, and hurling it on the floor and crushing it under his sturdy hand-lasted boots.

When one reads of Slocum's later wrecks and strandings, his dismastings and gale-shredded sails, it is as tempting to imagine his shock at the first devastation to a vessel under his command as it is instructive later to learn with what equanimity he accepted calamity. Victor wondered why Joshua's recollection of his father's brutality never seemed "greatly resented by his son . . . who rather regarded it as a just exercise of parental authority . . . I have heard him tell his mates about it at the cabin table. They thought it was pretty rough."

Rough was how it was in "Nova Scarcity," up there in extremis, with hard soil, hard weather, and hard Bay of Fundy tides. The Slocombes—originally settlers in the Massachusetts Bay Colony from England—were among five hundred nominal Loyalist refugees banished to Digby Island in 1783, where they were granted five hundred acres. The Slocombes

---

*Victor Slocum, *Capt. Joshua Slocum: The Life and Voyages of America's Best Known Sailor* (Sheridan House, 1950).

were in fact Quaker pacifists—enemies of war—rather than supporters of King George, but according to whatever principle or purpose, they were naysayers even to Revolutionary naysayers. They were tough and needed to be. Self-reliant and hardy, they accepted with pride the ethnic and cultural tag "bluenose," applied to Slocombes. (Joshua's grandfather was known as "John-the-Exile" after fleeing Massachusetts and the prospect of being drafted into either the Continental Army or King George's Redcoats.) It is a testimony to Slocum's empathy that at fifty-four he wrote an uncharacteristically revealing outburst to his cousin Joel: "Poor father! What a load he carried and how he grubbed a living, for us all, out of the old clay farm. And how I've seen him break down when he came back to the 'Family Altar' after the season of laying it aside . . . and cry Father, Father!"

Born into a stoic culture, he wasn't about to complain, yet as Walter Teller,* his earliest biographer, concluded, he was "one of the breed who struggle against the world's arrangements." This characterization requires modification, for Slocum not only accepted but welcomed that branch of cosmic governance ruled by nature. A boy growing up within sight and smell of the ferocious Bay of Fundy tides—violently ebbing and flowing as much as forty-eight feet between low and high, the oceans' most extreme rise and fall, stirred by whirlpools and beset by standing waves—couldn't walk along the beach without learning quickly to understand the consequences of such immense pulls of moon and sun. He would have been alert to the effects of wind blowing across water, heard the far-off "rote" or roar of seas breaking, read signs in the sky for premonitions of trouble, accepted the menace of fog, smelled the aroma of seaweed at low tide, experienced the dangers of hypothermia, heard stories of sailors lost to bad luck or bad judgment.

Bad luck was a tricky question, and some born sailors tried to dodge happenstance by ritualized superstition while others accepted it with an attitude akin to sangfroid, if not derision. The polar explorer Vilhjalmur Stefansson, taking a hard line on roller-coaster rides of luck, maintained that the experience of "adventure" at sea was merely a confirmation of incompetence and improper preparation.

---

*Much is known of Slocum's history, owing to his books and letters, the biography written by his eldest son, Victor, and notably Walter Teller's works. Teller's research for the first version of his biography—*The Search for Joshua Slocum*—was prodigious; after that book was published in 1953, new material flooded to the author, who used it to publish a revised version in 1978.

Instruction in kismet was quotidian along the Bay of Fundy. Like most of his fellow dwellers on the Nova Scotia shore, Slocum purposefully did not learn how to swim, on the theory that pathetically dog-paddling against the sea's freezing inhospitality was folly, and that being unable to swim would encourage a sailor neither to fall overboard—likely weighed down by oilskins and seaboots—nor to err in seamanship and sink. How to keep his footing aboard, and how to understand where in the world he happened to be, were the lessons he set out to learn at sixteen, when he left for good both his father and Nova Scotia, escaping to sea. Unlike Orpheus fleeing Hades, he needed no warning: Joshua Slocum would not look back.

TWO

Coming Aboard Through the Hawse-Hole

> The wonderful sea charmed me from the first. At the age of eight I had already been afloat along with other boys on the bay, with chances greatly in favor of being drowned. When a lad I filled the important post of cook on a fishing-schooner; but I was not long in the galley, for the crew mutinied at the appearance of my first duff, and "chucked me out" before I had a chance to shine as a culinary artist. The next step toward the goal of happiness found me before the mast in a full-rigged ship bound on a foreign voyage. Thus I came "over the bows," and not in through the cabin windows, to the command of a ship.
>
> —*Sailing Alone Around the World*

JOSHUA SLOCUM BUILT his first sailing vessel while he was still on the farm up on the windward side—the cold, barren, snow-holding side—of North Mountain, from which he was forcefully reminded of the theatricality of the Bay of Fundy. Sea smells were stirred by the tide and driven to him by gusts, and he could sometimes hear waves breaking against the rocky headlands. When the dense fog burned off, he could even see the sea. No older than eight, by the shore of a tiny millpond set a mile downhill at the edge of the farm, he lashed together three stout fence rails to make a raft and rigged this with a fence-rail mast, to which he attached bed-linen rags. Thus, downwind, he made his first shore-to-far-shore crossings. (Transatlantic sailors refer to their enterprise, when successful, as "crossing the pond.") This was his introduction to boat building, and to the lesson that sailing "downhill," as they say, was fun and fast; poling back upwind was a drag.*

Later, when he got a rare break from pegging boots at the Westport

---

*Up on North Mountain, local tradition holds that Slocum made an even earlier voyage across the millpond paddling a washtub.

Joshua Slocum's Liverpool

Joshua Slocum's San Francisco

shack, he would fish for cod or mackerel in local waters aboard neighbors' smacks, affording many an opportunity to be drowned. Slocum was determinedly ironic about his inability to swim. In *Sailing Alone Around the World* he wrote about an event that occurred forty years after he became a professional sailor, when he ran the *Spray* aground off the coast of Brazil; trying to kedge her off using an anchor that he had rowed to seaward and hurled from a dory, he managed to capsize the dory, an alarming development: "I grasped her gunwale and held on as she turned bottom up, for I suddenly remembered that I could not swim."

To live in such a busy harbor as Westport at that time was to be soaked in maritime history, lore, diction, and tempting opportunity. Along the Nova Scotia coastline were riggers and coopers, blacksmiths and fish brokers, sail lofts and chandleries, the whole culture dominated by seamen. It can't be overstressed how busy maritime commerce was in the mid-nineteenth century. Down the coast and up the Penobscot River at Bangor, Maine, three thousand ships arrived in 1860, sixty during Bastille Day of that year on a single incoming tide, in the space of two hours. These were mostly lumber schooners, akin to the deal drogher Slocum would presently board. "Sail was everywhere," as Peter H. Spectre wrote in the magazine *Maine Boats, Homes & Harbors*. "Cargo carriers, passenger packets, fishing craft—there were so many at any one time that the waters were white with sails. The coast was like a huge highway of sail." The lighthouse keeper at Owl's Head, on Penobscot Bay, counted during 1876 more than sixteen thousand schooners from his vantage. "Just schooners. That figure does not include sailing vessels of other rigs." Spectre doubts the accuracy of that census, hypothesizing that the keeper stepped outside once an hour to count. Becalmed schooners, or those breasting a tidal current, would have been counted more than once, especially on a clear day. So Spectre halves the number, and halves it again. Four thousand schooners in one year, more than ten each day, summer and winter.

But more crucial than the ubiquity of vessels in fashioning Joshua Slocum's ambition would have been his contacts with neighbors and the sons of neighbors returned from voyaging. There were so many opportunities to go to sea—fishing, whaling, coastal carriage, long-haul trade to India, China, the West Indies, and Europe, not to mention naval service—that a Westport boy would have had to search for a reason to reject the call. In *Live Yankees: The Sewalls and Their Ships,* W. H. Bunting quotes a man who grew up during the age of sail on midcoast Maine's Kennebec River: "Many boys that we knew went off in the ships and came back perhaps in a year or two for a little stay in town, swaggering a good deal and telling . . . tales of spice-lands and strange foreign cities— of Lima and Callao, and 'Frisco' and South Seas, and adventures in the 'Roaring Forties.' " And for the young adolescents of Westport, who might a century later have traded opinions and debated the merits of a Chevy flat-six against a Ford V-8, their preoccupation was with the sail plans of barks and brigantines, the properties of oak versus cedar for planking.

At thirteen, sick of tanning hides and of having his own tanned for building his ship model, he ran off to sea as a so-called peggy (probably from having to peg away at menial chores) on a fishing schooner, having claimed he could cook, not that it mattered much to the vessel's master. In the nineteenth century, cooks—at the bottom of the shipboard pecking order—were often sailors who had lost a limb or an eye, fitting them for nothing useful. But even by these lax standards, Slocum's performance at the cookstove was derisory (he "couldn't cook hot water for a barber's shop," in a contemporary taunt), and when his ship returned to port in Westport he was jettisoned, to return hangdog to his mother, yet another thrashing from his father, and three more years of pickling and whacking.

For an ambitious boy perched on the tip of an island on the quiet side of the Bay of Fundy, the options were few. He could try farming, but he'd seen more than he wanted of the back end of a worn-out plow horse. Working in the boot shop was a bitter daily lesson in the limits of commerce in Nova Scarcity. He could fish, if only he could afford to buy his own smack. When his mother died in 1860—four days before he turned sixteen—he made good his escape. His failure as a peggy had taught him that seagoing was drudgery. But anyone with a hobby, or a weakness for playing solitaire, will understand that to impugn an experience of drudgery—without specifying its precise nature—is less than useful. Gathering eggs from chickens is drudgery marginally less taxing, for some, than feeding chickens. Pegging boots is drudgery, for sure. So is beating upwind, tacking back and forth against a foul tide, but many people dream about spending every discretionary dollar they possess— and usually more—to make that drudgery possible.

Going to sea was a fine education for many kids from Nova Scotia and New England. In Saigon or Manila, Yokohama or Batavia, Archangel or Calcutta, the Fijis or Rio, the Moluccas or the Spice Islands, they might expect to run into friends from Searsport or Bath, Halifax or Digby Island. They were rescued from provincialism, not that white-man's-burden jingoism wasn't epidemic in the nineteenth century, when North Americans collided with Heathen Chinee and ignoble savages inhabiting the wild waters of Tierra del Fuego. British sailors especially were quick to describe East Indians as "tinted Baboos" or "snuff and butter jelly bellies." But young sailors—those with open eyes and ears—learned to cook and eat foreign food, to wear and appreciate foreign clothes, to play foreign games, to understand the singularity of the world's people.

As Slocum elliptically summarizes his situation in the sketch above, he began his career "before the mast," though "full-rigged ship" might leave a grander impression than the facts warrant. In Saint John, New Brunswick, Slocum and a friend from Brier Island shipped aboard a deal drogher, bound for Dublin, as ordinary seamen. There was great demand in Europe—whose forests had been felled relentlessly—for wood from North America. Millions of board feet from Port Medway, Nova Scotia, were rafted downriver in spring or skidded over the ice to be loaded aboard square-riggers, scores at a time loading in ports within a hundred miles of Westport.* "Deal" was rough-cut dimensioned lumber (fir or pine timber, nine by three inches, to be cut to the required length at its destination), and "drogher" was a term of contempt—"half-tide rock" was another—for a cheaply cobbled, worn-out, and leaky ship, despised by sailors not only for trying unavailingly to sink (failing only because of the buoyant cargo stacked in the hold and chained on deck) but also because an ordinary seaman, in order to keep the sea from swamping his bunk, had to spend more than a little time manning the pumps. At that, Slocum's first ship was better than many deal droghers, some no better than rafts with trees for masts and rags for sails. Some coastal tubs carrying long lumber down the Penobscot River from Bangor were so overloaded that they barely made it to port, their hulls submerged and the

*See Joseph E. Garland's *Lone Voyager,* his account of the remarkable solo sailing feats of Howard Blackburn, for detailed descriptions of conditions in the Maritime Provinces during Slocum's boyhood.

helmsman—who couldn't see forward over the woodpile—up to his knees in water.

Slocum went to sea with relish. After all, during his most impressionable years of boyhood, he had listened to sagas not only of the young sailors visiting home in Westport but also of the heroic and record-breaking passages of Cape Horn clippers carrying prospectors to the gold fields of California.* He would have heard the warnings—that to break those speed records masters ran hell ships, driving their vessels mercilessly and their crews brutally—but also of the fabulous paydays earned by captains who rounded the Horn. And he meant to be a captain. He knew himself. He *would* be a captain. Yet what Joshua Slocum could not have known in 1860 was that the glory days of sail—fleets of rake-hulled, towering-masted, overcanvased, overdriven clippers—had already ended.

As his son Victor writes, from the perspective of an American merchant seaman, halfway through his biography of his father:

> Our proud fleet of clipper ships was an anachronism. It was out of date as early as the fifties, for while American investors in marine securities were sentimentally applauding skysails, stunsails and fast passages around Cape Horn, the only importance of the clipper ship to us was that it was the culminating expression of our own national sea-mindedness before it went into decay. It is true that this was a glorious period of marine supremacy, but that is all the good it did us; and the sweeping of the seas with unrivaled tonnage and of the skies with unmatched clouds of towering canvas was only an idle boast.

The years of great prosperity for American (and maritime provincial) shipbuilding ran from 1840 to 1858, two years before Slocum's embarkation. Across the Bay of Fundy in New Brunswick, at Saint John, they were cranking out miles of wood deal droghers, clumsy "Saint John's Spruce Boxes." But in Europe, by 1860, iron was replacing wood in shipbuilding, and steam was replacing sail. Nothing in Joshua Slocum's

---

*Herman Melville wrote a five-line cautionary poem—"Old Counsel of the Young Master of a Wrecked California Clipper"—addressed to young sea-struck romantics:

> Come out of the Golden Gate,
> Go round the Horn with streamers,
> Carry royals early and late;
> But, brother, be not over-elate—
> *All hands save ship!* has startled dreamers.

history suggests that he could have tolerated the culture of the iron steamship, stinking of coal, burning the eyes with cinders, and requiring the ordinary seaman to chip rust hour upon hour in the dank prison of the hold. No: Slocum's craft had to be fashioned of wood and driven by wind.

In 1924 Joseph Conrad, in one of the pieces collected in his *Last Essays,* sounded a sentimental elegy for the life to which Slocum had been called:

> The last days of sailing ships were short if one thinks of the countless ages since the first sail of leather or rudely woven rushes was displayed to the wind. Stretching the period both ways to the utmost, it lasted from 1850 to 1910. Just sixty years. Two generations. The winking of an eye. Hardly the time to drop a prophetic tear. For the pathos of that era lies in the fact that when the sailing ships and the art of sailing them reached their perfection, they were already doomed. It was a swift doom, but it is consoling to know that there was no decadence.

Citing only the abuse of sailors by shipmasters, there was decadence aplenty, but even if Slocum had been able to foresee the death of his chosen life at its commencement, what might he have done differently? Doesn't everyone know that in our beginning is our end? But *So what* doesn't account for his plunge off the deep end. Almost any calling that might be considered—poet or autoworker or jazz pianist—seems from the perspective of common sense to be quixotic and probably doomed. Maybe it *is* enough to say *So what?*

Still, to reach the head of the worm-eaten mast soon destined to break off at its base, Slocum had to begin to climb. In contrast to midshipmen in merchant shipping (apprentice sailors who had paid to come "in through the cabin windows" and learn the ropes), ordinary seamen ("in by the hawse-hole," referring to the foul place in the bow through which the anchor chain passed) were the roughest of grunt laborers. This made Slocum's rapid rise through the ranks notable. He would later take greater pride from his rapid elevation at seventeen to second mate than from anything else in his career.

One of the first to have boarded quayside in Saint John, Slocum watched his fellow ordinary seamen delivered drunk to the drogher by a shipping agent, wheeling them piled like cordwood on an open cart. This forecastle crew were recruited or shanghaied by so-called crimps, who used booze and gambling and whores to put them in debt, and they made rough companions. Hungover and seasick during their first days at sea, they nevertheless knew how to keep a ship afloat.

Samuel Eliot Morison, in his *Maritime History of Massachusetts,* describes the society Slocum had just joined. In 1860 potential seamen with grit and ambition—perhaps less parochial than Joshua Slocum— had options conceivably more attractive than being bounced around the hard ocean: to the west fertile land could be cultivated and gold found for the grasping in California and Australia. Steam was replacing wind as a motive force, so extreme methods were used to gather sailing men: "boarding-house keepers [made] it their interest to rob and drug seamen in order to sign them on," pocketing a fee of three months' advance wages. "The percentage of foreigners and incompetents increased. Men of all nations, and of the most depraved and criminal classes, some of them sailors but many not, were hoisted, literally dead to the world, aboard the clippers. Habitual drunkards formed the only considerable native element in this human hash."

In 1860 Slocum's merits and steady temperament immediately stood out from the rude cohort with whom he bunked, ate, and slaved. He had shipped aboard because he wished to, with his eyes open. In his *Journal of a Tour to the Hebrides,* Samuel Johnson asserted that "no man will be a sailor who has contrivance enough to get himself into a jail; for being in a ship is being in a jail, with the chance of being drowned . . . A man in a jail has more room, better food, and commonly better company." This chestnut has the sour taste of a last word on the subject, yet young men continued to flock to harbors from inland farms and cities as well as coastal settlements. For all the notoriety of crimps, for all the warnings of misery publicized in Richard Henry Dana Jr.'s runaway best seller, *Two Years Before the Mast* (1840), North America had not run out of suck- ers or quixotics. In 1860 much commerce was still done by small coastal schooners run modestly but considerately, like family businesses, so that shipping out on a deal drogher might be said to be akin to volunteering to work on a chain gang, with the supplemental hazards that Johnson specified, and perhaps this argues against the liveliness of Slocum's wits. But in fact the young sailor soon showed himself to the ship's officers to be intelligent and ambitious. He was invited to steer the yawing, sluggish vessel, a mark of respect and confidence that freed the nominal helms- man to perform other chores, and was trusted with the wheel as the cumbersome ship picked up Poolbeg Light and entered Dublin harbor.

Determined now to see the world, Slocum signed off the drogher in Dublin and embarked by paid packet to Liverpool, hub of the world's shipping commerce, crowded with every kind of ship and sailor. He spent two weeks along the River Mersey, sightseeing as far as London, and looking to find a berth aboard an East Indiaman, the ships that traded between England, India, and China, across every ocean that had harbors with people selling or buying, ships routinely doubling Cape Horn and the Cape of Good Hope, well named "Cape Stiff" and "Cape of Storms."

If it sounded romantic, it was. It also bristled with menace, almost worse ashore than at sea. Slocum, young as he was and so lately without a horizon wider than what could be seen from atop North Mountain, nevertheless knew enough to shun brotherhood in the prevailing society of "packet rats," those Victor Slocum described as "a degenerate type of seamen who swarmed on the emigrant and clipper ships" of the day. These gathered in Liverpool's Merseyside singing houses and grog shops, at fandangos and donkey races, patronizing the whorehouses of every major port, each well equipped to skin a fellow seaman of his wages and bleed him white—often literally—into "buckets of blood," waterfront saloons. To understand the image that this sort meant to project in their self-celebration, it is useful to recall some of the tamer verses of Barnacle Bill's address to a fair young maiden:

It's only me from over the sea,
Said Barnacle Bill the Sailor
I'm all lit up like a Christmas tree,
Said Barnacle Bill the Sailor.
I'll sail the seas until I croak
I'll fight and swear and drink and smoke
But I can't swim a bloody stroke,
Said Barnacle Bill the Sailor.

I'll come down and let you in!
I'll come down and let you in!
I'll come down and let you in!
Cried the fair young maiden.

Well hurry before I bust in the door,
Cried Barnacle Bill the Sailor.
I'll rip and rave and rant and roar,
Cried Barnacle Bill the Sailor.

I'll drink your wine and eat your pies,
I'll spin you yarns and tell you lies,
I'll kiss your cheeks and black your eyes,
Said Barnacle Bill the Sailor.

"Me and my crew, we're here for a screw; I just got paid and I wanna get laid" is the gist of this bawdy ballad, created in honor of a very ordinary seaman of the 1850s variously believed to have shipped from Liverpool or San Francisco.

It is tempting to deplore the character of sailors in Slocum's time. But years later, writing the ending of *Sailing Alone Around the World,* Slocum recalled fondly that aboard ship "I did not live among angels, but among men who could be roused. My wish, though, was to please the officers of my ship . . . and so I got on." As to the nature of those "men who could be roused," Alan Villiers, an Australian master mariner who went to sea at fifteen in 1918 and wrote as well as anyone about his calling in *The Way of a Ship,* lovingly idealized the ones who were happy with their low status and articulate only among their own kind:

> Whatever the hardships of the life and regardless of the amount of heartless exploitation they might have suffered, those men were of a type which has now [1953] been destroyed . . . They asked very little and they were prepared to give a great deal, even their lives. The amount of work they did and the degree of hardship they accepted, in the movement of wind-propelled cargos about the free waters of the world, is now incredible. They responded magnificently to reasonable treatment, and a ship and her officers had to be bad indeed before they thought of giving anything but their best. They were fearless aloft and fearless on deck, indefatigable and splendidly competent . . . Good ships they swore by, and poor ships they cursed.

A corrective is necessary. While to bring a huge sailing vessel safely around the notorious capes of the extreme latitudes—dodging icebergs and such—inspires awe, Conradian literary conceits too often rise to the extravagant occasions of gales and sixty-foot seas, no less in the literature of experienced seamen than in the bloated rhetoric of adventure romancers, who are left without a treasure store of metaphors when the sea is well behaved.

A hard line is taken against the nature of shipmates by Jan de Hartog, the Dutch fisherman and sailor (and, later, theologian), who ran away to sea five years younger than Slocum. In *A Sailor's Life* (1955), looking back at the putative tragedy of steam's ascendancy as a degrading influence on the culture of the seaman, he rises to a high pitch of invective:

> The glory of the square-rigged ship has been immortalized by poets writing sonnets about long tricks at the wheel, and artists with beards singing sea-shanties in a jersey, accompanying themselves on the Spanish guitar. The advent of steam is considered to have been the advent of grime, trade unions, and class hatred between the bridge and foc'sle. It has corrupted the salts of yore from iron men on wooden ships into wireless-operators in flowered dressing-gowns . . . I sailed under canvas as a boy and in my memory the stalwart salts with the hearts of oak were moronic bipeds dangling in the branches of artificial trees in constant peril of their lives.

One learns from Villiers and de Hartog alike that generalizations are reliable only for their failure to capture the quiddities of human character and experience. Slocum was an ambitious and serious student of seamanship. If not a teetotaler, he was uncommonly restrained in his vices, although he couldn't have displayed much priggishness or he wouldn't have survived his two weeks in Liverpool. Rather imagine him as wary and observant, a good listener and quick study.

At nineteen, within three years after going to sea, having risen the year before to second mate, Slocum attained the rank of first mate. This was a position of authority and responsibility exceeded only by that of master, entitling him to be called "Sir" and "Mister" by the crew and to eat his meals aft in what Richard Henry Dana Jr. calls "the world of knives and forks and tea-cups." Youth was no impediment to his promotion (minimum ages for certification by the British Board of Trade were seventeen for second mate, nineteen for first mate, and twenty-one for master), so performance alone earned respect and the chance of elevation. Many sailors were drunks and reckless brawlers ashore but did well at sea—"able seamen" by rank. To be trusted with authority, Slocum had to be exceptionally and manifestly reliable. His son Victor describes a (lost) photo from the family album showing his father at this time, a "husky youth rigged out in checkered flannel shirt and with trousers tucked into cowhide boots, the very kind used on the Bay of Fundy to this day."

It is daunting to study what this unschooled boy was obliged to learn in order to pass the formal and practical tests required even of a second mate, much less a first. His early promotions would have been impossible had he been unable—like most of his shipmates in the forecastle—to read and write. Indeed he read hungrily throughout his life. But that alone wasn't enough. Learning the ropes—lines, braces and cordage, buntlines, warps, reef points, cringles, lanyards, ratlines, footropes, sheets and halyards, hawsers the circumference of pythons, and guys and shrouds and topping lifts—wasn't the half of it. Cordage needed to be rove through blocks, belayed, snubbed, knotted appropriately, spliced, downhauled, whipped, hauled and coiled in a Flemish fake. One had better distinguish between the working end and the bitter end. Rigging and its nomenclature were a spider's web of interacting parts, all titled and ranked: spankers and topgallants and royals and skysails were fixed to masts and yards, to be raised or reefed or furled, and none of it was intuitive. Remembering the names of things and their uses was such a crucial skill that when a novice sailor of Slocum's era was discharged, his papers either did or did not include this crucial testimony above the shipmaster's signature: "knows the ropes." On a full-rigged ship there might be as many as two hundred running lines, as opposed to fixed or "standing" rigging; these had to be manipulated by sailors, and the sailor had to know which was which—they looked much alike—and whether to haul them in or slack them off.* Setting the main topsail, a principal sail on a square-rigger, required the simultaneous manipulation of eleven lines. Anyone who has struggled—from the comfort of a cozy easy chair in front of a cheering fire—to comprehend the names and purposes of the parts aboard one of Patrick O'Brian's ships will appreciate the complexity of a novice seaman's task. Dean King's *A Sea of Words,* a four-hundred-page nautical glossary, is a necessary companion to O'Brian's idiomatic sea stories. Slocum had a more capacious and intricately interconnected maritime lexicon to memorize, much of which he would have taken in growing up on Digby Island: customs to absorb, chains of command to honor, sea legs to be found, seasickness to overcome. A sailor had to climb tall masts on a bucking ship, to tame clouds of flapping wet canvas trying to shake him loose, and he had to do this in all weathers, during

---

*As Spencer Apollonio, editor of *The Last of the Cape Horners* (2000), notes, "The order 'lee fore clew-garnet' . . . while meaningless, perhaps, to landsmen, tells a sailor precisely where to go and what to do (and always with an implication to be quick about it)." Remember that such an order would often be shouted into the teeth of a nor'easter screaming through the rigging, canvas thundering, waves crashing aboard.

Cape Horn howlers and sleet storms. Think of the perils of a high-wire walker 150 feet above the deck, with his wire swaying and its anchoring platforms pitching and rolling. A sailor had to hear orders accurately, then execute them. Any able seaman was expected to perform these tasks, but to rise in rank it helped to have a loud voice and clear enunciation, the better to be heard aloft above the shriek of wind.

The specific regulations—or house rules—had been codified in a handbook titled *The Seaman's Vade Mecum* (1707). Much knowledge of the peculiarities of the sea was passed from generation to generation and could be taken on faith. The accepted trade routes—from west to east around the Cape of Good Hope and Cape Horn, "running the easting down" as it was known—were refined and buttressed with historical data and hydrographic theory in 1851 by Matthew Fontaine Maury's *Sailing Directions*.

For Slocum, though, practical experience was indispensable. An officer was required to know the most crucial thing of all: Where in the world was his ship? It seems safe to suggest that nobody during Slocum's lifetime excelled him at the art of navigation. In his writing he's laconic, sometimes even coy, about the ease with which he found a route to this or that landfall, so much so that a landlubber might write off his successful arrival at destinations sometimes thousands of miles distant across open waters as dead reckoning—from "deduced" rather than "deadly," the estimation of location by relying on observation of speed, modified by tidal set, current, and leeway—or serial good luck. It wasn't chance that brought Slocum's vessels home, but rather his exercise of the art of shooting and reducing solar and lunar sights by sextant and azimuth compass, refined by the complex application of mathematical formulas and nautical tables.

To pass Britain's Board of Trade examination for certification as a second mate, Slocum had studied problem sets from J. W. Norie's *Epitome of Navigation,* which demanded that this teen with a third-grade education master not only Euclidean geometry but also, owing to validation of explorers' postulates that the earth is not flat, the spherical geometry of curved surfaces. Not to mention trigonometry, advanced algebra, the use of logarithms, and, above all, learning to admit it when he didn't know what he didn't know. To navigate "by guess and by God"—as sailors said of blind wandering—or to figure wrongly was not to fail in Latin at a proper declension or conjugation; it was to be shipwrecked.

Slocum became proficient in lunar observation, a particular kind of navigation whose practitioners were known as lunarians, fixing their positions by determining the distance and angle between the moon and a planet or fixed star. The great advantage of lunar navigation is the accuracy—within as little as a quarter of a degree, the distance from which a lighthouse set on a bluff might easily be sighted from offshore—with which it can establish longitude. Because the process required to fix one's position by observation of the night sky required exceedingly tedious and numerous calculations, three experienced navigators, working together, were generally required to execute it. For this reason the alternative means of fixing longitude—by observation of the noon sun together with a precise knowledge of Greenwich Mean Time—became the default method after the introduction of accurate shipborne chronometers.*

How it happened that Slocum became so proficient at lunar navigation had much to do with his grasp of the science's theory—all self-taught, his study snatched between watches at sea—and the reliability of his calculations. But his facility with the quadrant and sextant was the master skill on which all this depended, giving him the ability to read angles of arc from the deck of a pitching, rolling platform and have confidence in their outcome. Much of such an art can be learned and refined with practice. Slocum, though, clearly had a gift as arbitrarily bestowed as that of whistling with perfect pitch, or pitching a hundred-mile-an-hour fastball or hitting such a pitch out of the ballpark.

After shipping out from Liverpool, Slocum spent his first two years at sea being educated in social customs, astronomy, biology, physics, geography, the laws of cause and effect, and abnormal psychology. From the polyglot crew he must have learned foreign phrases. He learned carpentry and sewing as naturally as any student at trade school or a home-economics course. Sailors, necessarily subject to the commandments

---

*An apprentice learning the lunar method might require as many as four hours to complete his calculation. With practice, this could be reduced to thirty minutes, but a high-quality sextant (or, before the common use of sextants, an octant, which was itself actually a quadrant) was necessary. In *Sailing Ships of New England,* John Robinson and George Francis Dow quote the navigator of a square-rigger, presented in 1897 with such a pig's-yoke quadrant as Slocum used: "I have no idea how to use it and I do not believe that there is a shipmaster sailing out of Boston today who does."

and codicils of maritime justice, became sea lawyers. Slocum also read widely, literature as well as sea texts. Herman Melville's Ishmael is often quoted as testifying that a whale ship had been his "Yale College and my Harvard," and no wonder. Consider, too, the commonsense judgment needed to keep a ship on an even keel, the stamina demanded by voyages lasting many months, the bursts of energy necessary to take down sail in the face of a waterspout or typhoon, the patience likewise to slat list-lessly in the doldrums with the temperature in triple digits.

In 1861 Slocum shipped aboard the British ship *Tanjore* (for Tangiers) to China, around the Cape of Good Hope. Thirty-six years later, writing to the editor of *Sailing Alone Around the World,* Slocum vividly recalled the master of the *Tanjore* as a skilled navigator and a domineering mar-tinet so insistent on asserting his place in the chain of command that he conveyed a letter to Slocum (standing at his side) by first delivering it to the first mate, who then handed it to the second mate, who set it on the capstan from which the ordinary seaman was permitted to remove it.

In *Chance,* Joseph Conrad describes a master's Olympian distance and authority: "The captain of a ship at sea is a remote, inaccessible creature, something like a prince of a fairy-tale, alone of his kind, depending on nobody, not to be called to account except by powers practically invisible and so distant that they might be looked upon as supernatural for all that the rest of the crew knows of them . . ." Though Slocum couldn't recall the Christian name of the *Tanjore*'s master—he would have had no occa-sion to speak it—he remembered Captain Martin, "who talked through his nose," as sadistic, obliging his sailors to work with the ice cargo in the chill of the mornings and evenings and then, in Hong Kong, to work aloft, "or worse still, over the ship's side," in the heat of the summer days, so hot that "several of the crew died." When the *Tanjore* sailed from Hong Kong for the Dutch East Indies, Slocum, gravely ill, was put ashore "hove down with fever," as he later remembered, and sent to a hospital in Batavia (now Jakarta), a pestilent hellhole. He recovered from what was probably malaria ("Java Fever"), and in the first of the many disputed torts he would experience as a plaintiff or defendant, he sued Captain Martin for three months' pay, at fifty dollars per month (an unusually high wage at the time, paid only to crew signed at Liverpool), which he won. The only avenue to redress in a foreign port was through the adjudication of a consular officer, in this case the British consul hear-ing a complaint against a British master of a British vessel. It was rare that an ordinary seaman's word would outweigh a master's, so that Slocum's victory against Captain Martin must have been persuasively supported by witnesses.* Slocum was rescued from Batavia by Captain Airy, the merciful British steamship captain of the *Soushay,* who signed the boy aboard as an able seaman, knowing that Slocum—confined by fever to his berth—would be useless as a member of the crew.

To have endured these trials and be honored for mastering them must have been heady for a young man still in his teens when he was elevated to first mate. He was lucky to reach twenty-one. Before he did he had twice doubled Cape Horn and sailed around the world. The so-called Clipper Way (route of the wool and grain clippers) might commence in Liverpool, progress south well offshore of the western coast of Africa to round the Cape of Good Hope, and carry on to Australia, where cargo would be discharged and new materials loaded for delivery around the tip of South America to Liverpool. Sir Francis Chichester, in his book *Along the Clipper Way* (1967), describes the passage:

> Like a broad path curving down through the North Atlantic and the South Atlantic, passing between 300 and 800 miles south of Cape Town and then running down the Easting for 6,600 miles to Bass Strait either keeping within the Roaring Forties or south of them . . . After leaving Sydney, the clippers either passed between, or south of, the New Zealand islands, then again they ran their Easting down in the Forties or the Fifties. The next landmark was Cape Horn, 5,000 miles on from New Zealand, and once they had doubled the Horn the sailors reckoned they were as good as home, though in fact they had another 8,000 miles to sail through both Atlantics.

The *Tanjore*'s Captain Martin was a benevolent despot compared with many hard-driving and pitiless masters who pressed on despite the looming ascendancy in merchant shipping of steam power. By the time Slocum went to sea in 1860 the glorious days of clipper ships like the *Oriental* and the *Cutty Sark* were soon to pass. Racing around Cape Horn to

---

*It is characteristic of Slocum—in keeping with his clemency toward his father's violence—that years later, himself having been a shipmaster charged with cruelty, he wrote to the editor of *Sailing Alone Around the World* that "I may have been a little severe on Captain M of the old 'Tanjore' but it is my only revenge for years of broken health brought on by the Captain . . ."

deliver gold prospectors to the California frenzy of 1849,* or later to Australian gold fields in 1861, fast and nimble ships—"hell ships" and "murder ships" and "blood ships," their crews driven by the infamous "bucko mates" of lurid sea yarns†—had been displaced by beamy and overladen and overcanvased behemoths carrying coal and coffee and wool and lumber. While it lasted, the gold-driven golden age of sail had been gorgeous to behold, particularly from ashore at Boston or San Francisco or Sydney, as sightseers regarded with awe the greyhounds straining sleekly at their heavy chain leashes, about to weigh anchor and fill the sky with canvas and go to the other side of the earth at speeds more appropriate to a locomotive than a boat.

The clichés summoned by the sea—from the security of a beach, say—are wholesome: fresh, salty air, cleansing water, the play of sun on sea, perhaps some vigorous exercise among gentle waves. The reality was often almost too grim to be endured: sixty-foot seas pounding over the deck and washing everything not secured, including sailors, overboard. "Breaking" seas are well named, for that's what they do to human bones and crucial gear. Some captains lashed helmsmen to the wheel to keep them aboard, and others rigged canvas blinds (think of a horse's blinders) behind the helmsman so that he couldn't see and be terrified silly by the massive waves gathering astern and about to overtake them, thereby jumping into the rigging (if his legs hadn't been broken) and abandoning the wheel.

During the 1850s, when a dozen eggs brought round from Baltimore to San Francisco might fetch ten dollars, clipper captains were extravagantly rewarded. The master of a British ship, sailing from Liverpool to China or India, might command as much as £10,000, a fortune; a Cape Horn clipper master during the gold rush might be paid $3,000 for sailing from New York to San Francisco, and $5,000 if he reached the Golden

---

*It was a shaggy-haired native of Saco, Maine, who arrived excited in the spring of 1848 in the Plaza of San Francisco shaking in his hand a horseradish bottle enclosing several yellow lumps. "Gold! Gold! Gold! From the American River," announced Sam Brennan, the manager of Captain John Sutter's store near Sacramento. News traveled east, disbelief waned, and in 1849 there sailed from East Coast ports 775 ships bound around Cape Horn for the Golden Gate. A year later believers motivated the building—from 1850 until 1856—of the Yankee clippers, a glorious intersection of greed and speed that created beautiful ships and ugly behavior.
†Samuel Eliot Morison, warming to his work in his essay "The Clipper Ships of Massachusetts," remarks that "we have all been entertained by yarns of Yankee mates who struck men dead for a little cheekiness, and of captains who shot members of their crew off the yardarms for mere sport . . ."

Gate in fewer than a hundred days. Let's call it $100,000 in today's money. Fifty years later a captain would be lucky to be paid one-tenth as much, and pinching pennies was all the cry, with skinflint masters "keeping the Sabbath," as the saying went, "and everything else they could lay their hands on." (It was common practice for them to mistreat their crews so awfully that the sailors deserted as soon as they reached port, forgoing the balance of their wages.)

But cultures change more slowly than markets, and the slave-driving masters—"blasted boy-killers," one sailor named them—measuring their time and distance around the Horn with the reckless fanaticism of modern ocean racers, trained the next generation of martinets too well. One such instructor was the notorious "Bully" Forbes, whom Robert Foulke describes as "the prototype of the swaggering, hard-driving captain." He was said to have locked his sails' sheets (the equivalent of welding the pedal to the metal of a race car) and carried a pair of revolvers, one in each hand, to prevent the crew of the *Marco Polo* from shortening "tremendous presses of sail through heavy gales." He is quoted as having announced to his passengers at the outset of a voyage: "Ladies and gentlemen, last trip I astonished the world with the sailing of this ship. This trip I intend to astonish God Almighty!"

One of the most deadly offenses charged against abusive shipmasters was their custom of punishing sailors for minor infractions by ordering them aloft, needlessly, in harsh weather. Think of scurrying up the ratlines, spray-lashed and deafened by the howling din, with cold-numbed hands, chapped and bloody, fingernails mashed (gloves weren't used: too clumsy), during a thunderstorm, to serve as a lightning rod. It was rare that a deepwater passage did not take the life of at least one sailor.

Slocum did not complain when, in 1864, as a mate on the *Agra*, strong and nimble at 180 pounds, he was sent aloft in mid-Atlantic to the upper topsail yard to tame a sail.* The words "upper topsail" should convey the impression of perilous altitude. An ordinary seaman of the era recalled being sent aloft for the first time with the second mate shouting at his back, "Never ye looks down, sonny!" Herman Melville's narrator in *Redburn* describes the sensation: "I could but just perceive the ship below me, like a long narrow plank in the water . . . Though there was a pretty smooth sea, and little wind; yet, at this extreme elevation, the ship's

---

*A full-rigged ship might also fly skysails, known as cloud-rakers, or even a moonsail, higher still.

motion was very great; so that when the ship rolled one way, I felt something as a fly must feel, walking the ceiling . . ." Aboard the *Agra,* a gust set Slocum's sail flapping like an untethered circus tent, and he was hurled off the yard. According to Alan Villiers, an eyewitness to what generally happened next: "Men who fell from aloft had little chance, whether they fell on deck or into the sea. The only chance for them was if they struck lines on the way down to break the fall." In *White-Jacket,* Melville writes that "a seaman fell from the main-royal-yard of an English line-of-battle ship near us, and buried his ankle-bones in the deck, leaving two indentations there, as if scooped out by a carpenter's gouge." Slocum's head struck the main yard (a horizontal member attached to the mast) as he fell, cutting a gash over his left eye but slowing him. The vivid scar was noted—as was his survival—by a Boston newspaper reporter in 1895, as he sailed alone from Gloucester around the globe.

Virginia Albertina Walker

THREE

Master Slocum

To face the elements is, to be sure, no light matter when the sea is in its grandest mood. You must then know the sea, and know that you know it, and not forget that it was made to be sailed over.

—*Sailing Alone Around the World*

CERTIFIED AS A SHIP'S OFFICER, he became *Mister* Slocombe, and in 1865, electing San Francisco as his hailing port, he became a United States citizen. During the following decade most of his cousins and siblings would return from exile in Nova Scotia to Massachusetts, but Slocum's decision to anchor at the edge of the Wild West was in keeping with his restless avidity for chance. He had visited San Francisco a couple of times, carrying coal from Liverpool and Cardiff and wool from Australia, returning to the British Isles with grain and sometimes gold.

The most pedestrian-seeming cargo concealed hazards. Coal, with its danger of spontaneous combustion if tightly packed and damp, was one of the riskiest of freights, and a coal fire at sea, resulting in the loss of all hands, was not uncommon. (In 1891, during the single month of November, six vessels that loaded coal at Birkenhead, across the Mersey from Liverpool, burned at sea instead of delivering their cargo to San Francisco.) Wheat, which Slocum would frequently carry, was also subject to spontaneous combustion, and for this reason it was often carried on deck, where great vigilance was required to keep it dry. Manganese ore from Chile was heavy and dangerous. Railroad tracks, shipped to San Francisco while the transcontinental railroad was being completed, were prone to shift in the hold during heavy seas, upsetting the trim of the carrying vessel. In brief, merchant shipping—whether the cargo was coal, ice, gunpowder, iron rails, live cattle on the hoof, lumber, guano, jute, copra, or immigrants—was risky business.

Sailing as a whaler had always been an option for Slocum, but unlike conversion to steam shipping, a sea change he emphatically rejected, whaling seems never to have crept even hazily into his field of vision. His repudiation of whaling certainly owed nothing to his scruples as a lover of nature's creatures, which he happily slaughtered until one day late in his career when he decided abruptly to be done with killing fish and fowl, let alone mammals—but always excepting sharks, which like most sailors he loathed with fervor.*

Blubbering was awful, brutal work. The manners and temperament of Ahab would have made him recognizable as a type to those gullible unfortunates who shipped aboard whalers out of New Bedford or Nantucket or San Francisco under the illusion that they would come home rich from their share of sperm oil and whalebone. Many whalers went to sea straight from the farm, having been tempted by allotments advertised by recruiting agents on behalf of rapacious shipowners. A notorious instance—not possibly apocryphal—has a young hayseed offered 1/250th of the net profits earned by his ship during its voyage of undetermined hardship and duration. (Three years constituted an easy trip; four was more usual.) Balking at such a paltry share, the recruit leaped at the agent's counteroffer of 1/500th: *Now, that's more like it!*

Samuel Eliot Morison writes stirringly of the outrageous situation of American whalers in Slocum's time, how resourcefully they were cheated by the machinations of outfitters (who kicked money back to the whaling masters) and by sales of tobacco and such from the masters' slop chests. He reports cases of sailors returning to port so deeply indentured to their masters that they had to pay in order to disembark. Morison's special contempt, as a lover of fine ships, is reserved for the whaling vessels themselves, their voyages prolonged by greed until at last "the old hooker crawled around the Horn with a yard of weed on her bottom and a crew that looked like shipwrecked mariners."†

No: whaling was not for Joshua Slocum. But the dominant constant in his many changes of career and circumstance was his steady connection to the sea; another was his relish of enterprise. At various times Slocum sold fish, seashells, self-published books and pamphlets, autographed

*In *The Voyage of the "Liberdade"* (1890), he still held "these monsters," with their "rows of pearly teeth," to be the sea's most awful peril. Amplifying his indifference to the skill of swimming, he muses: "How it is that sailors can go in bathing, as they often do, in the face of a danger so terrible, is past my comprehension."
†Samuel Eliot Morison, *The Maritime History of Massachusetts, 1783–1860* (Northeastern University Press, 1961).

photos, lecture performances, pieces of coral, ships, and furs. He was at one time or another a trader, gillnet fisherman, shipwright, carpenter, lumberman, charter captain, and trapper. And San Francisco, in the decade following the gold rush, was as good a place as any—with the possible exception of Sydney in the years immediately following Australia's own gold rush—to grab at chance or be crushed by hazard.

Not every idea hatched in a boomtown was a good one. If those eggs brought round Cape Horn to gold diggers hungry for an omelet fetched ten dollars per dozen in March 1852, a shipper might be lucky to get a dollar a dozen nine months later, when the hungry prospector might not be hungry anymore, or might be broke, or might have decided to take time to raise his own chickens. Passengers from America's East Coast typically paid $150 to $200 to come around the Horn, but the really big money was to be made from the unpredictable yearnings of suddenly and hugely wealthy prospectors. The market was capricious: the bark *Suliot,* sailing from Belfast, Maine, to San Francisco in 1849, carried such varied merchandise that her manifest, or inventory, was entered on a roll fifteen feet long. Dry goods, prefab shacks, groceries, medicine, and—as a last-minute addition to fill the holds—a lot of hemlock boards. By the time the ship entered the Golden Gate 117 days later, only the hemlock proved profitable, bought for ten dollars per thousand board feet and sold for three hundred. Yet a year later the bottom dropped out of the lumber market. Joshua Slocum, having by now sailed for five years aboard ships trading in wool, lumber, coffee, and coal, knew the vagaries and perils of long-distance trade, as well as some of the dramatic rewards. The sure bet in a port like San Francisco, its Barbary Coast already legendary for outlaw excess, was vice, but that—like so-called blackbirding, bearing Rudyard Kipling's "taint of a musky ship, the reek of the slavers' dhow"— was never his calling.

Slocum at first used San Francisco as a home base from which to hug the shore. Following the Civil War, during the glory days of the wheat trade, San Francisco was the red-hot center of world shipping, surpassing even Liverpool in comings and goings. Hundreds of great ships lay alongside its wharfs and crowded its ample anchorage. Here was the social as well as commercial hub of maritime trade, masters showing off their ships and judging the lines of their rivals' vessels, approving this captain's Bristol-fashion spit and polish, condemning that one's laundry-sack harbor furl. A gaudy figurehead would surely invite disdain.

Slocum wasn't ready to join such an exalted fraternity. As soon as he became a citizen he designed and with a partner built a gillnet boat up north on the Columbia River and used it to fish for salmon. The boat was double-ended, twenty-five feet long, and to provide shelter partly decked. It had a small spritsail attached to a stubby sixteen-foot mast, which doubled as the pole of a tent used during inclement weather. Again and again, when Slocum found himself in a fix he would boat-build his escape. His ungrudging praise of his father's ability to fashion a vessel with only a jackknife and a tree must have been offered, given his sensitivity to idiom, with the knowledge that "jackknife carpenter" was a dismissive description of a handyman indifferent to finish work. Indeed, excepting a period in the 1870s when he was in the business of selling ornamental Philippine hardwood to Chinese boat builders, and using his trading vessel the *Amethyst* as a floating display case of inlaid brightwork, he took no interest in joinery as an art.

Now, with his partner in their rough vessel, he gillnetted salmon on the Columbia in a process known as "shooting twine," stringing fixed nets from the river's surface almost to its bottom in the path of fish heading upriver to spawn, and sold them to a cannery in Astoria, which then bought their boat at season's end.* Having returned to San Francisco with only a modest profit, the partners next ventured farther north to hunt seals and sea otters in the waters along the Pacific coast of the Oregon Territory and around Vancouver Island. Fur trading was potentially very lucrative: a sealskin would fetch $10 on the market in Hong Kong, and an otter hide from $50 to as much as $350. Fortunes were made in what sailors termed the "Nor'west Coast and Chiny" trade, the pelts sailed from the Pacific Northwest to Canton (closed by local trade restrictions to the importation of American goods other than furs and hides) and bartered for nankeen fabric, tea, silk, and porcelain, the lovely Canton ware so cherished in New England.

The sea otters, already remorselessly thinned by Russians during the early settlement of Alaska, weren't lolling around in the waves begging to be translated into coats and hats. Having been hunted in the surf, otters were wary of the scent of humans along the beach. Slocum and his partner needed sharpshooting skills to kill them at a distance from the water's edge.

Admirers of Slocum should be less impressed by his marksmanship

---

*The Columbia River Maritime Museum in Astoria, situated where canneries once stood, has exhibited an old wooden drift boat, one of thousands comprising the Pacific gillnetting fleet, the design prototype of which the museum credits to Joshua Slocum.

than by his boat-building skill (which would yield him his two vessels of self-rescue, the *Liberdade* and the *Spray*) and his writing. Victor Slocum read the journal that his father kept to detail his explorations of the Columbia River, Gray's Harbor (an estuary south of the Olympia rain forest), Puget Sound, and British Columbia. He recollected "humorous allusions" to the vagaries of the fishing and trapping life, together with accounts of encounters with bears and wildcats, but no copy of this, his earliest narrative, has survived. Nevertheless, it is notable that Slocum, without formal schooling, had from his teenage years been drawn toward literary record making, storytelling meant to please strangers.

In 1869, at twenty-five, he got his first command, a seventy-five-foot coasting schooner plying between San Francisco and nearby Half Moon Bay, from which he carried pumpkins, potatoes, and barley back to the city. Sailing the *Montana* must have been a breeze for Slocum, but now, prepared by his experience selling fish and pelts, he also became a trader, the owner's agent in the matter of selecting goods and setting a price for their transport. Soon Slocum stepped up in responsibility by becoming the master of a larger coasting schooner carrying wheat to Seattle and coal back, a position that he received owing to his experience carrying grain from San Francisco to Liverpool and Cardiff. Local cargo carried by fast coastal schooners was shipping for fees only recently unheard of, from sixty to a hundred dollars per ton.

During the 1860s the worldwide desire for California wheat—"so hard and dry," according to William Hutchinson Rowe, "that it would stand the 14,000-mile voyage around the Horn and arrive in the European ports in prime condition"—had a more lasting impact on the prosperity of California than had the payday in 1848 at Sutter's Mill. Hard-grained California wheat was in high demand from British and Irish millers, and the great grain races to Liverpool from San Francisco and Australia, carrying each new harvest, were followed avidly by landlubbers as well as seamen. But as W. H. Bunting writes in *Live Yankees*,* "the fastest ship was not necessarily the most profitable ship—a damaged cargo was remembered long

---

*This is a trove of first-person accounts and original documents culled by Bunting from the papers of the Sewall family, the most prominent shipping family of Bath, Maine, "City of Ships." The Sewalls accounted for an astonishing percentage of the vessels—wood and metal—that comprised the American merchant marine of the nineteenth century. Three of the most profitable were named *Harvester, Thrasher,* and *Reaper.*

after a quick passage had been forgotten." The sunny Sacramento and San Joaquin Valleys—connected by waterways to San Francisco—produced grain exports from the Golden Gate that increased in value in a single year from $1,750,000 to $6,718,000. No small potatoes, 400 percent. Carrying grain was tricky and could be dangerous; poison gas from decaying wheat blinded and killed members of more than one crew. (Perhaps it is best to stipulate that carrying anything aboard a piece of wood floating on an ocean—and certainly human beings—could be dangerous.)

Slocum's third command was the 110-foot barkentine *Constitution.* Ann Spencer specifies this ship carried "cotton seeds, lumber, machinery and shingles" to Guayamus, Mexico, and from there salt to Carmen Island in the Gulf of California.* Having returned to San Francisco, Slocum was sent in the *Constitution* to the Antipodes, specifically Sydney.

It's tempting to oversell the significance of someone so young being trusted to command a valuable sailing ship and its crew and freight on a voyage to the ends of the earth. Slocum's rapid advance from ordinary seaman to master was not that exceptional in a transient culture where so many were speculating, hopping from chance to chance. Anybody could look for gold, and anyone with a bag of gold dust could try to buy cheap and sell dear. But few could command a sailing ship, and the ones who wished to but couldn't were either found out or sunk by the time the first gale hit them.

Slocum sailed for Sydney in early November, and less than three months later—on January 31, 1871—he was married. He met Virginia Albertina Walker by the happy circumstance of being in a lively port city at the same time that a lovely young woman with an adventurous spirit was out and about at the kinds of dances and dinners to which promising young sea captains would be invited. Like San Francisco, Sydney was energetically evolving socially as well as economically, and was hospitable to outsiders. How could it have been otherwise in a refugee colony settled about fifteen minutes ago by exiled criminals?

---

*In her biography of Slocum, *Alone at Sea,* Spencer makes coherent sense of the chronology by which Slocum came to his second command. Her account was made possible by the New Bedford Whaling Museum, which holds in its Walter Teller Collection the results of records researched in daunting detail by Leon Fredrich, a maritime scholar intrigued with dates and weights and shipping manifests. Before Fredrich pinned down which vessels were in fact Slocum's second and third commands—the *Constitution* and then the *Washington,* both owned by Nicholas Bichard, a San Francisco immigrant from Guernsey—Victor Slocum's sometimes shaky memory and Walter Teller's good-faith inference got the sequence and ports of call reversed.

Virginia Walker was twenty when she met Slocum, and was like him a wanderer on the earth. She had been born on New York's Staten Island at the height of the California gold fever, to which her father, William, succumbed. A disappointed forty-niner, he then moved his family to Australia just after 1852, hoping to find gold in New South Wales and Victoria. Australia's prospectors—the so-called diggers of song and legend—found tons of the stuff, but Walker returned in Sydney to the trade he had previously practiced in New York, becoming the owner of a stationery store that was prosperous enough for him to indulge his love of amateur theater. (Victor Slocum remembered that his "genial" grandfather Walker "could repeat any speech in *Hamlet* if given the first line.") He was a volunteer fireman, an estimable hobby that seems to call forth a better class of eccentrics, and Victor reports that he owned a cockatoo that liked to shout out, when bored, "Fire, fire, Walker, fire!" Virginia's sister was a successful opera singer, a contralto; they had a younger brother named George.

It wasn't unusual for fluid societies with tons of ore and banknotes loose on the streets to ape such expressions of grandeur as London and New York displayed. In addition to theaters and opera houses, the citizens of Sydney liked to have grand balls in honor of visiting ships' officers from around the civilized world, and at one of these Virginia—costumed as Columbia, America's own Gem of the Ocean—was photographed leading the grand march; at the "tuckout," as locals called the banquet, William Walker was the toastmaster. These celebrations were memorialized in a red plush album carried by his mother, as Victor remembered, and when it was brought out to impress (or more likely amuse) visitors aboard one or another of Slocum's ships, "I noticed that my father always put on a bored and disinterested look."

Slocum had been on his own in an almost exclusively masculine world since his mother's death—which seems to have so wounded him that he never brought himself to write about her, or talk to his children about her, save to praise the flapjacks that emerged from her fireplace on North Mountain. And bearing in mind his increasing inclination toward solitude (that *Alone* in the title of his magnum opus deserves emphasis), it is startling that his encounter with Virginia Walker swept him off course so suddenly and completely that they were married scarcely two weeks after they met.

By this time, Slocum had been at sea for eleven years, experiencing the striking lonely-in-a-crowd inwardness of his chosen calling. Not for him the theatrical roller-coaster rides of his fellow sailors, the drinking, brawling, and whoring in port followed by hangovers and perhaps the disgrace of being shanghaied. Slocum was either on watch or studying his craft or reading or looking around with his eyes wide open. He had elevated himself to a person of consequence, someone electing to stand out and above and apart. No wonder, as Samuel Eliot Morison writes with piquant chauvinism, that "a promising sea captain generally had the pick of the pretty girls in his home town. 'She's good enough to marry an East Indian cap'n!' was the highest commendation for a Cape Cod damsel."

Being at sea for months at a time—without the ameliorating drama of a dangerous hunt that invigorated whalers' experience—imposed, in Robert Foulke's nice phrase, "an inexorable captivity" and a sense of isolation on the crew. To have chosen such a life, as opposed to having been drugged or crimped or hoaxed aboard, was almost defiant in its acceptance of alienation.

In *Two Years Before the Mast*, Richard Henry Dana describes the consequence of what Foulke describes as "intellectual poverty," the outcome of "constant propinquity," during a long voyage around Cape Horn:

> Any change was sought . . . [to] break the monotony of the time; and even the two hours' trick at the wheel which came round to us in turn, once in every other watch, was looked upon as a relief. The never-failing resource of long yarns, which eke out many a watch, seemed to fail us now; for we had been so long together that we had heard each other's stories told over and over again till we had them by heart; each one knew the whole history of each of the others, and we were fairly and literally talked out.

Though the British merchant marine—its ships known familiarly as lime-juicers—was more highly esteemed on the seven seas, and better supported by its government and investors, its vessels better crewed by superior masters and at more generous pay, American custom was more casual in the matter of so-called hen frigates, ships with masters' wives aboard. This indulgence defied sailors' stubborn superstition that bad luck inevitably followed the boarding of their ship by a woman, despite sailors' counterintuitive conviction that Neptune could be calmed by a ship's figurehead of a naked woman fashioned from wood. Although there's no record that Slocum took acceptance of voyaging couples into account when—having previously shipped on Her Majesty Victoria's ships—he became a citizen of the United States, why else choose a circumstance that would put him aboard American hell ships, shorthanded and brutalized by bucko mates?

For Virginia's part, she told her first child, Victor, that she knew as soon as she saw Joshua that he "was just the kind of a man she wanted, not the stuffy sort she saw in conventional Sydney society." Perhaps owing to the class anxieties fostered by a convict society, stuffy Poms did their best to domesticate the rough-and-tumble Down Under of diggers, swagmen, and jackeroos, but Virginia's notion of the good life was obviously fueled by her love of adventure. Described by an admirer as "regal in bearing but light-hearted too," an excellent rider, she liked to take her horses into the Blue Mountains outback on camping trips, sleeping under the stars. She boasted that her mother was descended from Native Americans of the Lenni-Lenape (Delaware) tribe of New Jersey and southern New York.

Slocum's appearance was stern and sober. Prematurely balding, he appeared and behaved older than his age, with sunken cheeks and a deliberately fixed gaze. Virginia Walker's features in contrast were frank and welcoming, and her eyes remarkable, as golden as an eagle's in her children's memory. It is clear that this couple, rationally suitable in tastes and ambition, were right—maybe even "destined"—for each other. But from its beginning their marriage was much, much more than a wise and lucky match. Everyone who reported having watched them together remarked that they were so absorbed with each other, so palpably affectionate and love-struck, that they created an aura of exclusion around themselves. A young female cousin described Joshua as "an ardent person," in Virginia's company, "certainly demonstrative in showing affection." The couple liked to laugh, even—or especially—if the jokes were private. (No small matter, especially given the isolation of a ship in mid-ocean. One shipmaster's wife, quoted in Hen Frigates,* complains of growing "so lonely at sea, I almost forget how to laugh.")

They must have agreed to forgo the formal wedding and jamboree sought by her father, who gave his formal consent that "Virginia Albertina Walker, Spinster . . . being under the age of twenty-one years,"

*Joan Druett, Hen Frigates: Passion and Peril, Nineteenth-Century Women at Sea (Touchstone, 1999).

be married to "Joshua Slocum, Master Mariner of Massachusetts [*sic*]," in a family ceremony by a Baptist minister. And then, almost immediately, she kissed her mother, father, and sister goodbye, boarded the *Constitution* carrying her riding outfit—whip most definitely included—and sailed off carrying coal and tomatoes to San Francisco (roughly seven thousand miles away, given the deflections of the sailing route) with her twelve-year-old brother aboard. They arrived May 4 and departed two days later on the *Washington,* a bark of 110 feet also owned by Nicholas Bichard.

This was to be their honeymoon trip, a voyage to Cook Inlet near Kodiak Island to fish the chinook salmon runs—just the sort of adventure Virginia Slocum relished, into the wilderness and exposed to extreme conditions. Her husband saw it as greatly raising the stakes of his previous fishing ventures: fortunes could be made from selling salmon in the port cities of the Pacific Northwest.

The risks were at least as great as the rewards. Victor Slocum's biography claims that his father was "the first American to enter Cook Inlet when the Russians left after the Alaska Purchase," made by U.S. Secretary of State William H. Seward in 1867. However unbeckoning this territory—variously known as Andrew Johnson's polar bear garden, Seward's Icebox, and Seward's Folly—actually was, that claim cannot be true. New Bedford whalers were taking bowheads and right whales from the Kodiak grounds more than a decade before Tsar Alexander II sold out to the United States. What was true was that these treacherous waters, almost as tide-scoured as Slocum's native Bay of Fundy, had only primitively been charted by the Russians. Cook Inlet, a 180-mile glacial fjord, is subject to tidal bores, waves as high as six feet traveling as fast as fifteen knots. Portions of the silted, muddy, and foul bottom—exposed at low tide—have the baleful characteristics of quicksand, winds are chill, and fog is frequent, with rocky ledges abounding.

Victor Slocum, who later visited these waters without his parents, characterizes their nature and situation: "At the head of the inlet the rise and fall of the tide is greater than anywhere else in the world except in the Bay of Fundy. It is forty feet during the springs, making a five or six knot ebb which carries with it huge blocks of ice, tree trunks and every kind of fluvial debris that could be emptied out of the headwaters." The one hazard the newlyweds would have been spared, thanks to the summer season, was ice.

What young George Walker later described as the greatest experience of his life must have been all that and more. Herds of fur seals—known as sleepers for their custom of floating on their backs with their flippers across their snouts—could be seen in the company of beluga whales. On Kodiak Island roamed the bears of the same name, which, because they do not hibernate and eat a steady diet of salmon, are the largest in the world. Sailing up the Pacific coast from San Francisco, the *Washington's* crew had prepared for the salmon run at Cook Inlet's Kasilof River by building several gillnet punts from Slocum's design. Meantime, the master and his bride settled into their constricted quarters, which were far superior to any he had enjoyed as an ordinary seaman, able seaman, or mate. Their cabin—paneled in satinwood or perhaps bird's-eye maple— would have been equipped with a washstand, desk, sofa, bookshelves (for Slocum was always well stocked with fiction, poetry, books about the sea, and natural history). Walter Teller speculates that what natural light penetrated the cabin "came from a transom through which Virginia might have an excellent view of the legs of the man at the wheel, and perhaps a little sky beyond, criss-crossed by the ship's rigging." The Slocums' sleeping berth would have been swung on gimbals, likewise the dining table. Meals would be taken with the ship's mates, some of them rough as cobs, indifferent to hygiene and often surly, resentful of a woman aboard.

If "hen frigate" sounds derogatory, it was meant to. Putting aside until later the frustrations imposed on sailors by infants bawling and toddlers scampering underfoot and even aloft, ships—especially those as small as the *Washington*—were unfriendly places for women. Exceptions were made, as Teller notes, for a few wives who showed "sportsmanship and usefulness," by caring for the sick, mending clothes, and learning to navigate. "It was a rarely courageous wife who accompanied her husband on more than one voyage." From the time she married until her death thirteen years later off Buenos Aires, Virginia sailed wherever Joshua sailed, learning her ropes and how to box the compass—putting a name to each direction from due north 360 degrees back around to due north—as well as nautical taxonomy.

It wasn't that their fishing venture to Cook Inlet was all fair winds and gentle seas. They had timed their arrival to coincide with not only the June chinook salmon run on the Kasilof River but also the midnight sun; this lent the crew both the opportunity of working day and night and the drawback of working night and day. They anchored the *Washington* in what seemed like a protected spot two miles offshore, and on the lee side of rocky Karluk Reef, setting up camp along a beach at the mouth of the Kasilof River, not far from where the Kenai entered the inlet. Slocum and his crew socialized and traded lore with fishing members of the Ninilchik tribe, among whom lived mixed-race descendants of Russian convicts who'd been transported here during Catherine the Great's reign to hunt sea otters. Unfazed by such rough yobbo neighbors, Virginia was awed by the country's extreme natural menace, with volcanoes, moose, lynx, wildcats, and bears in abundance. She liked to shoot her .44 Henry rifle and should perhaps be forgiven as a creature of pre-enlightened sensibilities for having bagged an eagle on the wing. (As late as 1962, Alaska paid a bounty for the claws of our national emblem.) Family legend has it that she also came close to bagging her husband the night he returned prematurely and stealthily toward their tent after gathering supplies aboard the *Washington*. According to Victor, his father was on the right end of a Sharps .50-70 carbine when he was menaced along the banks of the Kenai by an ill-tempered Kodiak bear: "He had once been clawed and bitten by a bear while in British Columbia and knew bear nature better than to take another chance. The pelt of this particular bear was one of the largest ever taken from Kenai, and it was long afterwards stretched out on the floor of a bungalow in Sydney, to the astonishment of the natives."

Such stories, whatever their grounding in fact, are reward enough for reading children's biographies of their parents. One can imagine young Victor, on a visit to his Sydney grandparents, wrestling with the bearskin rug—claws and yellowed teeth preserved—and learning (or believing he had) about these hairbreadth escapes. His summary of the Cook Inlet adventure, however, is less dramatic, a laconic declaration followed by a qualifying throwaway that characterized his father's literary style: "The fishing was carried out successfully except for the loss of the vessel." The *Washington,* light in ballast in order to welcome a huge load of fish, was buffeted so mercilessly by williwaws—explosive gusts peculiar to mountainous fjords—that she "snapped at her [anchor] cables, which were veered out to the bitter end." On the summer solstice, the longest day of the year, while all were ashore, a brutal gale at high tide drove her high onto the beach. "The bones of the *Washington,* bleaching in the sands," as Victor wrote in 1950, "are still a warning."

What happened beginning the following morning was a tamer version of the many accounts that astonish readers of Ernest Shackleton's heroic rescue in 1915–16 of his crew from Antarctic ice. First, the crew agreed to continue fishing through the chinook run. Meanwhile Slocum, with the assistance of a ship's carpenter, constructed a thirty-five-foot whaleboat from bits and pieces of the stranded *Washington,* adding to his fleet of gillnetting punts and two lifeboats, with a view toward not only seeking the comparative safety of Kodiak Island, two hundred miles distant, but also carrying their haul of salmon to market. So as the carpenter and his apprentices built the whaleboat, the rest of the crew continued to fish.

Trading bad luck for good, they'd just finished fishing when a U.S. revenue cutter (precursor of the Coast Guard) steamed into Cook Inlet, offering rescue to Slocum and his crew but not—understandably—to his fish. He accepted passage to Kodiak only for Virginia, electing to remain (with young George Walker at his side) until the abundant catch had been made ready for shipping. Then, posting an armed member of his crew "to keep off Indians and bears," as Victor puts it, he set out with his makeshift fleet, using the power of ebbing tides to carry him four or five hours at a brisk pace from beach to beach. Then they crossed from the mouth of Cook Inlet to Kodiak Island, with the help of a favorable wind pushing the jury-rigged sails of the three largest boats.

There they discovered a couple of Russian sealers with empty holds, which Slocum chartered to fetch the salmon catch from the Kasilof; the fare was then loaded, with his crew, aboard the bark *Czarevitch,* which for the right price detoured from its mission to harvest and ship natural ice to warm ports, instead carrying the happy survivors and their treasure to San Francisco. There, adding the loss of the *Washington* to his other expenses, the vessel's owner sold the fish and pocketed a profit. Slocum's reputation seems to have survived without grave injury the loss of the *Washington.* Though he would not again command a ship owned by Nicholas Bichard, he and Virginia were invited to live aboard Bichard's *Constitution*—berthed alongside Hathaway's Wharf in the port of San Francisco—while he sought his next posting. And here, on January 10, 1872, Victor was born, the first of seven Slocum children born on vessels, most at sea.

Victor Slocum in China

FOUR

Love Stories

Two of my children were born on this voyage [aboard the *Pato* at Petropavlovsk]; they were two months old when we arrived at Oregon— four days old when we began to take in fish . . . Yes Sir, we had a stirring voyage and altogether a delightful time on the fishing grounds [off the Sea of Okhotsk] for every codfish [of 23,000 total catch] that came in over the rail was a quarter of a dollar—clear . . . a great success.

> —JOSHUA SLOCUM, in a letter to John W. Edmonds
> dated May 3, 1890, failing to mention that
> the unnamed twins died in infancy in Portland,
> soon after the fish were landed, in September 1877

My hand shakes so now I can hardley write. Dear Mother my Dear little baby died the other day . . . Every time her teeth would start to come she would cry all night if I would cut them through the gum would grow together again. The night she died she had one convulsion after another I gave her a hot bath and some medecine and was quite quiet infact I thought she was going to come around when she gave a quiet sigh and was gone. Dear Josh embalmed her in brandy for we would not leave her in this horid place she did look so pretty after she died Dearest Mother I canot write any more.

> —VIRGINIA WALKER SLOCUM, in a letter from
> Lagumanoc, Philippines, dated July 17, 1879

QUOTING INFORMAL PROSE of the nineteenth century, it is tempting to regularize writers' spelling and punctuation; the biographer realizes that the conventions of usage and syntax were less constrictive then, and it's nasty to *sic* the grammar of purloined letters and diaries never meant for publication. But in Virginia Slocum's agonized letter to her mother in Sydney, the gathering storm of grief is perfectly conveyed in her run-on sentences and abrupt tonal shift from panic to hope to ghastly resignation.

So, too, does her husband's jolly letter about the months during which their unnamed twins of unspecified gender died of untold causes capture utterly the imperviousness of Slocum's emotional bulkheads, tightly sealed against the penetration of despair or complaint. He refuses to speak of the voyage and its aftermath as having been anything other than "a great success."

To have lost three of seven children in infancy would seem to anyone born after the general use in privileged societies of penicillin—and vaccines protecting against measles, mumps, diphtheria, whooping cough, scarlet fever, and smallpox—unendurable. Indeed, the grief was no doubt as intense for Joshua as for Virginia, but a world where such losses were unremarkable must be understood to be vastly different from our own. Samuel Eliot Morison writes of the *Phineas Pendleton* returning to a New England port from Peru with her lower masts painted black. A widowed captain's wife was aboard, her husband and their three children having died of diphtheria. Grief is not date-stamped. Lines written by John Donne or Ben Jonson or Anne Bradstreet cannot be surpassed in controlled agony, but the Slocums—having lost aboard ship three of their first five children—did not on that account desert nor even rebuke the sea. Neither did they leave off adding to their family.

The reality facing a merchant seaman such as Joshua Slocum was that just as he couldn't guarantee the delivery of goods by timetable, neither could he expect to be paid to move freight if he was unwilling to spend long periods away from home. He had to take whatever was offered, often loading at out-of-the-way ports goods destined for ports similar but distant. Although merchant mariners were not at sea for such protracted terms as whalers (it was not unknown for a Nantucket wife to wait five years for her husband's return), two years was a common period of separation. That the Slocums could not afford to buy and maintain a home ashore, whether in San Francisco or Sydney, was secondary to their delight in each other, so they made their home afloat, aboard whatever vessel from whichever hailing port offered the most attractive deal. It is certain that Virginia approved of this life, embraced it with a whole heart, and though there were other masters' wives who shared her enthusiasm, none could have exceeded it.

And this despite discomforts and perils. Homesickness was exacerbated by the anxiety of receiving family news while traveling halfway around the world, and the uncertainty of this news ever catching up. It could take more than a year to convey a letter from an exotic port to its San Francisco or Boston or Westport or Sydney destination. To keep abreast of bad news as well as good, holding a family together aboard ship might have seemed less distressful than leaving immediate family ashore. Joan Druett, in *Hen Frigates,* tells the awful story of a shipmaster receiving news that "one of his children had died, but his correspondent had neglected to tell him which one."

Children delivered by stork aboard hen frigates sometimes specified their birthplaces in latitude and longitude rather than place-name, the place being simply the sea (or, more specifically, the Bering Sea or the Sunda Strait).* Imagine being offshore during a full term of pregnancy. Morning sickness was compounded by seasickness, from which almost every deepwater man or woman suffered at least occasionally. "Paying homage to Neptune" was the jocund euphemism for the black comedy of puking, but nothing can adequately account for the despair provoked by that malady suffered so routinely by human beings who cast off from shore. There can't be many readers who haven't experienced the astonishing willingness of a person in the full throes of seasickness to die. If the cargo was stinky—fish, let's say—or the bilges dirty or the weather severe enough to drive the sufferer belowdecks: oh, dear! It was so bad, so sapping of energy and will, as to "unfit one for every effort," inducing "a feeling of extreme indifference to everything," in the words of a shipmaster's wife describing the first week of a long voyage from Boston in 1853. Yawning segues into dizziness, cold sweats, shortness of breath, drooling. In *Women of the Sea* (1962), Edward Rowe Snow quotes from the log his mother began in January 1883 aboard her father's bark *Russell,* bound for Santos, Brazil, from Liverpool. An American girl of fourteen at the time, she was exhilarated by her first day at sea: "I feel so happy; I just want to shout right out and tell everybody I am going on a long sea voyage with Father and Mother. All the boys and girls I know think I am lucky and want to come, too." Next day the plot shifts, like the deck underfoot, and her prose with it: "Our ship is rolling. Mother and I are awfully seasick. I can't write any more, and perhaps I never can." But she

---

*Joan Druett reports that during the nineteenth century more than seventy citizens of the small town of Searsport, Maine, were born at sea.

can, and does: "I feel terribly bad! I will climb into my bed, or bunk as the sailors call it, and stay there forever, maybe. Oh, dear, I said good-by to the land today, but now I guess I'll say good-by to the world." The ship plows and bucks west across the North Atlantic, and another day dooms: "If only the ship would stay still one minute, but she tosses and rolls, creaks and shivers and makes us all miserable. Lucky are those boys and girls who didn't come. The wind has increased to a gale." She lives, of course, to tell the tale, heard around her Winthrop, Massachusetts, hearth with many a knowing nod and reminiscing grin.

Seasickness is a bit like gout in its failure to evoke an empathetic response from those not suffering it. But so grave was the immediate consequence of the affliction that sailors new to the sea were routinely pampered by even bucko mates for the first few days, allowed to lie groaning in the fetal position in the yawing, pitching, rolling hell of their donkey-breakfast bunks. In "My First Voyage," an essay by J. G. Bisset, the veteran sailor and shipmaster remembers with painful vividness how it was for his apprentice self on his first day out of Liverpool, on the bark *County of Pembroke,* bound for Melbourne, Australia, around the Cape of Good Hope: "I threw myself into the bunk, fully dressed, and fell asleep." What seemed only minutes later he was turned out to go on watch, "but after a violent spasm of seasickness, climbed back again, and prayed that the ship might go down quickly and take me with it."* While it was a danger to the ship and its crew to send such a sick boy aloft, a mate's patience was notoriously limited, and this one's cure for Bisset was a pint of seawater scooped out of scuppers awash with heavy seas, up on deck where he had been dragged by the scruff of his neck. " 'Drink that; it'll make a sailor of you.' " It seems it did.

At least the water forced down Bisset's throat wasn't contaminated. Many afloat were not so lucky, with drinking water polluted by bilge-water or worse leaking into the casks and tanks. Organisms thrived in the heat of the tropics, and a sulfurous stink was the least of the water's offenses. After all, in those days "fresh" water would be pumped aboard directly from such noxious sources as Buenos Aires's muddy (and quixotically named) Rio Plata, or from the alligator-teeming and fetid canals of Batavia. Typhoid fever, known also as cesspool fever, was a common hazard of drinking—while holding one's nose and averting one's eyes—water from such sources.

---

*Included in Charles W. Domville-Fife's *Square-Rigger Days: Autobiographies of Sail* (1938).

Then add pregnancy to the situation. The peril of miscarriage was acute for storm-tossed expectant mothers sailing through extreme climate zones, erratically nourished and stress-inducingly detested by the crew. Virginia Slocum had to rely on her husband to attend her as midwife; he was also required to act as ship's doctor, setting fractures, sewing gashes, diagnosing tropical diseases. There is no record of Slocum's record as a diagnostician and healer, but a popular treatment of his time was purgation by castor oil and / or enemas and / or bloodletting. A more drastic cure was blistering by mustard or caustic pitch, perhaps on the principle of curing a headache by smashing one's thumb with a hammer. Given the haphazard state of nineteenth-century seaborne medicine, a healthy dose of benign neglect might have been the tenderest care an ailing sailor or pregnant woman could receive.

Now imagine that the mother thrives and gives birth. Stormy seas could break through a skylight and drown a baby in its crib. (Like most awful things, it happened.) Newborns died from insufficient mother's milk, those who weren't kept alive (temporarily) on a diet of rice water, sugar, and crushed ship's biscuits. Some children, the daughter Virginia lost in the Philippines among them, died of infections caused by teething. And as dangerous as it was for babies afloat, there is evidence—witness the Slocum twins dying in Portland—that ashore they would be subject to diseases from which they had been effectively quarantined at sea, where they developed no immunity. Cholera was a common horror, carried by ships from port to port, killing one in five of those who contracted it, and those died horribly and within a day: the victim might awake feeling fine, be bent double by cramps and dehydrated by diarrhea before lunch, and dead by dinner. (Slocum would experience the ravages of cholera off the east coast of South America in 1887, most of his crew killed off within a few days.) And there was dengue fever, accurately reviled as "breakbone fever" by the tropical sailors who suffered its agonizing joint pain. There were also—to rattle off a few alphabetically— appendicitis, beriberi, the croup, malaria (which had almost killed Slocum himself in Batavia), scurvy, typhus, and yellow fever.*

Put aside the dire possibilities and consider the domestic dailyness.

---

*W. H. Bunting quotes a master's letter home, Captain Joe Sewall aboard the *Edward Sewall*, regarding a winter storm off Cape Hatteras, following an easy passage from Hong Kong: "In the height of the blizzard Feb'y 9 Mrs S[ewall] was confined and gave birth to a fine large hearty boy. Everything went well, except the cold was severe and the ship tossing about on large seas. Feb'y 14 the baby suddenly took an ill turn and in a few hours strangled to death with croup."

Imagine cleaning diapers, or being a sailor forced to accept on intimate terms the challenge of changing diapers. Who would care to be that sailor off watch, trying to sleep through the caterwauling of a baby crying for milk or from colic? Imagine being a sailor dodging the master's toddler on deck, as the child learns to crawl and to walk and—inevitably—to climb in the rigging. (Kids got thrown around in heavy seas and were always in danger of being swept overboard, so a sailor might need to grow an extra limb: one hand for the ship, one for himself, and one for the captain's little girl.) Children born on warships got the cursed title "son of a gun," and there was good reason for sailors to expostulate about their miniature shipmates.

On the other hand, it's not for nothing that Rudyard Kipling's *Captains Courageous* is a classic of social and generational collision, hauling by literal accident a spoiled boy aboard a Grand Banks fishing schooner that rescues him from death at sea. And who could fail to envy Jim Hawkins's education by Long John Silver and his parrot in *Treasure Island*? Joan Druett tells of children learning to curse and tell yarns; one six-year-old, in reaction to being spanked, nearly broke his mother's wrist. And, while little boys and girls on deck were treated as almost indistinguishable creatures by the crew, the former learned especially quickly from their shipmaster fathers the privileges of command: "[Seven-year-old] Harry has been amusing himself hauling ropes and giving the sailors orders to haul . . . then to belay and then telling the man at the wheel to shake her a little so they can haul the sheets home, and with his hands behind his back, resting on his heels looking aloft (his favorite attitude)." Instead of running away to sea, inasmuch as they were already there, bold children often violated boundaries by going forward to the ordinary seamen in the forecastle, where presumably they would be subject to the baleful influences of irreverent yarns and corrupt chanteys. These visits were no picnic for the sailors, who often resented being put in peril of the master's wrath. But many actually liked hanging out with kids, when they had the leisure, and whittled model ships or carved scrimshaw for them or taught them knots.

What might seem peculiar to shorebound chauvinists and feminists—that masters often joined their wives at knitting and embroidering and sewing, or helping with the laundry—was a wholesome product of the unquestioned masculine power exerted by a ship captain "running his easting down," rounding Cape Stiff before a full gale with all sails flying.

Expressions of sadness—weeping—came easily to many sailors, and even Slocum was scrupulous to record in *Sailing Alone Around the World* several times when he gave way to his emotions, as he chose to phrase it.

Following the births of Victor (1872) and Benjamin (1873), daughter Jessie was born in the Philippines in 1875. Unlike her unlucky twin siblings born in 1877 and her sister born in 1879, she survived, like her brothers, into old age. In 1881, the Slocums' youngest child and third son was born aboard ship in Hong Kong. Slocum's first command after he lost the *Washington* was the *B. Aymar*, a so-called packet—that is, a fast-sailing carrier of passengers and of timely packages and mail—of 128 feet that was named for its owner, the prominent New York merchant Benjamin Aymar. (She was capacious enough to have carried more than 180 passengers to New York from Antwerp in 1857.) After some pleasurable passages shuttling between San Francisco and Honolulu, a milk run with abundant opportunities for the couple to socialize in the civilized ports of call at both ends of the voyage, the Slocums decided in 1873 to venture east as far as Japan and Australia.

Virginia eventually had four young children to raise and educate aboard various vessels, and her children and kin testify that she did a crackerjack job. She lavished love on her husband and children, and this affection was returned without the formality natural to their standing and the era's mores, with abundant storytelling, singing, and teasing.

Daughter Jessie, in a letter to Walter Teller, remembered her mother as "a remarkable woman. Not many had the stamina she had. There are none today [1952] would live as she had to. She lived truly as the Book of Ruth says." ("For wherever you go, I will go," saith that good woman.) But duty was only the bedrock of Virginia Slocum's tough and tender virtues. She played the harp, guitar, and piano, and several of her husband's vessels were equipped with pianos on which she taught her children songs. (Stephen Foster's "Oh! Susanna" was a favorite, along with any of his "Ethiopian" songs.) She conducted Sunday-school lessons and created scrapbooks from found art discovered from Saigon to Montevideo. The family experienced a floating geography lesson, arbitrary in its details but as inclusive as the ocean's limits.

Growing up aboard ship was peculiar, of course, and mothers especially fretted that it would leave their children ill prepared for life ashore.

Well and good for a daughter to know how to reef a topsail or a son how to use signal flags to communicate from the stem with the helmsman. "He is all ship, can't sing a note but knows considerable about a ship," complained one shipmaster's wife about her little boy. Another mother at sea reported that her fourteen-month-old daughter "can pull on the ropes, and sing out like any old sailor . . . and she pulls on every string or anything else she can get hold of." Joan Druett tells of a particular pair of young sisters so "black with sin" (in a kinsman's view) that they were known as Pot and Kettle; they climbed the ratlines and swore like, well, sailors. Many children who learned to walk at sea, with that wide-stanced gait produced by "sea legs" to keep upright on a rolling deck, remarked on how difficult the first days of walking instead on land were by comparison, and it was customary that sea kids' speech would seem curiously archaic, infused as it was by the cadences and lexicon of an antique culture, untutored by idiomatic landlubber influences.

But the deficits of growing up in a constricted space only a hundred feet long by thirty wide and traveling with very imperfect strangers, by fits and starts and through extreme weather, had to have been outweighed by the adventure of it all. An analogy might be the lure for many of whaling: despite the noisome and deadly nature of the work, despite the exploitation of its laborers, despite the years of separation from land suffered by crews, it was undeniably thrilling. The brief bursts of adrenaline triggered by the sight of a whale, the harpooning, the contest with a huge creature, the rush of surviving a Nantucket sleigh ride—these kicks made many seamen return willingly to endure a lot worse than penal servitude. Nevertheless, of the Slocums' children only Victor devoted his life to sailing vessels and steamships.

An offhand detail in Victor Slocum's brief *New York Times* obituary in 1949 refers to his mother as having been "a school teacher." The Slocum children spent their early years in the Pacific, between Australia and the coast of Siberia, with extensive visits to Honolulu, Manila, and Canton, and from 1872 through 1883 Virginia strictly observed, during the three hours before noon of every weekday, lessons in spelling, reading, and arithmetic. (Mathematics—like astronomy—was vividly practical, a necessary set of rules applied to the problem of determining the ship's position.) Discipline was enforced, in Victor's memory, "by a switch stuck over a picture in the cabin and the culprit had to fetch it himself when it was needed, but that, as I must say, was not often." On deck they learned to splice and to tie knots, and studied sewing with the sailmaker. On Saturdays they did chores, cleaning their quarters and mending their own clothes. They amused themselves with whist and dominoes, and above all they talked. At Sunday school, a matter of indifference to Joshua, Virginia set a lesson to be memorized from the Bible, and memorization—as was the happy custom of Victorian schooling—played a principal part in their brood's education. The Slocums' taste was catholic, and Victor remembers with fondness his parents' amused instruction in a foreign language using a German comic book they bought the children in Hong Kong. Virginia's experience of her father's passion for Shakespeare inspired her to infect her own offspring with the bug, which she already shared with her husband.

And his shipboard library was extensive. Victor recalled many volumes about the sea: histories of battles and explorations, reproductions of ancient charts and mathematical tables, books of natural history, botany, and ornithology (Darwin and Huxley). Victor vividly remembered animated discussions at the galley table about Washington Irving's popular biography of Christopher Columbus, "the great navigator's triumphs and misfortunes as well as the shameful treatment of the Indians by the gang of cruel adventurers at their heels."

This recollection reflects the confusion of conflicting images, not only of Joshua Slocum but also of all the other Americans and Europeans venturing to the edges of the world, not to discover or conquer but to trade and often to exploit and cheat. Exploitation was race- and color-blind, and if pirates abounded in Malaysia and the South China Sea, cannibals were known to satisfy their appetites with missionaries chancing to wash ashore and fall captive during mealtimes in the Solomon Islands and the New Hebrides. It was for no fanciful reason that Slocum had fake gunports painted on both the *B. Aymar* and the *Amethyst*. Readers of *Sailing Alone Around the World* will find vigorous contempt for the wily "savages" of Tierra del Fuego a few pages distant from Slocum's paean to the sweet-voiced singing of brown-skinned children during his romantic idyll in the South Pacific.

In addition to studying texts devoted to the technical aspects of his calling—navigation and marine design—Slocum favored the work of essayists like Lamb, Addison, Twain, and Macaulay, as well as such historians as Gibbon and Hume. Victor observes that his father "was always looking [for] models of style" to develop his own writing. He loved fiction and poetry: *Pickwick Papers* was a special favorite—testimony to his nice sense of the ridiculous—and in verse he had of course memorized Coleridge's "Rime of the Ancient Mariner." Given Slocum's extraordinary adventures, it is tautologically fitting, even charming, to learn from his son that he "simply reveled in the tales of Sinbad the Sailor."

As soon as Victor was old enough to understand a story, he shivered from fright at his father's enlargement of the child's dimly recollected encounter with Bully Hayes, a theatrically notorious pirate, at the Malaysian island of Oulan. After enjoying a postprandial promenade with Virginia around the deck of the *B. Aymar,* Slocum would often tell stories to his two-and-a-half-year-old son. "By this time," Victor writes, "I had acquired both the faculties of observation and memory. I soon began to remember things because there was always so much going on worth remembering." His own dreams were troubled by accounts of the cunning Chinese and Malay brigands too cowardly to "attack a foreign devil merchant ship in a brisk breeze, but instead lurking on the horizon waiting for a vessel to be becalmed or grounded on a sand bar, usually near the mouth of a river." Then they would man their oars, "swarm aboard, murder the ship's people and tow the whole thing inshore for plunder."

Bully Hayes was a white devil, the last of the buccaneers, born in Cleveland in 1829, in his prime active in the New Hebrides and the Loyalty Islands of the South Seas. He captured natives, transported them to Australia, and sold them to Brisbane planters—the old and familiar trade of "blackbirding" or man-stealing. Another of Hayes's trades was so-called filibustering, a nice term for piracy. Joshua Slocum recalled that that "resourceful ruffian . . . hove across my course" in 1873.* At that time Hayes was posing as a missionary, a ruse to save himself from hanging, and in the lagoon of Oulan he came alongside the *B. Aymar* paddled by a crew "amazingly tattooed and fairly belted with knives." Fully bearded, tall, and massively muscular, the pirate wore "an air of great

---

*Slocum's final published work, "Bully Hayes, the Last Buccaneer," appeared in *Outing* in March 1906. It's an as-told-to adventure yarn, only infrequently told in Slocum's understated idiom. Hayes deserved the hype: he once attended a play in Sydney devoted to exaggerations of his misdeeds, including pillage and rape, and declared himself—moments before eluding capture by the police—to be well pleased with the performance. The story as reported in Victor's biography is unintentionally a jamboree of fabulation, with Slocum retailing the lies of the buccaneer to conform to a Sinbadish narrative plan concocted by *Outing*'s reporter, whose version Victor then consulted as an aide-mémoire.

dignity and authority. His speech was slow and sprinkled with godly phrases." And what booty did he demand in return for the boatload of bananas he had brought Captain Slocum? A Bible, of course. " 'My own copy of the Holy Scriptures has been worn out by much use,' he explained, 'and my natives are sitting in darkness waiting for the reading of The Word.' "

Hayes complained that on the Micronesian island of Ponape, as the outcome of a dispute with "a tattooed savage" (the island's king), Hayes's first mate, "Lanky" Pease, plundered the island of timber and buffalo, and loaded the cargo aboard their vessel, crewed by "wild-eyed Mongolians." The pirate/missionary didn't neglect to observe that "the old packet needed a washing out after those coolies." Hayes then told Slocum of his mate's rascality and, forgetting his missionary manners, exclaimed: "I wouldn't have been so put out about it if he had been content with a fair cargo of buffalo, but, God damn him, he took so many that he had to cut holes in the deck to let their horns stick up through. By the Great Shark, when I meet him, he dies!"

In fact, another mate—one "Dutch Pete"—murdered Hayes four years later, after a quarrel, and dumped him overboard, where he was no doubt taken as salvage by Beelzebub.

The Slocums' children had fond memories of Christmas in Asian ports. The stockings, hung one year from the mizzenmast, were filled by Santa with Japanese toys and Chinese treats. Jessie remembered a carved Melanesian doll. Victor recalled being excited to receive a fanciful kite and a paper rooster in China. There was always a roasted turkey or goose dinner, and plum pudding for the crew. The kids—dressed in Chinese suits, tasseled caps, and turned-up shoes—would be photographed, then rowed around the harbor to other hen frigates to celebrate with any children present while their mother socialized with other shipmasters' wives.

Because Slocum, like other merchant captains, was busy in port with customs officers and consignees and suppliers and shipwrights and riggers and consular officers, Virginia was left to her ingenuity. During an age of formality and rigid class distinction ashore, on-the-fly get-togethers between masters' wives dispensed with decorums. Local lore was precious, and methods for discovering and paying a fair price for clothes and fresh fruit were as important as techniques for dealing with hostile seamen were potentially life-and-death. (No evidence suggests that Virginia took much interest in the exotic food—curries and guava and bouillabaisse, say—to which her travels must have introduced her. Her children remembered her as a rough-and-ready cook, with a range extending from chowder to blueberry pie.) Many journals of captain's wives during this period detail these rare social occasions, much as a novelist of manners or an anthropologist might observe the speech and furnishings of others. Whether got up in simple bed-ticking dresses for comfort in tropical ports or fully rigged out in floor-sweeping skirts and shawls, enhanced (as Druett describes) by "mittens, tippets, fringes, beadings and bonnets so beloved by Victorians," they assumed themselves to be women of consequence.

So starved were sailing wives and children for company while at sea that they even (briefly) envied whalers, who stayed at sea for so long that they never missed an opportunity, when spying another whaler at sea, to heave to for news, an exchange of food, and a gam. Joan Druett tells in *Hen Frigates* of shipmasters offering rewards to any member of his crew spotting a ship at sea, the sight of "someone in the world beside ourselves." Afforded such luck, the ships might approach closely enough—risking and not always avoiding collision—to exchange messages chalked on blackboards. Virginia Slocum was so sociable a woman that it might have been an insupportable burden to be separated from her friends and extended family in Sydney, but no evidence suggests that she ever complained.

And nothing in her husband's writing expresses any concern for her experience or emotions. About his mother and Virginia, Slocum's reticence seems pathological, but efforts to put him on the couch are insolent and unavailing. For all his goodwill, fine manners, and common sense, Walter Teller commissioned a graphologist to study Slocum's penmanship, principally to unravel the mystery of his refusal to make any but the most glancing—and grief-burdened—allusions to Virginia's death, and none at all to her life. Readers are directed to their imaginations to see and overhear the couple together, perhaps on a calm night at sea, leaning over the rail, discussing in voices pitched low to assure privacy their ambitions or fears or elemental affection for each other.

Her children vividly recollected a series of caged canaries, a popular shipboard diversion. Monkeys were common aboard the Slocums' larger ships. Cats were also sometimes taken aboard, but the time would inevitably come—often in the worst of weather—when they decided to climb aloft, thus claiming all nine lives in a fell swoop. Benjamin fondly noted another arrow in his mother's quiver, the pleasure she took from killing sharks: "To spend a few hours with sharks, in mid-ocean," as he wrote Teller, "Mother and I teamed up. It was my job to get the shark interested in coming close up. I used a new tin can with a string on it to attract the shark close under the stern where Mother dispatched it with her .32 caliber revolver with which she never needed but one shot. How I loved to see her do it."* Even if the unerringness of her aim was exaggerated by a loving son's memory, her competence is as impressive as her enthusiasm was robust, and on several occasions she would need to aim her revolver at human beings. Yet, as her daughter wrote to Teller, even then it was known that "her heart was not strong."

Despite shooting sharks and playing the piano and teaching her children lessons and assisting her husband with navigation and listening to her birds sing, Virginia Slocum's lot at sea was monotony. Rockwell Kent wrote in *Voyaging,* his remarkable account of sailing in the roaring forties, that before any roaring began there was a steady, less dramatic hum.

> With the disappearance of land the ship at sea becomes a planetary body moving in the orbit of its prescribed course through the fluid universe of the ocean . . . The true record of a voyage on the sea must be a record of those illusive imaginings of the almost unconscious mind responding to the hypnotic monotony of the ship's vibrations, of the liquid rustling of the water streaming past her sides . . . and the even seething pattern of her wake. The memory of it is of prolonged and changeless contentment.

Well, for the landbound, that's the conundrum, isn't it? Did this constitute the ecstasy of a natural rhythm or the drip-drip-drip-drip of a water torture? It seems that Virginia and Joshua Slocum never asked, bless them. If love cannot conquer all, it can surely confound conventional expectations of what is tolerable. As a kinswoman wrote Teller, the Slocums "were deeply in love and could be completely oblivious of everyone and everything if they could be together."

---

*Hatred and fear of sharks were universal among seamen. In *Sailing Alone Around the World,* when Slocum encountered "wolves of the sea," he took time from solitary sailing to "shoot them through the head." It was believed they could smell death before it arrived, and that a shark following in a ship's wake announced that someone aboard would soon die, and that, if caught and brought aboard, their stomachs would contain sailors' remains. Let's assume they generally didn't, though a French naturalist of the sixteenth century asserted that sharks adored eating white men, and Englishmen above all.

The B. Aymar

The Amethyst

FIVE

Enterprises

My mother, with her three children, made the best of jungle life during the construction of the steamer. The air was heavy and damp and there was the poison of vegetation as well as the peril of venomous creeping things. Up through the cracks in the split bamboo flooring could crawl centipedes, scorpions, and even a small boa if it took a notion to come in at night, and hang down from the rafters, tail first. We found that both centipedes and scorpions had a habit of crawling into our shoes while they were not in use, so it was routine to shake and search everything while dressing in the morning . . . Nearby was a swamp filled with crocodiles, and their barkings were added to the singing of locusts. Only in forests like those in the Philippines can one hear such a nocturnal roar. It affects the superstitious tendencies of the natives. It will get a white man if he is alone too long in such a jungle.

—VICTOR SLOCUM, *Capt. Joshua Slocum*

THE SLOCUMS' THIRD CHILD, Jessie Lena, was born in June 1875 while the *B. Aymar* was at anchor in Subic Bay. The New York merchant who had given his name to the vessel was brought low by the Panic of 1873—caused by the burst bubble of America's exuberant enthusiasm for railroad stocks—and his East Indies trader was sold, marooning the family on the beach. And what a beach it was!

Still, Victor Slocum's elaboration of the perfect ghastliness of the flora and fauna at Olangapo on Subic Bay requires some modification. Boa constrictors there were, though of moderate size and pacific disposition, despite his memory of them being ten to twelve feet long and his claim to "have a picture of one thirty feet [with] a body as thick as a man's." But he failed to mention the cobras and Wagler's pit vipers native to the region. Scorpions there were and centipedes so venomous that one of the few deaths attributed to the pest's bite occurred in the Philippines, the victim a ten-year-old child, the same age as the Philippine schoolgirl who was attacked and decapitated by a crocodile while she was paddling her canoe to school.

Olongapo, sixty miles from Manila and contiguous with Bataan, is now a city of a quarter million, and until recently adjacent to a huge United States naval base. In 1875 it was the site of preindustrial shipbuilding enterprises, affording access to good timber on the inland slopes—where the boa constrictors were kept company by hordes of chattering monkeys—and having the advantage of a perfect launching beach, with deep water near to shore.

The Slocums came here owing to a meeting between Joshua and Edward Jackson, the English entrepreneur and naval architect who had brokered the sale of the *B. Aymar* to a Shanghai shipping firm. A go-getter, Jackson wanted to build a 150-ton steamer of his design to be used in the Philippine Islands for the transport of passengers and freight. Commissioning Slocum to supervise the construction was not a hard sell, given that he was high and dry with three children and shipbuilding was, after sailing in deep water, his favorite calling.

His first challenge was to build a native nipa hut at the inland edge of the beach. Bamboo, with a thatched roof, nipa huts are elevated (those crocodiles!), and for stilts Slocum used molave, a fine-grained hardwood resistant to rot, uninviting to ants, and also used locally for ships. To support his hut against the assaults of inevitable typhoons, Slocum applied his skill as a rigger to stay it, as though the center-pole were a mast, with what Victor describes as "stout ropes of twisted rattan secured to stakes driven into the ground." This precaution had never before been displayed at Subic Bay, and it drew attention—and resentment—to Slocum and his family, particularly from the Chinese, who until then were the go-to cohort when a ship needed building. They in turn were resented by native Tagal laborers, whose character Victor esteemed more greatly than that of the "Chinamen," despite what he took to be Tagal fecklessness: "any native would much rather go to a cockfight than work."

Beneath the floor of their hut the Slocums kept pigs and those fowl not in the fight game. The tropical climate—today a plus for tourists—was frequently as oppressively damp and suffocating as a barber's hot towel. Joshua busied himself getting Jackson's steamer hull built—the engine and fittings would be installed at Manila—and Virginia kept her sons and infant daughter out of danger, and in Victor's case out of mischief. They spent a year at this adventure, as constructing the vessel was slow work. "It was as though," Victor reports, "this was the first vessel ever to be built. Monkeys screeched and scampered from the trees as they fell to the woodsmen's axes. Tagal sawyers ripped the timber into scantling and plank by hand, using a single frame saw." Of the writers who have memorialized Joshua Slocum's history, he is the most specific about the processes that excited his father's ingenuity and dismay. A reader will learn from Victor's *Capt. Joshua Slocum* exactly how fishermen's boots were hand-lasted in his grandfather's shop on Brier Island, as well as the difficulties and the virtues of building a hull from timber native to Olongapo. John McPhee would approve of Victor's avidity for sequence and procedure. It's fair to assume that by the time he was five years old, and witnessing the work at Olongapo, he had begun to absorb the habit of studying the nature and uses of things and techniques from the example of his father's emphatic competence. There is pleasure to be taken from reading about the hardwoods available on Luzon for such construction. The molave mentioned above was impervious to sea worms and "came in logs thirty-five feet long by twenty-four inches square, often crooked, which made it all the more suitable for ship frames. There was . . . Dugan, the ironwood, which sinks like a stone . . . together with Luan, which was used to plank the Manila galleons because the Spaniards discovered that it did not splinter with shot . . . [and] the tall Mangachpuy, springy and durable for masts and decks." In addition, because his father later bought Philippine timber to sell in China, the inventory is named—"Ebony, Camagon, Narra and Tindalo"—perhaps as much for the music of the nouns as for their value in fine joinery.

The heavy logs, having been felled in the jungle, were skidded to the beach by carabaos, domesticated water buffalo weighing as much as a ton and—when docile—able to haul daunting loads. Trust Victor to excite even these ponderous beasts: "Though apparently clumsy, carabaos can be very quick and sure with their horns; a cow, to protect her calf, was once known to hook a shark out of the water and to rip it open." Shortly before the hull was completed, humans rather than carabaos, crocs, boa constrictors, scorpions, or centipedes put the family in deadly peril. Virginia, whose prescience was displayed again and again (beginning at Cook Inlet during the fiasco and triumph of their salmon-fishing adventure), had been wary of the sullen Chinese muttering near her at Olongapo. One night, while Joshua was conducting business in Manila, she heard shouting near the hut and went to the doorway to find a crowd carrying lit torches. There had been rumors that the Chinese meant to murder the Slocums in their sleep, as a warning against other foreigners ambitious to build boats in their precinct. The torch-lit crowd was made up of Tagals who'd worked on the Slocums' hut as well as Edward Jackson's steamship, and they had installed themselves— unbidden—as bodyguards.

In the end, the Chinese contented themselves with sabotaging the boat's launching by pulling the tracks out of alignment, thus derailing the heavy vessel in the sand. The Tagals—orchestrating a veritable rodeo of buffalo—managed to drag her afloat at high tide, whereupon she was towed to Manila to be fitted with boiler, engine, and conveniences.

Now it was time for Slocum to be paid by Edward Jackson, who declared himself pleased with the mariner's work. But—as was to happen all too often to this square-dealing man—his employer's contract had fine-printed codicils. Giving an excuse that has gone unrecorded, Jackson offered Slocum in place of the money he'd been promised—take it or leave it—a forty-five-ton schooner named *Pato*, the Spanish word for "duck" (the noun rather than the imperative verb).

Slocum's logs, journals, and incoming correspondence were lost with him when the *Spray* disappeared in 1908, so it is impossible to reconstruct either the extent of his Olongapo losses or his attitude toward Jackson. But Victor Slocum is emphatic about his mother's haste to get her family off that muggy and pest-ridden beach, away from "venemous creeping things" and Chinese shipwrights—"a savage lot," descended from pirates—scheming to seize or destroy the steamship. Almost as an afterthought, he adds that so fierce and unabated was the hostility of the leader of this Chinese mob "that his son, six years afterwards, attempted to stab the Captain while ashore in Manila." (Indeed, attempts on Joshua Slocum's life, usually at knifepoint, became almost routine during the following dozen or so years.)

The *Pato* was more yacht than drogher. Designed and built by Edward Jackson, she was inspired by the schooner *Sappho*, defender of the second America's Cup and holder for thirty-six years of the record for the fastest west-to-east transatlantic crossing—twelve days—which she set shortly before the *Pato* was built in the Philippines. Seventy-two feet long (shorter than the *Sappho* by thirty) and forty-five tons, the Slocums' new home afloat still lacked a cabin-house when they boarded her, but what work had been completed was of high quality. While she was much smaller than the *Washington* or the *B. Aymar,* her fine lines and impressive turn of speed inspired admiration and even envy among Slocum's fellow shipmasters, and he soon reckoned that he had landed on his feet after Jackson's breach of agreement.

He put their new boat to work right away, transporting general cargo interisland through the Philippines. The Slocums took a cat aboard named Flagstaff, owing to the determined verticality of her tail in all winds, and soon the *Pato* was chartered by the insurance underwriters of a British bark run aground on a coral reef (prophetically named on the Admiralty chart as North Danger Reef) almost five hundred miles from Manila, a valuable cargo of Chinese tea and silk in her hold. The salvage mission required three round-trips between Manila and the wrecked bark to transfer and deliver the goods, and such was Slocum's resourcefulness during the process that he immediately got a commission to carry cargo from Manila to Hong Kong.

During that voyage he had a bright idea, and Virginia, pregnant again, leaped at its boldness. They would go fishing again! And thus it was that Joshua Slocum embarked on one of his most stirring adventures: a voyage from Manila and through Hong Kong and Yokohama to Kamchatka and the cod-fishing grounds of the Okhotsk Sea.

Bound on the west by Siberia and on the east by the Kamchatka Peninsula, with the Kuril Islands barring its southern mouth, the Okhotsk Sea was remote and forbidding, iced over much of the year. Its isolation and hostility excited Slocum's practical as well as venturesome motives. The fishing grounds, only recently discovered by Europeans and Americans, were rich and lightly exploited. Whalers were sailing into the sea to take bowheads, and the salmon runs rivaled what Cook Inlet had provided, but Slocum was on the hunt for cod.

He got the idea aboard the *Pato* while sailing toward Hong Kong and sorting through sea chests that had accompanied him and Virginia since their misadventure in Alaska. One of his chests held knives used to split fish, and handling them after six years was enough to change the course he had charted for his family aboard their trim schooner, fast enough to deliver light cargo but surely not designed to carry fish in her hold. Nor was the crew he hired in Hong Kong suitable for yacht racing; "flotsam of the North Pacific," as Victor characterizes them, they must have seemed a rough gang to ship aboard a small vessel carrying three children and a wife six months or more pregnant with twins. "Enough seal poachers, sea otter hunters . . . were found on the beach [at Hong Kong] to make a fishing crew willing to go on shares. These were of the type that the Captain had come to know on the Northwest Coast and they got on well together."

In the event, the adventure that summer was as thrilling as discovering gold nuggets strewn for the taking, "a stirring voyage and altogether a delightful time on the fishing grounds," as Slocum would write after it ended, even if the aftermath—the death of those twins in Portland—caused the Slocums' second son, Benjamin, to write Walter Teller that "the ocean is no place to raise a family." His older brother disagreed, recalling this excursion in enthusiastic detail. Victor was old enough at five to remember the events vividly and young enough to have their drama amplified by their very novelty.

Victor's account of that summer is lavish, detailed, and for the first time in his book he doesn't rely on what his father later wrote or told him. He elaborates every aspect of the adventure—the geography, history, biological diversity, and culture of the Okhotsk Sea—with his research as a grown writer, fueled by his thrill at having been there, seen that, and done so in the company of his parents and young siblings. For Slocum's later biographers, Walter Teller and Ann Spencer, the codfishing episode was an interlude in the busy to-ings and fro-ings in a merchant seaman's itinerary, and they each devote roughly a dutiful page to the events that began with the Slocums' boarding of the *Pato* in Manila and ended with her sale two years later in Honolulu. Victor's account runs sixteen animated pages, starting with his father's purchase in Hong Kong of four fishing dories, nested in pairs and strapped to the *Pato's* deck as she voyaged almost three thousand miles north to the Siberian port of Petropavlovsk.

This route took them through the Formosa Strait, where they sailed among what Victor characterizes as "the great fleet of trading and fishing junks," an encounter worth remarking inasmuch as the speed, stiffness, and dry decks of these Asian vessels deeply influenced Joshua

Slocum's later design of his self-built rescue vessel, the *Liberdade*. The journey continued north through the Korea Strait, with Japan to the southeast, and after twenty-five days and two thousand miles, the *Pato* entered the Okhotsk. Three days later, "my mother, all aglow with excitement, called me on deck to see the high conical peak of Mount Vil-luchinski, white and glistening in the morning sunlight, high above the fog drifting upon the sea." Seven thousand feet high and twenty miles distant, "it was one of the sights never to be forgotten in one's lifetime." (For such outbursts of wholehearted astonishment and affection, *Capt. Joshua Slocum: The Adventures of America's Best Known Sailor* should be val-ued above what could have been merely an opportunity to cash in on having a famous father.)

By the time Slocum and his family and speculative crew had wet their lines in the Sea of Okhotsk, the process of taking and cleaning and salt-ing cod had been refined—if that's the best word for a mess of scales and guts—off the coast of New England. First, everyone worked on shares determined by formulas bearing on ownership of the vessel, the cost of fitting her out, and the purchase price of salt to cure the fare (as the total catch was termed). Slocum found the best fishing grounds by in-formed trial and error, every now and then casting a baited line over the rail near the shoreline of Cape Lopatka. Victor earned the privilege of claiming to have caught—by happy accident and in defiance of his father's command to keep his hands off the fishing gear—the first and one of the biggest of the twenty-five thousand cod they were soon to haul on board.

As soon as the captain was satisfied that this was the place, he anchored in twenty fathoms (120 feet) and the dories nested on the *Pato*'s deck were launched and rowed, trailing trawls 1,200 feet long with baited hooks every twelve feet. This was hand-over-fist work, and everyone joined in, most eagerly Virginia, four days after delivering her ill-fated twins. They soon realized that they had grossly underestimated their haul, bringing along only enough salt to cure a small catch for the Manila market. But luck ebbed and flowed like a Fundy tide for the Slocums, and here, sailing over the horizon at this isolated spot on the Okhotsk, loomed none other than the *Constitution*, the vessel on which Victor had been born. She, too, had been hauling cod, and was loaded to her gun-wales with fish and about to shovel her excess salt into the ocean, but instead it went free of charge into the *Pato*'s holds.

Then the fun really began. There's nothing like price-per-unit scavenging to get the blood running hot, and in addition to whatever share each crew member would receive when the fare was sold in port, each cod caught by hand line from the mother vessel drew a bounty of twenty-five cents, with Victor's and Benjamin's catches tallied along with Virginia's. As Victor remembered, "the sinker no sooner touched bottom than you had one . . . In two weeks the schooner was loaded to her marks." There was a bit more to the process than dangling bait on a hook and hauling in money. The catch had to be salt-cured to arrest the natural process of decay caused by enzymes and bacteria, but for dry-curing each fish had to have the greatest amount of its meat salted down. Once taken aboard the cod moved along a gruesome assembly line, described in detail by Elijah Kellogg in *The Fisher Boys of Pleasant Cove* (1874)*: a "throater" slit the fish's throat and pulled out its tongue before slicing open the belly and cutting grooves on each side of its head. Next a "header" broke off the head and tore out the liver (saved for oil) and entrails, moving the remaining body along to the "splitter," who stripped out the backbone and dropped the rest into the hold to the "salter," who did what his name suggests, with a fine judgment as to how much salt to apply and how most efficiently to "kench them down," arranging them in tiers, alternating napes and tails.

Having already abandoned his plan to take their fare to Manila's paltry and pinch-fist market, Slocum decided to sail it to Victoria, on Vancouver Island in British Columbia, a distance of 2,900 miles following the curve of the Aleutian Islands along the great circle route, requiring more sophisticated navigation—constant shifts of heading as opposed to straight-line (rhumb-line) sailing—and the prospect of cold and dense fog. For Victor, the adventure continued, as landing parties in the Aleutians came back aboard with geese, and a member of the crew asked to be put ashore with his rifle to bag the *Pato* a bear. "In an hour he hailed us from the beach and when he tumbled over the rail he was covered with mud and badly shocked from fright . . . No one could get anything out of him further than that he had found the bear."

After months at sea in uninviting waters, with a rough-and-ready crew and a hold full of dead fish, Victoria must have been a tempting place to

---

*An eloquent account of the details of cod fishing and many other marine practices of Slocum's time is *The Maritime History of Maine: Three Centuries of Shipbuilding and Seafaring* (1948), by William Hutchinson Rowe.

rest at anchor, with its colonial civility, snug harbor, and rose gardens. But Slocum and his crew disdained the price offered for their haul and quickly set sail for the Columbia River, where the *Pato* was towed to Portland by a stern-wheeled steamer. Upon arrival, Slocum continued to speculate: using his catch as collateral, he borrowed enough money to pay off his crew, based on the price quoted for the San Francisco market. Virginia's share was sixty dollars, with which she bought a Singer sewing machine. The children, too—baby Jessie included—were paid, according to detailed records kept by their mother.

Their father, alert to chance, had decided to cut out the middleman in his sale of what he knew to be the first full fare of salt cod brought to Oregon. The final curing and packing in tins was done across the Willamette River in East Portland, and the family lived ashore near the *Pato*'s wharf during the following months, giving Victor his only experience of formal schooling. The owner of their boardinghouse became friendly with Virginia and gave her a canary named Peter, who as her son wrote would "live longer than his mistress."

Portland was already a lively city in the late 1870s, with a bustling red-light district, rough saloons, and many restaurants. Sailors routinely ignored warnings to be careful and stay sober lest they wake up with a broken crown, shanghaied on a derelict vessel (justly referred to in slang as an old hooker), and in debt to the shipmaster who'd paid a crimp two months' wages to buy them. But a lively city is a hungry city, as Slocum was not slow to appreciate.

He quickly went about his business, and few of his enterprises better dramatize what a carpe diem kind of fellow he was, remarkable even in such a carpe diem period in our carpe diem country's history. Like a costume-jewelry salesman showing off his wares on his wrists and fingers, Slocum went from restaurant to fish market carrying one of his "Cape Cod turkeys" by its tail, but was surprised to encounter frank skepticism. It seemed his cod was too dark, since Portland diners were accustomed to white meat that had been bleached pale by astringent alum. A lemonade-from-lemons idea formed in an exclamatory bubble above the entrepreneur's head, and he bought one of the bleached cod and thereafter went forth to potential buyers bearing one of each, preaching against the bitter evils of alum bleach and thus introducing to the people of Portland—soon to become the greenest good citizens of all—the benefits of natural, pure, organic, and dark food.

Having wintered over in Portland, the Slocums sailed for Honolulu at the end of March 1878, with an eye to selling the *Pato* there. Fast and elegant, she was too small for carrying cargo, and Slocum had resolved to join the timber trade between the Philippine forests and Hong Kong boat builders. During the comfortable passage to Oahu, Slocum and his crew holystoned the decks, varnished the brightwork, and polished the brass. He rightly hoped to present her as a yacht rather than a codfish smack, though what she smelled like belowdecks has not been told.

Slocum had a genius for putting himself in the way of opportunity. After a few interisland passages with general freight he and his family found themselves docked in Honolulu shortly after the departure of what Victor describes as "the crack mail schooner, *Hilo*," which was "well out of the narrow coral entrance to [the harbor], when a belated sack of mail was rushed down" to the docks too late, to the postal official's dismay. Victor quotes his father as calling out, " 'Heave aboard here, I'll take it out to her.' Beat the *Hilo*? Nothing like that was ever heard among the Islands." The throng ashore saw the race was on, and a favorable gust, combined with a calm that slowed its rival, enabled the *Pato* to drive down upon the fabled mail schooner "like a train of cars." Catching up, Slocum—with a pretty display of seamanship—sailed close enough to toss the mail aboard the *Hilo*.

Soon after, word of the impromptu race was published in the *Pacific Commercial Advertiser* and a local planter offered to buy the *Pato* for $5,000 in twenty-dollar gold pieces. The Slocums booked passage to San Francisco on the German bark *Christine*. Shortly before sailing the planter tried to pay in silver rather than gold, a proposition Slocum refused. Victor recalls that his father held up the *Christine*'s departure more than an hour while negotiations were concluded. At last the captain was striding down the dock and up the gangplank with a sack in his hand. "It was gold. My mother was sitting on the after-deck in a wide rattan chair when the bag was tossed into her lap with—'Virginia, there's the schooner.' "

In San Francisco Slocum soon singled out the *Amethyst* among the huge fleet anchored and wharfed in the harbor, many for sale. She was a bark of one hundred feet and four hundred tons (four times the *Pato*'s carrying capacity), oak-built and copper-fastened and with exquisite finish work by Thatcher Magoun in Medford, Massachusetts. The *Amethyst* had been launched in 1822, in a series including *Topaz, Sapphire,* and *Emerald.* She had been a passenger ship with the Jewell Line of Boston, carrying passengers to and from Liverpool, notably on one passage west of seventeen days. Even though the *Amethyst* held the round-trip transatlantic speed record for thirty years, the popularity of even speedier clippers had eclipsed her favor with passengers. After being used to hunt bowhead whales in the Bering Strait, and then unromantically to carry coal from Puget Sound to San Francisco, she was put up for sale at a price that Slocum could afford.

As old and abused as she was, the *Amethyst* was in fine condition. Victor remembers especially the luxurious finish of the owner's stateroom, "handsomely fitted up in mahogany and horsehair." While Slocum refitted her for the timber trade, coppering her bottom (to protect against sea worms and delay the adhesion of speed-robbing algae and mussels) and cutting a hole in her bluff bow as a pass-through for lumber, his family lived ashore for a few months at the Clipper Hotel, at the foot of Market Street. Victor's memories are as usual vividly narrated: the bustling waterfront and especially the arrivals and departures of the Sacramento ferry, her steam calliope releasing the pressure of her boilers by ear-splitting renditions of Verdi's "The Prison Song" from *Il Trovatore.* Less nostalgically he recollects the virulent prejudice against "Celestials," the "Heathen Chinee" brought to America's West to build railroads and, once they were built, disdained as interlopers. After the Central Pacific had used up their labor, it was proposed they should be forcibly repatriated or, failing that, put to sleep. Victor recalls a night at the Clipper, as a boy of seven, being terrified by a torch-lit lynch mob passing beneath his hotel windows, led by followers of Dennis Kearney, a rabid racist and nativist (himself born in Cork County, Ireland, a sailor who jumped ship in San Francisco). He claims that his father had prepared himself at an open window to rotten-egg Kearney, "but my mother dragged [him] away from the window by his coat tails and told him that if he threw it and hit Kearney . . . the mob would burn down the hotel."

Joshua Slocum's tender feelings for the Chinese (despite his friction with them at Subic Bay) must have owed more than a little to his dependence on their eagerness to buy the Philippine timber he hoped to sell them. During the three years he was the owner and master of the *Amethyst,* she traded exclusively "out east" in the Pacific. But before the

Slocums sailed for Manila, Joshua made a trip by rail, alone, back home to Nova Scotia. En route he wrote dispatches for the *Sacramento Bee,* which clippings were lost with Slocum's other papers; but reporting put a busy bee in his bonnet, his first venture as a freelancer. According to Victor, on his way east he found himself defending the honor of a lady whose privacy had been violated one night in her compartment, confronting the villain on a railway station platform in Altoona, Pennsylvania. Victor repeats his father's account: "It was a biting, frosty morning and he said he felt extra athletic. He knocked the intruder cold."

Victor also reports that the captain did not visit his own father, the curmudgeon having remarried and moved to Lunenburg, on the Atlantic shore of Nova Scotia; but the failure of a reunion after a separation of eighteen years cannot plausibly be put to the hundred or so miles between Brier Island and his father's new home. Did Slocum think better of reconciliation? Some family feeling provoked the visit, because when he returned by train he brought along his youngest sister and brother, Ella and Ingram, who would sail with his family aboard the *Amethyst,* Ella to help pregnant Virginia with the children and Ingram to cook for the Slocums and the ship's officers in the ship's caboose galley, with headroom a foot lower than his six-foot-two height. To compound his discomfort, during the first leg of the *Amethyst*'s voyage she carried poorly stowed railroad iron, the shifting of which caused the vessel to roll sickeningly.

From Honolulu they sailed to Guam, to take on water and fresh fruit and vegetables. Slocum was unimpressed by the islanders, describing them to his family as yahoos (he had been reading *Gulliver's Travels*): "He found the natives," Victor writes, "very like the Malays of the Philippines, indolent by nature and cruel to their animals." On the scale of intolerance, Slocum's prejudices fell well short of the British and Dutch colonials' pukka-sahib vocabulary of disdain, with its "sea monkeys" and "cocoanut niggers," but he was quick to generalize from isolated experiences. One might wish that a sea captain—intimately in contact with such polyglot fellow hostages aboard ship as Scandinavians, Irish, Chinese, Russians, Indians, and Pacific Islanders—would be educated in the futility of extrapolation, but one might wish many things.*

*For perspective it is fair to mention that Charles W. Domville-Fife's *Square-Rigger Days* (1938) anthologizes a personal essay by William Deal titled "The Nigger of the *Chelmsford*," which details a voyage from Sydney to London in 1893. Deal, described by Domville-Fife as "a fine sailor of the

From Guam Slocum sailed the *Amethyst* to Lagumanoc, a mountainous and rich lumber source on the north side of Tayabas Bay in the Philippines. He obtained a line of credit from a Manila banking house and began his trade between Luzon and Hong Kong to satisfy the demands of the Chinese emperor, who was determined to build a modern navy. But the forward motion of sailing ships is glacial contrasted to the jittery speed of economic markets, and before Slocum could make his fortune off the Chinese shipbuilders of Camagon, Narra, Tindalo, Betis, Ebony, and Dugan, the British seduced the Chinese from hardwood to iron, from mandarin junks to gunboats. In the meantime Slocum used the *Amethyst* as a showroom, improving her constantly to advertise the refinements of Philippine hardwood in whatever port he called. Her hull was dull black, and if her bluff bow and abrupt stern didn't allow for the kind of elegance of line that black can encourage— "like a black velvet dress on a beautiful woman," as Samuel Eliot Morison has it—she made a good show, scrubbed and freshly painted, her brass polished and her teak, mahogany, and rosewood varnished, her joiner work exquisite from stanchions and fife rails above deck to library shelves and cabin tables below. Victor recalls that his father, whose eyes were always open for a new market, drew a Hong Kong timber buyer's attention to some especially beautiful rosewood filigree, suggesting that it would nicely adorn the man's ornate coffins.

It was in Lagumanoc in July 1879, when the *Amethyst* was taking on timber, that the Slocums' little girl died soon after being born at sea and was embalmed in brandy, because—as Virginia wrote her mother in such anguish—"we would not leave her in this horid place."* Where they in fact left her is not known, but it is clear that whatever calamity fate delivered, they kept moving. During the winter they sailed ice from Hakodate, on Japan's Tsugaru Strait—where the *Amethyst*'s deck and rigging were coated with ice—to Hong Kong,† and coal from Nagasaki

---

old school," writes with such casual unselfconsciousness about the "nigger" of the title and his blockhead Swede and "dago" shipmates that Slocum's slurs seem almost politically correct.

*In *Alone at Sea*, Ann Spencer writes that embalming kin in liquor was a common European and American seafaring practice, except aboard temperance vessels, whose method of preservation "was to coat the child in tar."

†Ice was a hot commodity during the latter half of the nineteenth century. Its traffic by sea may be said to have been invented on the Kennebec River, north of Bath, Maine. Shipments of "Kennebec Crystal" went as far from Maine as Calcutta—more than half the load arriving after half a year unmelted. New York market speculation on ice from Maine—complete with Tammany Hall

to Vladivostok and Shanghai, from which they carried gunpowder to Formosa—destined, as Victor writes, "to blow up some rebels."

It was at Atimonan, near several active volcanoes in the Philippines' Lamon Bay, that the Slocums witnessed an earthquake. "The first sign of disturbance," Victor reports, "was the rattling of the [anchor] chains in the hawse pipes and then the vessel began to vibrate . . . The water was boiling all over the bay." And it was in the Philippines where—at the island of Bantigui—two of Victor's most vivid childhood memories unfolded. While loading there the captain, "who always did a bit of timber cruising of his own," noticed a huge rosewood tree growing on the slope of a hill above the beach and resolved to cut it down. The tree was so tall and thick that it required three days for the chopping gang carried on board the *Amethyst* to fell it, and then it had to be cut in half in order to drag it to the water to be floated to the mother ship. Still, the tree was too ungainly to be managed and had to be abandoned, which weighed heavy on Slocum's heart, for he had estimated that it would fetch "five thousand dollars in San Francisco for bar tops."

This misbegotten enterprise was followed closely by an encounter with a couple of natives who paddled out to the anchored ship in their outrigger canoe with an item for sale. The merchandise was an impressively huge, perhaps zoo-sized, boa constrictor, but let Victor tell the tale: "[Their boat] was a small *banca* with the crew at each end and the boa, lashed head and tail and coiled around the outriggers, occupied the middle. The boa was lively and strained [at its] lashing . . . It was a fearful thing and the sight of it threw my little brother, Ben, into a fit of hysterics."

Benjamin wrote to Walter Teller that his father had longed to buy the snake, but that his mother was not persuaded this was a prudent investment. Closing his discussion of the episode, he noted: "Anything to make a dollar, danger or no. Father was a trader in any line."

Virginia's influence on Joshua's actions was often decisive; he trusted her absolutely to know his gifts and their limits, to protect him against

bribes and cornered markets and unconscionably high fixed prices from New York to Baltimore—eventually drew the attention of the trust-busting Teddy Roosevelt, who sent Bath's own Charles Morse to federal prison in Atlanta.

the temptations of rashness but also to stir his boldness. Teller relates a story by way of illustration, set in late 1880 at Hong Kong in a harbor crowded with ships, though without tugs available to tow the *Amethyst* to a mooring. With his wife by his side at the wheel, Slocum entered the harbor under full sail, "heading for a narrow passageway between three British warships on the starboard side and a full rigged merchant ship on the port side," as Teller quotes Benjamin's letter of recollection. The *Amethyst* was coming down directly toward these vessels at such speed that the British deckhands and the admiral of the fleet of Her Majesty's ships prepared for "a very severe smashup . . . looking for a crash of spars and torn sails." Benjamin's father kept coming—"Mother stood by him. Her silence gave him confidence." Having threaded the needle and avoided collision "by inches," Slocum found a vacancy, put the helm down, and "swung into the wind, and 'let go the anchor' order was given." But then he realized that by failing to dip his ensign he had committed a breach of etiquette. So he wrote a note of apology to the admiral, who replied by commending Slocum for his bravura seamanship and inviting him to join him aboard for dinner, together with "the lady who stood beside you."

The next time the *Amethyst* entered Hong Kong harbor, in March 1881, Virginia was at full-term pregnancy with their final child, James A. Garfield Slocum, born on President Garfield's inauguration day, and less than four months before the president was assassinated by Charles Guiteau.*

On June 23 of the same year, back in Hong Kong, Slocum sold the *Amethyst* in order to buy a one-third interest in the *Northern Light,* at the time one of the most magnificent ships afloat, 233 feet in length, 44 feet wide, 28 feet deep in the hold, and registered at two thousand tons with three decks.

*Jessie Slocum Joyce, telling her story to Beth Day for *Joshua Slocum, Sailor* (1953), remembers that owing to her birthplace she was known by her siblings as "the Filipina," Ben "the Australian," Victor "the American," and Garfield "our Chinese brother."

The Northern Light

SIX

Northern Light

I had a right to be proud of her, for at that time—in the 1880s—she was
the finest American sailing vessel afloat.

—Sailing Alone Around the World

T RAGIC IRONY IS EMBEDDED in Slocum's description of the *Northern
Light* as "my best command," the kind of blindness that characterizes Oedipus before he plucks out his eyes. The sequential unraveling of
the shipmaster's overreaching pride in the *Northern Light* isn't compelling
tragic drama merely because it's congruent with a kind of story formal-
ized by Aristotle, but also because Aristotle's description reveals such
fundamental truths about human ambition, performance, and outcome.
And just as Oedipus, a blind ex-king, recovered from his fall to experience consolation at Colonus, so did Slocum rise from his ruin to achieve
heroic refreshment.

It's unknown whether Virginia encouraged the sale of the *Amethyst* to
finance Slocum's stake in the *Northern Light,* but it's likely that she did.
The *Amethyst,* so much smaller than their new vessel, was possibly the
oldest then afloat among American merchant ships; she was showing her
age, having been battered in a five-day typhoon in the South China Sea,
during which the captain lashed himself to the helm and Virginia locked
the children below.

Boat envy is a universal malady, and the *Northern Light* was as "beautiful as her name," as Slocum wrote. (She was named in honor of a previous *Northern Light,* a clipper launched in 1851, two years later sailing
around Cape Horn from San Francisco to Boston in seventy-six days, a
record that held until 1993.) The new *Northern Light,* with twice the carrying capacity of her namesake, had also been launched near Boston. At
the time Slocum bought his interest in her, the so-called medium clipper,

a three-skysailyard windjammer, had been at sea for eight years. She had been sailed to Hong Kong by John E. Kenney, an American commander who—for reasons unspecified—was eager to sell his ownership share. The transfer was overseen by the duty-free port's U.S. consul John Singleton Mosby—*that* Mosby, the Mosby's Rangers' Confederate Colonel Mosby. Mosby had filed the birth certificate for the newborn Garfield on the Slocums' previous visit to Hong Kong, and like Slocum he had risen through the ranks from private to his exalted place; the two hot-tempered men warmed quickly to each other, though Virginia—notably unsqueamish—could not endure the sight of his disfiguring saber scars.

But let us relish Victor's eloquence on the subject of the new ship:

> No one of the present generation [mid-twentieth century] can form any sort of an idea of the majestic grandeur of a ship of the *Northern Light* class, not only as a picture, tearing along under a cloud of canvas, but even when lying quietly at anchor with a forest of yards correctly squared and harbor stows on the sails. It was a sight to compel a feeling of awe merely to look aloft to trace out the massive hempen shrouds and backstays, to say nothing of tracing out the leads of the running gear. To know that was in itself an education, and to be master of all was a big job . . .

How big a job, and how vast its psychological complexities, would become one of the two most argued and unresolved mysteries of Joshua Slocum's character and reputation. There existed among many forecastle crews a farcical resentment of their master's perquisites, living a carefree life on the bounding main, all moonlight and gentle breezes, while they struggled with tempests and cobbly seas. While it was true that the captain of a sailing ship by strict custom delegated all executive duties of running his vessel to first and second mates, leaving himself seemingly free of responsibilities, in reality he had an unrelenting liability to keep the crew alive and well, the ship afloat, the cargo safe. The master had to understand, and often calculate on the spot, the weight and bulk limit of cargo he could carry without causing his vessel to be crank or slow, to pitch or yaw.* He had to grasp better than any stevedore the art of loading: what to carry deep in the hold, what between decks, what on deck,

---

*For a vessel to be "cranky" is to be unbalanced, tending under sail to tip to one side, confounding her natural and wind-driven inclination to heel to the other, or exacerbating her natural heel near to the tipping point. It is a dangerous condition, sometimes caused by cargo having shifted and sometimes—and more consequentially—by a flaw in the ship's design.

and whether forward, aft, or amidships. He had to comprehend what were the properties of such freight as cotton, sulfur (whose fumes could blind a crew member as surely as the methane emitted by a cargo of rotting bananas), guano, pianos, nitrate (whose great weight came with foul odor), locomotives, and even rice (a weevil-ridden and hateful cargo that, if wet, produced a steaming and unendurable stench). Moreover, he had to be alert to changes—that is, future values—in the commodities market. In addition to seamanship, crowd psychology, medical practice, the code and common laws of ships and sailors, and the nature of commercial exchanges, the master, believed by his ordinary seamen to be lounging in his deck chair by day and banqueting at night, had to write coherent business letters, keep meticulous accounts, and have the social grace to mingle with merchants and consuls in any seaport in the world. Few sea urchins from Nova Scotia could fit this bill.

And now consider the scale of the *Northern Light*. By one measure she was five times greater than the *Amethyst,* requiring a crew of forty-five and difficult indeed to handle. Robert Foulke describes the cohort of modified clippers to which she belonged: "Larger, heavier and clumsier than the clippers, these ships were not thoroughbreds: they were often over-masted to make up for increased weight; their length sometimes made them cranky in maneuver and unmanageable when running before heavy seas; their low freeboard made work on decks which were almost constantly awash exceedingly dangerous."*

Foulke refers to vessels of the latter *Northern Light*'s class as belonging to a period of "decadence" in deepwater shipping. If, as her subsequent history shows, there was a fatal flaw—the outcome of cheapjack construction—at the heart of his huge new command, how could as experienced a mariner as Slocum have missed it? All too easily, comes the ready answer. His own son's estimation above of her "majestic grandeur" is blindingly seductive, and ship surveys during the heyday of merchant shipping in the late nineteenth century were no more reliable than house inspections during the subprime mortgage boom of the early twenty-first.

To stretch the analogy, one should not discount the granite counter effect, the in-ground pool effect, the cherry cabinet effect. The Slocums

*Robert D. Foulke, "Life in the Dying World of Sail, 1870–1910," *The Journal of British Studies* 3, no. 1 (1963).

weren't merely investing in a long-haul cargo carrier; they were buying their dream house, and as a dwelling the *Northern Light* was extraordinary. From her figurehead to her rounded stern, she had plenty of the "wow" factors that real estate agents like to sell. But even more tempting must have been the master's quarters, with room for Virginia's piano and Joshua's library. Victor remembers his father's reading chairs and volumes of Gibbon and Macaulay, Cervantes and Dickens, as essential furniture. "One of the cabins of the *Northern Light* contained a library of at least five hundred volumes representing the standard works of the great writers. Such company at sea made an ideal atmosphere . . . The cabin, with its orderly and well fitted bookcases, looked very much like the study of a literary worker or a college professor."*

Writing to Walter Teller in her old age about visiting the *Northern Light* in New York as a girl in 1882, Slocum's half-sister Emma recollected that "everything was there as in a modern apartment. There was a pantry boy, a Philippino . . ." And writing for the *New York Tribune* in June of that year, a reporter described the *Northern Light* in his headline as "An American Family Afloat."

> No one, to look at the graceful lines of this vessel, her Yankee rigging and sails, her bold cutwater and her noble stern, could mistake her for any other than an American ship.
>
> This vessel is the clipper ship Northern Light, owned by Benner and Pinckney of this city . . . The tautness, trimness, and cleanliness of this vessel, from keelson to truck and from stem to stern, are features not common on merchant ships . . . The neat canvas cover over the steering-wheel bearing the vessel's name and hailing port, worked with silk, is the handiwork of the captain's wife. Descending to the main cabin, one wonders whether or not he is in some comfortable apartment ashore.
>
> When a Tribune reporter visited the ship, Mrs. Slocum sat busily engaged with her little girl at needlework. Her baby boy was fast asleep in his Chinese cradle. An older son was putting his room in order and a second son was sketching. The captain's stateroom is a commodious apartment, furnished with a double berth which one might mistake for

---

*A shipboard library was not a customary appurtenance of a shipmaster who shared ownership of his vessel with land-based investors. W. H. Bunting tells of the response of Arthur Sewall to an invoice for a walnut bookcase ordered by the captain from the builder of *Indiana*, a full-rigged Cape Horner being prepared for the command of John Delano: "I do not allow such ornaments in our Sewall ships. We do not intend our captains to be reading story books at sea. We intend our captains to spend their time on deck reading the weather and trying to make quick passages. Take your hatchet . . . and convert that thing into kindling wood."

a black walnut bedstead; a transom upholstered like a lounge; a library, chairs, carpets, wardrobe and the chronometers. This room is abaft the main cabin, which is furnished like a parlor. In this latter apartment are the square piano, center table, sofa, easy chairs and carpets, while on the walls hang several oil paintings.

In front of the parlor is the dining room, which, together with the other rooms, exhibit a neatness of which only a woman's hand is capable.

Going on deck, the captain showed with great pride the cleanly kept steam engine in the after end of the forward house. It was used for handling cargo, condensing water, extinguishing fire, pumping the bilges or for other emergencies. The carpenter shop was next visited. In this was a long bench with vise, a lathe, saws and other tools for new work or repairing.

But before the *Northern Light* docked in New York, she sailed from Hong Kong, where the Slocums took her over, to Liverpool. It would be helpful to have some record of the survey that was performed on her while negotiations proceeded for Slocum to purchase Captain Kenney's interest in the newish vessel. The age of a boat can tell little or reveal much, and even more perplexingly a new ship may be the worse for her youth and an old one the better for her maturity. If the *Amethyst* was the oldest American vessel afloat, she had also been lovingly fashioned from first-rate materials and fastened extravagantly with copper fittings. Just as the earliest fiberglass yachts are often still afloat, having been extravagantly overbuilt (in part due to ignorance of the new material's strength), so did innovative construction techniques for such modified clippers as the *Northern Light* often encourage overconfidence in the durability of vessels soon to be burdened by huge cargoes and expected to carry acres of sail while driving through extreme seas at extreme latitudes.

When Slocum sold her, the *Amethyst* had been sailed for almost sixty years. But ships of the *Northern Light*'s class were estimated to have a useful life of from merely eight to eleven years; by one reckoning the grace period between launching and "disaster and deterioration" might average ten years. When the Slocums bought in at Hong Kong, their vessel had been sailed hard for more than eight years. It was customary to have a ship surveyed from stem to stern, from masthead to keel bottom, every seven years. This was crucial for ships of such extreme size: the longer a ship, the greater the stress on the hull's integrity, especially on her bow, stern, and rudder mechanism. Examination of ships' records at the times they changed hands—the *Northern Light* had been sold for $95,000 a few years before Slocum bought his share at a now unknown price—reveal widespread chicanery. Even if the surveyors weren't bought off, the sellers or their agents were good or even masterful at disguising flaws (many of them hidden underwater) in the hull, mechanisms, rigging, and keel bolts of huge contrivances being advertised as in A1 condition.

While there's no way of knowing whether Slocum was gulled into trading up to the *Northern Light,* it's certain that hardheaded prudence often enjoys a holiday when sailboats are being considered. And it's also certain that the most costly and dangerous crises that the *Northern Light* would suffer under Slocum's command—her rudder breaking away in Long Island Sound and her rudderhead completely twisting off and her topsides springing huge leaks during a storm off the Cape of Good Hope—were structural failures that render his boast that she was the "finest American sailing vessel afloat" at best wishful, at worst delusional.

But structural problems paled before the grief soon to be suffered by the ship's crew, and by the Slocums on account of her crew. Aboard what her master titles "this magnificent ship, my best command," the early signs were auspicious. Having, in Walter Teller's estimation, struggled to "the top of the tree" at age thirty-seven, with Virginia and their four children comfortably installed aboard, Slocum sailed from Hong Kong to Manila, where he took on a load of hemp and sugar to be delivered in Liverpool, going west near Sumatra, through the Sunda Strait to the Indian Ocean and around the Cape of Good Hope. Victor recalls a stop in Java for produce and livestock, and that aboard the *Northern Light* during that voyage to the Mersey River there were pet monkeys and civets to set against the rats. The crew was disarmingly competent, British sailors taken aboard in Hong Kong after their passage from Cardiff carrying coal. This was a singing crew, handy with such chanteys as "Hanging Johnny" and "Blow the Man Down." Song, which encouraged the rhythmic pulling of lines and hauling of cables, was always a good sign, the equivalent of a miner's canary tweeting happily away. When this crew grumbled it was because they wearied of chicken and eggs in their diet, and longed instead for their customary salted mystery meat.

Tempting as it is to delay explaining what sailors ate aboard ship, it is now the time for an account. The meat, salted pork or beef or horse, was often high-smelling and always coarse with gristle. Dried beans were favored above pea soup, in which maggots floated to the top. Ship's biscuits harbored weevils. Figs and raisins were home to white worms. And as awful as the food was, there was never enough of it.

After six months at sea, the *Northern Light* entered the Mersey on Christmas Day of 1881, church bells sounding through the fog, and delivered the largest shipment of sugar ever to have been off-loaded at Liverpool. Even before she was docked much of the crew left their ship to waste their pay, never to appear aboard again. She then had her bowsprit replaced and bottom recoppered after the removal of such an accumulation of barnacles from the tropical seas that even these experienced ship repairers were amazed by their profusion. (Victor believed that the awful condition of the *Northern Light*'s bottom accounted for the unusually slow passage of 160 days from Manila.)

Meantime, Virginia used the time dockside to take her children on educational excursions to Liverpool factories, where the Philippine raw sugar was made ready for teacups and Philippine hemp fiber became twisted rope. And it was also dockside that there occurred a prophetic altercation between her husband and the rigger commissioned to fabricate and install the new bowsprit.

Slocum had recently used his fists in Altoona, Pennsylvania, and many who knew him as a boy and young man testified that he was unwilling to shy from a fight. Back in 1871, soon after marrying Virginia, he had successfully defended himself against a charge in San Francisco of beating and wounding a crewman aboard the *Constitution*. Interviewing Slocum years later aboard the *Spray*, a reporter for the *Boston Sun* described him as a mature and settled mariner, "as tough as wrought iron and as lively on his feet as a chicken . . . His fist is not only big, but has a hard, horny Jim Corbett cast that inspires respect." As an afterthought, the reporter noted that Slocum was "a good shot with the pistol."

Now, back in Liverpool, the rigger failed to appear with his workers to install the new bowsprit, and Slocum instructed his first mate to assemble a crew to do the job themselves. Once this was done, the rigger came on board in what Victor describes as "a truculent mood. An altercation ensued on the main deck . . . and the Captain was cited to appear in court next morning." His son—displaying both a case of "my old man can whip your old man" and a wink to the knowing regarding the wiles of plaintiffs—tells with pride that the rigger appeared in court "very much bandaged and attended by both a doctor and a nurse." The case—no harm no foul?—was dismissed.

But what lingers, and provokes debate, is the temperament (and temper) of Joshua Slocum as a master at sea.* His children, who saw him daily and in trying circumstances during many long passages at sea, remembered him as gentle and witty with them and with their mother, a tease and sometimes a whimsical show-off. As Grace Murray Brown wrote to Walter Teller, Slocum's own father had been "too harsh to be taken straight," causing him to run off to sea after his mother died, but his rough experience as a child didn't necessarily smooth his edges as a father figure aboard ship. Mrs. Brown, who loved the memory of her much older cousin, remembered that Slocum's "contempt could be very potent," that he could be sarcastic and blunt, "crusty or cutting," and that "he was capable of letting his irascible side show up if sufficient provocation was given or even suspected . . . Small slights would rankle and never be forgotten or forgiven."

By Victor Slocum's account, the crew that sailed on the *Northern Light* from Liverpool to New York was a "typical Western Ocean hard case crew, with a bucko mate to match." This description, with amplification, might provide a context for the horror shows that would be played upon the *Northern Light*'s ample stage during her voyages over the next two years. The bucko mate to whom Victor refers was known as Black Taylor, a "swarthy down-easter," one of that breed of Maine coasters who were said to fear only God and Cape Cod. Slocum, according to his son, had a lifelong respect for Taylor, and trusted him. But "bucko mate" is no term of affection. As we have seen, aboard American "blood boats" and "hell ships" these men squeezed work from the crew by lavishing on them "belaying pin soup" and brass knuckles affixed to a "bunch of fives." The degree of brutality indulged by a bucko mate in service to his vessel's needs was governed only by the humanity and attention of his master, and Victor explains that Black Taylor's gave him a green light: " 'Mr. Taylor, you know what to do. And if you have any trouble with those soldiers and sea lawyers, I will pay the expense in New York.' "

"Soldiers" was a term of derision for sailors who weren't. "Larrikin"—

---

*The responses of book reviewers to subjects of biography are as unpredictable as the responses of a friend to someone introduced with the assurance "You'll love her." Or, in the case of Walter Teller writing *The Search for Captain Slocum* in 1956, "You'll love him!" Reviewing Teller's book for the *Saturday Review* (August 11, 1956), Robert Payne wrote of the man who beguiled Teller that he exhibited "a strange streak of sullenness and anger," that he was "irascible," a "crusty-tempered, hard-hitting and secretive old fogy" beneath whose external "canniness" there was "always something curiously rotten, something which has gone to seed."

a wise guy and loafer—was a synonym. During the leisurely forty-day passage to New York, following the northeast trade winds, Slocum meant to put the *Northern Light* in apple pie order to show her off not only to her two-thirds owners but also to his father, whom he had invited to travel to the city—all expenses covered—to regard the height to which Joshua had climbed at the age of thirty-eight. (This would be Joshua's first shipboard visit to New York.) But a leisurely sail, counterintuitively, is anathema to a crew. A sailor cannot be expected to holystone decks or polish brass or varnish brightwork during a gale, or even while rolling morosely in the heat of the equatorial doldrums, though when the weather abates, as in the trade winds, it was time to tar the standing rigging and scrape and paint the masts, bulwarks, and deckhouses. As Victor marvels earlier about his father's management of the *Amethyst,* "he could find more work for the mate in a minute than the mate could do in a day." In the event, work did get done on the *Northern Light* between Liverpool and Sandy Hook, performed however grudgingly by the crew or encouraged brutally by Black Taylor. If there was an ugly aftermath to this passage, it was recorded in the memories and on the bodies of those who made up what Victor denigrated as a "typical Western Ocean hard case crew." Sailors who had served on American ships of the time were easily identified by scars, a limp, or a mangled hand. And no doubt the pride-driven zeal indulged during that task-mastering passage to New York left an invisible scar on Slocum's reputation.

Joshua Slocum with Gilbert Islanders

SEVEN

Mutiny

There can be but one opinion as to the conduct of Capt. Slocumb [*sic*], of the *Northern Light*. Whatever may have been the offense of the unhappy wretch whom he tortured, the fact that Slocumb treated him with inhuman barbarity is past contradiction. The mere imprisonment of the man in the hole where he was found by the officer who arrested him is sufficient proof that Slocumb is a brute who deserves the severest punishment.

—*New York Times* editorial, November 29, 1883

T HE BROOKLYN BRIDGE would not officially open until May 1883, but when the *Northern Light* was towed up the East River to Pier 23 in Brooklyn, the structure had already ended the era of New York City's dominance as a home port to the tallest of tall ships. The final break in the spans of the marvelous suspension bridge was closed over by the spring of 1882, and the *Northern Light*'s topmost masts had to be removed—"struck"—in order for her to pass upriver to her wharf and later to her loading pier, where she would take on that Faustian-bargain modern cargo—case oil, or kerosene—bound from a refinery to delivery in Japan. Victor believed that he remembered the *Northern Light*'s remaining topmost masthead—at least 120 feet high—being dabbed with paint by a playful bridge workman as the boy stared up from the deck of his father's great ship to the overarching structure towering above her.

The two Roeblings, John and Washington, designed, supervised, and built—in the most intimate, hands-on, hanging-from-scaffolds way— what was then the modern world's most remarkable engineering feat. Washington's father, John, died in 1869 of complications from a construction injury when bridge timbers crushed his toes. The son then took over, only to be paralyzed by decompression sickness after he examined the suspension bridge's pylons. Many workers died fulfilling the dazzling vision of a soaring connection—a taming, as it was understood. And in 1885 the first jumper took his plunge to display its dramatic value as a place to fall literally from a great height.

The Brooklyn Bridge, besides announcing itself as a barrier to the evolution of ever higher-masted sailing ships, was also an emphatic monument to iron and steel, in the making of which wood seemed almost incidental. And busy on the East River below its spans were steamboats of every size and ambition, from tugs to pleasure yachts to oceangoing passenger ships, in a hurry, leaving and arriving on schedules no sailing vessel could guarantee.

Hart Crane's extraordinary poem "To Brooklyn Bridge" (1926) is an artifact of twentieth-century modernism, but had it been written in 1883, Joshua Slocum surely would have found its lines prophetic. He would have understood its epigraph, taken from Satan's response in the Book of Job when the Lord asks where he's been: "from going to and fro in the earth, and from walking up and down in it." Slocum must have marveled, and perhaps shuddered, at the din of construction, the glare of welding torches, the chainlike shadows cast by the sun behind its wires and cables, themselves a kind of grotesque caricature by magnification of his own ship's rigging.

> Down Wall, from girder into street noon leaks,
> A rip-tooth of the sky's acetylene;
> All afternoon the cloud-flown derricks turn . . .
> Thy cables breathe the North Atlantic still.

And he would have appreciated Crane's apostrophe to the achievement: "O harp and altar, of the fury fused . . ." It is in the shadow of the Brooklyn Bridge that a reader today considers the quaint romantic artifice of the *New York Tribune*'s article titled "An American Family Afloat," quoted above, its prose as plushy as the *Northern Light*'s upholstery. The feature's lead is blind to its surrounding realities: "At Pier 23, East River, lies a typical American ship, commanded by a typical American sailor who has a typical American wife to accompany him on his long voyages, and to make his cabin as acceptable a home as he could have on shore." Given that the modifier "typical" is always booby-trapped, the *Tribune* reporter seems ignorant even of what he knows that he knows: "A visit to her deck suggests two sad and striking thoughts, one that American sailing ships are becoming obsolete and the other that so few American sailors can be found." And this *was* a fact, whether or not it was also a fact that Captain Joshua Slocum, as the reporter assured his readers, "is one of the most popular commanders sailing out of this port, both on account of his general capability and his kindness to his crew."(It was notable that Slocum enjoyed working side by side with members of his crew at rigging, sail mending, and carpentry, and that this relaxation of formality was appreciated.)

Walter Teller describes John Slocombe's final visit to his son—their first meeting in twenty-two years, "like Joseph in Egypt sending for Jacob," the father obeying "the summons"—as cordial. Seventeen years later, in a letter to his cousin Joel, the captain wrote with his customary runic reticence about family matters that during the reunion the two men "didn't spend our time talking about fine large ships, our business was a quarter of a century back . . . 'Joshua' said he 'do you remember the night in the little boat when we rowed all night on a lee-shore and the fishing vessels came into port with close reefed sail?' Didn't I remember it!"

The old man, who died five years later, was "a fiscal failure" now past seventy, and he'd never met Virginia or his grandchildren by her and Joshua. He brought along his daughter by his second marriage, Emma, who visited with her half-brother for seven weeks. She described Joshua and Virginia as having been kind and attentive to the young country girl she had been, escorting her to museums and art galleries and on a tour of Harper's publishing house (which suggests the vitality of Joshua Slocum's preoccupation with writing). Emma's hosts bought her gifts and took her to Coney Island "to hear [John Philip] Sousa's band of one hundred pieces. I saw nothing but happiness between Josh and Virginia. I think there was nothing else. They seemed perfectly happy. Captain Josh was a kind, thoughtful and fine man." The extended family enjoyed a few jolly picnics at Manhattan Beach, in the company of other shipmasters the Slocums had met somewhere on the seven seas.

Akin to so many bucolic stories of the perfectly named Gilded Age, there was quicksand just beneath beachside band concerts and rot in those "black walnut bedsteads." To pay for the *Northern Light*'s conspicuous graces, case oil was to be carried from one of the more than a hundred kerosene refineries on Newtown Creek to Yokohama. Newtown Creek would become notorious even before Slocum set out to round the world on the *Spray* as perhaps the most foully polluted industrial site in the United States, if not the planet. Located on a tributary of the East River north of the Brooklyn Bridge, it was where John D. Rockefeller located his plants to refine Ohio and Pennsylvania petroleum—displacing coal—into kerosene to light the world, and the place where he was busy turning his Astral Oil Company into that octopus so tamely titled Standard Oil. Case oil was an appropriately standardized cargo, packed in five-gallon tins, two tins to a case, and in feverish demand in Asia, where kerosene was rapidly replacing plant oil, in turn liberating farmland for food production.

Already, in 1882, Newtown Creek's waters (if the fluid that floated boats there could be thought of as H_2O) corroded ship bottoms so quickly that masters found it prudent to load up with case oil and scoot on the earliest possible tide. But finding a crew to sail the *Northern Light* halfway around the world had become increasingly difficult. It wasn't merely that the wages offered were laughably meager, or that the discipline enforced by officers was frequently sadistic, or the food disgusting and the hazards awful. No, these days young adventurers were now fetching up out west in camps such as Deadwood, where the floor of a saloon in the Black Hills was steadier under the feet of a drunk prospector than the ratline shaking a hungry sailor two hundred feet above the bedlam of a boiling sea.*

Walter Teller, seeing the situation from Slocum's point of view, writes that "foremast hands were being recruited from the dregs of society." This is a recurring declaration in histories of whaling, mercantile shipping, and navies, as these pages have shown. But at this particular moment, on a ship that required a larger crew than the thirty or so finally recruited, it must be stressed that Teller wasn't exaggerating when he wrote that aboard the *Northern Light,* as she prepared to cast off from Newtown Creek, "one found not only roving adventurers, and men seeking to escape the restraints of civilization, but drunkards, vagrants, criminals and degenerates."

The exact names, nationalities, ambitions, and résumés of the crew delivered to Captain Slocum by shipping agents—crimps—are details lost to time. But it may be assumed that they comprised the usual motley cohort of desperate men shanghaied by a well-organized ring of thugs while bewildered, bewitched, blackjacked, or beguiled ashore at rum-

---

*In his *Maritime History of Maine,* William Hutchinson Rowe notes, "Very queer specimens were often brought aboard by the crimps. Three of the crew furnished to the *St. Stephen* at San Francisco in 1877 were cowboys who had never seen salt water until the week before."

pots, gambling dens, and bawdy houses. As custom would have dictated, the first two months of *les miserables'* wages—so-called advance notes—would have been paid to the crimps as a fee for digging up and delivering the near dead, who could be presumed to be hungover, seasick, or at the least suffering seller's remorse as they found themselves on an August afternoon being towed by a tug northward up Long Island Sound so that the *Northern Light* could avoid a return passage under the Brooklyn Bridge.

In the customary and disgraceful way of things, the exploited crew would shrug, sullenly, and work gratis for two months, an enterprise known as "working up the dead horse," and somewhere at sea (perhaps in the horse latitudes) a ceremony would attend the "burial of the dead horse," with appropriate chanteys and perhaps rueful resolutions to be wiser next time ashore. But what happened after clearing Long Island Sound and heading seaward, bound for Yokohama, was not in the normal course of things. Victor, then eleven, was an interested witness to what took place.

Having been signaled by Slocum that no further tow was needed, and some sails having been hoisted to carry the *Northern Light* to sea, the tug dropped the towing hawser and turned back toward New York. Too late did Slocum realize that his fine ship's rudder had quit functioning during the tow, and that without it he couldn't steer. Whether or not the mechanism had been sabotaged, the most urgent piece of business then was to ship the long hawser before the *Northern Light* ran over it, tangling it on her keel and further damaging her rudder. The steam donkey engine, used to turn a huge capstan that might have winched the hawser aboard, was in use raising the topsails. The machine's larger purpose, to reduce the size of the crew necessary to sail such a large ship, was for the crew more of a rebuke than a benefit, especially given the engine's nickname, so reminiscent of the loathed "donkey's breakfast" upon which they tried to sleep. The common term at the time for the capstan itself— "niggerhead"—suggests the atmosphere of fellowship enjoyed by shipmates.

But back to the loose end of that hawser. To the end of getting it in, at the best of times an onerous task, and in what might be imagined was a state of high excitement if not panic, Slocum's new first mate—a bucko of the "real down east bull type that 'ate 'em alive,' " in Victor's words—swept through the forecastle and "chased all hands, drunk or sober, out on the deck and lined them up on the hawser, going down the line with a belaying pin to get the slackers into action." Imagine the pandemonium: men abruptly roused from hangovers or worse, headaches induced by Mickey Finns or even blackjacks, to meet their chief mate and galley master, being force-fed belaying pin soup by a bellowing bucko bull. Imagine the din on deck, augmented by Captain Slocum's fury that his New York tug was ignoring his signals of distress.

The hawser having been successfully shipped, a signal was sent to nearby New London to fetch a pilot boat to tow the *Northern Light* in for repairs. This created a nice conundrum in maritime law, a spiderweb of evolving codes and contradictory subcodes that baffled attorneys around the world but was argued with unhesitating self-certainty by those ordinary seamen who made a specialty of knowing their rights, few as those were. Here was the question: Could the *Northern Light*'s voyage—putatively to Yokohama, Japan—be said to have ended here in New London, Connecticut, upon the master's order to enter that port, not 150 miles from the ship's embarkation point at Newtown Creek? And if the voyage had ended, were not the crewmen now entitled to leave the ship (and that "real down east bull type" mate) and to collect the full pay that they'd been promised?

So insistently did many members of the crew demand these entitlements that, while under tow from the pilot boat, Slocum and his officers raised the signal aloft: "Mutiny On Board," summoning the U.S. revenue cutter *Grant*. With this the crew, "armed with handspikes," rushed the quarterdeck, where Slocum intercepted them "with a drawn revolver and a cool, clear-cut order to 'Stop at peril of life.'" While it might seem churlish to doubt that anyone in such a situation—in the history of the world—ever said, exactly, "Stop at peril of life," it is certain that what happened next was seriously ugly. In a letter to Walter Teller, Benjamin testified that he saw his mother holding revolvers in both hands, covering his father while the crew was searched for weapons. The captain ordered the mutiny's ringleader to be put in irons. As the tough first mate was tricing the mutineer, the latter lunged at him with a sheath knife, stabbing him "furiously in the abdomen four times." He died two months later of his wounds.*

The revenue cutter having come alongside, the assailant was arrested

---

*Sheath knives were overwhelmingly the weapons of choice in episodes of grave shipboard violence, so much so that, as Bunting writes, it had been illegal since 1868 to wear such a knife aboard an American ship. Captains were required to "enforce the statute or face a fifty-dollar fine for

and the crew put under armed guard. The rudder was repaired, its securing pins having broken under stress. (Is it far-fetched to imagine that they had corroded while being soaked in that acid bath of Newtown Creek?) Then Slocum made what would prove the strategic error of appealing to the crew, "man to man," as Victor writes, to continue to Japan under a new chief mate, who had seen naval service in the Civil War, "which had given him fighting enough to last the rest of his days."

The embers of mutiny, in Victor's memory, continued to smolder as the *Northern Light* made her way south, crossing "The Line" with proper equatorial ceremony. Neptune climbed aboard to indulge stunts and cross-dressing in a spirit of Mardi Gras. (A favorite prank, designed to victimize greenhorn equator crossers, was to lay a hair across the lens of the telescope—horizontal to the horizon—and offer a prize to the first lookout who discovered The Line appearing out of the distance.) During the approach to the Cape of Good Hope the crew sang chanteys, but they must have been of the blues sort, because they were grumbling.

After a month at sea, the Great Comet of 1882 appeared, portentously, given the circumstances of the remaining passages to Japan and back to New York. Late 1882 found the *Northern Light* running her easting down in the roaring forties, sailing at a smart clip from the cape to Australia's Cape Leeuwin to Tasmania, where she headed north along Australia's east coast. Two weeks before Christmas, sailing through the "Cannibal Isles," known today more realistically as the Solomons, Slocum's lookout spotted in midocean a small boat adrift with five aboard, three young men, an old woman, and an old man, who was their leader. Together with their boat, they were hoisted aboard the *Northern Light* and managed—using a mix of common words and hand signs—to convey that they were the survivors of a twenty-one-foot open whaleboat that had set out forty days earlier with seven additional Gilbert Island mis-

---

every omission. But despite this severe penalty it is unlikely that any shipboard regulation has been more flagrantly ignored," since the sheath knife was considered an all but essential appendage to a sailor's hands while he worked aloft, not to mention its utility in his mess kit. In New London, after persuading the crew to continue on the voyage to Yokohama, Slocum had every sheath knife aboard confiscated and then returned to its owner with the tip struck off. As Victor argues, "The point of a sheath knife adds nothing to its proper use, and the best intentioned in the crew saw no injustice in an order which placed every man on an equal footing as far as suspicion went."

sionaries (the islanders' term for converts to Christianity). Returning home after an interisland business visit, they had been blown six hundred miles out to sea by a monsoon, and the fate of the seven who had died was unspecified (but to Slocum and his family, unsuspicious). All survivors—nearly starved and alive only because monsoon-driven rain had provided drinking water—declined medication with brandy, declaring it "taboo," a self-denial they soon learned to rationalize away.

A few years later, Slocum wrote a short recollection, "Rescue of Some Gilbert Islanders," which he meant but failed to append to the published version of his *Voyage of the "Liberdade"* (1894). It was finally printed, with a brief editor's note, in Walter Teller's collection of his writings, *The Voyages of Joshua Slocum* (1985). Like so many of Slocum's adventures, this rescue played out publicly and dramatically. After feeding and tending to his new passengers, he attempted to lay a course for their home island of Abamama, but wind and currents foiled this plan. Next he thought to put them ashore at Pohnpei (formerly "Ponape") in the Caroline group. At the terrified urging of the rescued survivors, who assured him they would be eaten by Caroline Islanders, the *Northern Light* continued another 2,400 miles to her destination, Yokohama, where the captain imagined this band of Christians would be welcomed, celebrated, and returned in comfort to Abamama. They arrived on January 15, 1883, and if the Gilbert Islanders were well fed and healthy, they found the snow-clad Japanese port bitterly cold.

Ashore, Slocum advertised their plight and by publicity managed to raise sufficient funds to rescue the shivering group from the paper house in which they had been installed by the local Bible society. Because the survivors were not American, the U.S. consul was powerless to pay for their homeward passage, but the Slocums circulated a subscription list and raised $750 on the first day, principally from European merchants but also notably from a private donation by the American ambassador to Japan. The money rolled in at such a rate that Slocum put an ad in the local paper begging that contributions cease. With the help of gratis passage aboard the Pacific Mail Steam Ship Company's *City of Tokio* to San Francisco, where they cashed a large letter of credit in their favor, the group steamed to Honolulu and thence by chartered schooner to Abamama, a total circuit of 11,000 miles.

Enacting Clare Boothe Luce's axiom that no good deed goes unpunished, the fate of the funds collected on behalf of the shipwrecked Christians was challenged by the aforementioned Bible society, provoking an investigative report in the *New York Times,* which inspired in its turn a letter from Slocum to the editor of that newspaper, published on January 11, 1884, a year after the events in question and approximately six weeks after the quoted *Times* editorial labeled Slocum a "brute." In reply to the question of where the money went, Slocum, aboard the *Northern Light* in New York, wrote:

> On our late voyage to Yokohama we had the good fortune to rescue a party of converted South Sea Islanders. This has been reported to the Christian world, and the Captain's account of their religious state has been made much use of for advertising purposes, to which it was not intended . . . [My] part in the rescue was a duty thrown upon [me] through circumstances. [My] duty was discharged—as any true sailor would discharge a duty—simply by doing it . . . It was a matter of no small concern to know what I should do with them:
>
> I applied to the missionaries at Yokohama for their relief; they gave me none. The Bible Society had nothing but Bibles to give . . . By telling their story through the press kind sympathy was raised. Then came funds for their aid . . . Of the uses to which the [cash] were applied I was to be informed. I handed the money over to the Bible Society man with the understanding that he would send me such a statement at this port. Apparently that gentleman has forgotten the agreement.

More consular business was afoot in Yokohama, concerning mutineers still aboard the *Northern Light.* Soon after rescuing the Gilbert Islanders, Slocum heard rumors from the forecastle that a Russian crew member—in defiance of the policy established in New London that possession of a pointed sheath knife was "a declaration of war against the government of the ship"—had been grinding the tip of what Victor calls a "villainous looking knife" and bragging that "it would 'be in the Captain's heart before they made Yokohama.' " Admitting as much under questioning, he was put in irons until he could be turned over to the U.S. consul there.

As has been noted, consuls had almost absolute authority over ships and crews of their flags while in port. Slocum's most recent consequential experience with such a personage had been in Hong Kong with John Singleton Mosby, who was famously fond of ship captains and the hospitality they offered. (He was just as infamously hostile to the complaints of ordinary seamen, and a terror to black crew members charged with offenses at sea.) When the ship anchored, Slocum requested that the shackled mutineer be removed from the *Northern Light* and face charges.

But the consul declared ex cathedra that the knife wielder instead be detained ashore in Yokohama but returned to the ship before Slocum sailed for Manila. This poured gasoline on the fire. The pent-up crewman brooded, Victor tells, fanning his "morose hatred into a blind fury." Meanwhile, the *Northern Light*'s chief mate was ailing and her second ashore and besotted by gin. As Slocum prepared to sail in ballast to Manila to pick up a cargo of sugar and hemp for New York, his crew grumbled and threatened not to work the ship. With the aid of the donkey engine, the anchor was brought short just as the consul's steam launch came alongside—in the spirit of *Captain, you seem to have left this ashore*—bearing the violent mutineer, who was meant, by prior agreement with Slocum, to have been disarmed. He wasn't disarmed, and when escorted up the gangway by two consular constables he broke free and "made a run at [Slocum] with a knife." Missing his mark, he was restrained and bound in irons to the backstay. Believing, correctly, that the mutineer had confederates aboard, Slocum went below and fetched from the ship's armory a repeating carbine, with which he ordered the two constables down the gangway to their launch. Then, from the wheelhouse, armed, he ordered the sails and anchor lifted. In Manila, where a cholera epidemic raged, the prisoner was accidentally on purpose allowed to escape from an open hatch, and finally—for just a little while—the *Northern Light* was at peace.

That is, if sailing through what Victor reasonably ranks as "the most appalling catastrophe since the dawn of human history"—the eruption and fallout from the volcano Krakatoa—may be termed peaceful. The *Northern Light* was passing through the Sunda Strait, between Java and Sumatra, during the late spring of 1883, while Krakatoa was in full eruption. The sea boiled. An American ship, the *William H. Besse*,[*] within easy signaling range aft and closely accompanied by the *Bourne*, came up hard aground on a brand-new lava reef raised in the exact spot through which the *Northern Light*, with a deeper draft, had just sailed. (The *Bourne*, hav-

---

[*]Shortly before, in Manila, aboard the *William H. Besse*, under the command of Captain B. C. Baker, Slocum had responded to a call for help from Mrs. Baker, whose husband was ashore. A member of the crew had fallen gravely ill, and Slocum went below to the forecastle to nurse the sailor. Removing his coat, he cradled the dying man's head in his lap. Later that night, two more sailors from the *William H. Besse* died of cholera. The vessel—together with her sister ship, the *Bourne*, and the *Northern Light*—fled Manila at the tail end of a monsoon storm.

ing touched bottom and bounced off, got to deep water and managed to tow the *William H. Besse* off the reef.) Fretting about the ever-changing depth, Slocum ordered the lead line cast, and it came up from the bottom with its tallowed tip melted. A bright column of fire threw up ashes and smoke to an altitude of seventeen miles. A volcanic explosion was heard in Perth, more than two thousand miles distant, and at Batavia, a hundred miles away, where the detonations were described as "deafening." At Mauritius, thousands of miles distant on the other side of the Indian Ocean, in response to what was thought to be the roar of heavy guns, naval artillery troops were ordered to their posts. Having been heard from approximately three thousand miles away, the noise is estimated—though who knows how?—to have been the loudest sound in recorded history. The air stank of sulfur and the sea near the *Northern Light* turned white with pumice ash, but she was nevertheless afloat and her crew—having slipped past yet another knifepoint—alive if not well.*

Borne west by the Agulhas Current, but against the force of a westerly gale, the ship now sought to clear the Cape of Good Hope the wrong way around, against the trade winds. This collision of wind and current kicks up mountainous seas in the extreme latitudes, and the *Northern Light* was forced to heave to, lower sails, and try to ride out the mess until the gale blew itself out. Unexpectedly—as such disasters always seem to arrive—her rudderhead twisted off, the same fatal flaw that had crippled her off New London in the placid waters of Long Island Sound. Here the situation was grave, potentially deadly, for with no means of steering the *Northern Light* was at imminent risk of being pooped, broached, or pitch-poled.

And like some sick-joke reprise, that wasn't all. As towering seas swept over her deck and lower rigging, the water's weight caused her to wallow, straining her planks, opening seams, and causing torrential leaks. Because any crewman manning pumps on deck would have been swept

---

*Krakatoa's "paroxysmal explosions," the final destructive blasts of August 26 and 27, have been estimated to have been two hundred megatons in force, a factor of 13,000 greater than the Hiroshima Little Boy and four times that of the largest nuclear test explosion ever recorded. It caused tidal waves, killed at least thirty-six thousand, and two years later was the cause of the so-called Yellow Days that blanketed much of the earth in dust, creating sunsets of heart-stopping beauty. Writing to Walter Teller, Benjamin Slocum believed that "had we been three days in that region we would have been suffocated by the fumes."

overboard, the captain had to rely on his steam donkey engine to pump her holds. And this at first seemed to work—a rare case of steam behaving as Joshua Slocum's friend—until it was noticed that the floodwater being pumped overboard was diminishing in volume and darkening in color. They were pumping molasses! The sea had mixed with the sugar, and just as a jury-rig had been completed to steer her, the *Northern Light* was getting crank, listing thirty degrees to port, the symptoms of a ship loaded with too much weight too shallow in her hold and not enough deep. The sugar that was now pump-clogging syrup had been stowed deep, so Slocum had to give the order to jettison as much of the hemp as could be thrown into the waters off the Cape of Good Hope. Borne by the current, "bales of hemp floated to windward as far as we could see," Victor relates.

Once more the Slocums had survived, and the captain's ingenuity and seamanship were audacious. Suddenly they were only twenty miles from land, and the safe harbor of Port Elizabeth, at South Africa's eastern cape.

Here begins the end of Joshua Slocum's tragic mastery of that "magnificent ship" that represented to him—in defiance of his miserable experience aboard her—the zenith of his career. The *Northern Light* spent two months in Port Elizabeth being completely overhauled. Her topsides and deck had to be recaulked to stop leaks. Her rudder again was repaired. She was rerigged, her hemp standing rigging—holding her masts in place—replaced by steel wire. Her remaining cargo of sugar and hemp was restowed. And finally, the ailing mate was replaced by a presentable new officer, Henry A. Slater, twenty-six, whose papers—later proved to be forgeries—commended him as a capable British seaman, visiting the Cape Colony to restore his health.

Not until the *Northern Light* was at sea, bound for New York, did Slocum learn that Slater was an incompetent hustler who had boasted even before signing aboard that he would murder the Slocums and together with malcontent accomplices seize the *Northern Light* and use her for purposes to be specified later. Or so Slocum's friends and admirers were later to declare. Attempting to sort out what happened on the troubled ship is like trying a case in court—appropriately enough, because that was where the so-called facts were determined. All parties claimed injury, and in fact all suffered. At this distance, of course, it is impossible to know what happened aboard the *Northern Light*.

The problem facing a judge of the events today is illuminated by the uncertainty surrounding America's most infamous and most laboriously recorded and eyewitnessed mutiny: the *Somers* incident. The hanging at sea of three seamen found guilty of plotting to seize the USS *Somers*—a navy training ship—occurred in 1842, forty-one years before the Slater debacle, steeping it in legend rather than blurring its memory. Like the 1789 mutiny on the HMS *Bounty,* the events leading to that crisis were disputed, aggravated by the high standing of the characters on both sides of the divide. The *Somers,* a hundred-foot brig, was commanded by Alexander Slidell MacKenzie, an esteemed writer. His first mate was Guert Gansevoort, first cousin of Herman Melville, whose *Billy Budd* was more than a little inspired by the case. The Henry Slater of the *Somers* incident was a seventeen-year-old trainee midshipman, Philip Spencer, the son of the U.S. secretary of war, John C. Spencer. The boy, with a record of nastiness and petty delinquency, occupied his free time during a training cruise in the South Atlantic hatching an elaborate plot to seize control of the *Somers,* murder any officers or crew who opposed him, sail the ship to Cuba's Isle of Pines, and transform her—fully armed as she was—into a pirate ship, idealized in a crude drawing by young Spencer as flying a skull-and-crossbones ensign! At first, as word trickled from the forecastle to Commander MacKenzie, thanks to Gansevoort, this scheme was regarded as too silly to cause alarm, but then Spencer and his closest confederates began asking questions about navigational details relevant to the nearby West Indies, and when MacKenzie had Spencer's cramped quarters searched a scarf was discovered on which the names of likely fellow mutineers were written in Greek.

Anyone who has been a party to a kangaroo court that can reduce ladies and gentlemen to the subhuman state of a lynch mob—searching for the locker room thief or the bathroom graffiti vandal—can easily imagine how a captain's mast (a military trial at sea) can build like a freak wave, overtaking all common sense and proportion. The hunt for a defendant's evasions and lies can have primitive fervor, and so it did during the court-martial of Spencer and two of his sidekicks, Samuel Cromwell and Elisha Small. On December 1, 1842, the ship's crew was called to attention and ordered to cheer the American ensign three times as the three were hoisted already hanged into the ship's yardarms, where they were left to dangle high in the rigging for almost two hours before they were cut down and buried at sea. Commander MacKenzie, who of course had attracted the undying enmity of his superior, Secretary of War John C. Spencer, was himself tried at a court-martial for murder, and acquitted, but his reputation was ruined. The U.S. Naval Academy was founded in 1845 in revulsion against the formerly haphazard practices of training military sailors aboard such vessels as the *Somers* (which was lost in a squall in 1846).

It is the question of haphazard practice as opposed to strict custom that creates the friction in the case of Slater versus Slocum. In the culture of crimps, slave wages, spoiled food, vermin-infested quarters, heart-pounding crises followed by brain-numbing doldrums, there must have been—somewhere in the wide world—happy ships commanded by wise and gentle masters providing delicious fresh food and plenty of it, lending their voices to singalongs on deck under the light of the moon, their sails filled by winds a little aft of the beam blowing at a steady twenty knots, as porpoises played in the bow waves. If Joshua Slocum stepped aboard or heard about such a ship, he never told anyone.

Instead, he exercised the power necessarily conferred on captains to rule and to overrule. Ten years after the Slater dispute, Slocum admitted to a reporter for the *Boston Sun* that he had not been "a martinet, but I have ideas of how to run a ship. The old shipmasters treated their crews like intelligent beings, giving them plenty of leeway, but holding them with a strong hand in an emergency." With a waterspout, say, bearing down on a ship, or a freak wave overtaking her from astern, or the sight ahead of waves breaking on a reef where none was meant to be, authority had to be reliably located. And, as Lord Acton famously declared a few years after the *Northern Light* disturbances, power tends to corrupt and absolute power to corrupt absolutely. In practice, the application of the power of an effective captain is subtly tempered by experience-tutored custom. After all, his authority—given that he is so outnumbered—relies on the consent of the governed. If the underlying authority is absolute, the executive management of the ship is delegated; with a crew of dozens working in teams hundreds of feet distant from one another, how could it be otherwise?

It was on this issue of delegation that Joshua Slocum and Henry Slater had their first confrontation, from which a serial debacle developed. The *Northern Light* was a week out of Port Elizabeth when Slater, as third mate, was directing a team of ordinary seamen to adjust the rigging of the mizzenmast, located aft near the wheelhouse. His specific commands, to hoist one thing above another, had led to a tangle of lines and a jammed halyard, inviting from someone aloft irreverent accusations that Slater didn't know what he was doing. These few facts seem to have been undisputed, but a reader may well wonder why it had taken a week for an impostor's incompetence to be revealed: to manage the rigging of a ship without knowing the ropes must be like trying to pilot an airplane without having flown in one.

Slocum, his attention drawn to the confusion at the mizzenmast, instructed Slater to correct his work. According to Slater's own testimony in one of the many versions of events that he narrated to newspaper reporters, the captain at the mizzenmast "found fault with my work. I pointed out that I was competent to do the work." To rebuke a mate in front of the crew was a provocative gesture, as Slocum understood, but according to Victor's version, "the mate told the Captain 'to mind his own damned business,'" upon which insubordination Slocum immediately broke Slater in rank, ordering him forward to the forecastle. (According to Slater's version, Slocum—in response to Slater's defense of his competence—produced a sheath knife and "rushed over and struck at me. I caught his hand, twisted the knife out of his grasp, and threw it overboard. He then went below." On the face of it, this sequence seems implausible.)

Other eyewitness testimony came from William H. Dimmock, who had joined the *Northern Light* as her carpenter's mate in New London. According to Dimmock's unfriendly-to-definite-articles account:

> Slater had replied to Slocum's instruction to correct his rigging mistake "that no man on the ship could tell him his business" . . . Slater told captain he was third mate of the ship, and knew his business. His language and manner were insulting, and he took a belaying pin out of the rail as if to strike the captain. Captain Slocum informed Slater that he was disrated, saying, "You are no longer an officer of this ship: take your things from the [officers'] cabin and go into boatswain's room." Slater refused to go, but after a few hours went forward among the men.

It seems incredible that hours passed between insults—let alone attempted or even threatened violence—and some resolution to what was unambiguously mutinous behavior. Other than fire aboard ship, no calamity was more feared than mutiny. Casual violence might have been a leftover from the barbarity of the Civil War's recent slaughter, but aboard ship it was even more hazardous than to hurl an insult haphazardly in a Wild West saloon to stir the latent hostility between the many governed and their few governors. An indecisive despot—a shipmaster who would either walk away from a violent confrontation and flee to the refuge of his cabin (Slater's version) or permit a mutineer to disobey a direct order for "a few hours" (Dimmock's version)—would be an intolerable peril to his crew.

Moreover, do not lose sight during these events of Virginia and the four Slocum children. Henry Slater's recent boast in a Port Elizabeth saloon, that he would seize the *Northern Light,* was as serious as a heart attack. While this might have been the effluvia spewed by a braggart drunk on gin and pirate yarns, it wasn't incidental that under United States articles of war at the time, talk of mutiny—even in jest—was a hanging offense, as Philip Spencer and his friends had learned aboard the *Somers.*

A subsequent episode, presumably "hours" later, placed Slater before Slocum, who ordered acting second mate William McQuaker, Dimmock's immediate superior, to trice Slater in irons. In Dimmock's elliptical account:

> McQuaker, the sail maker, was acting as second mate. When he told the men to do anything, Slater would order them not to obey, saying "I'm second mate of this ship." A pair of shackles was put on Slater's wrists, and he was placed down on the half-deck, where there was plenty of room. Boatswain carried down his dinner, but could not find Slater and reported the fact to the captain. A search was ordered with lanterns, and Slater was found stowed away in [a sail locker]. He had the shackles on, and he said he didn't want anything to eat, but wanted to be left there to die. The captain finally concluded to let him have his own way. He was offered supper, but refused. That night was very dark. Slater came out, his hands free, and went on the poop deck. No one on deck but mate and man at wheel. Slater went into mate's room and took revolvers, and cases of ammunition, and then went across to second mate's room, where McQuaker and boatswain were. Told McQuaker to hold up arms while he searched for firearms. Slater told boatswain that if he made any noise [Slater] would blow his brains out . . . We were called up with McQuaker and the boatswain by Captain Slocum, who said that there was more trouble. A consultation was held, and . . . the mate was ordered to place Slater in irons at all hazards, but not to hurt him, unless absolutely necessary.

Slater was found in the starboard forecastle . . . McQuaker told him that he must go in irons, and that it was useless for him to resist. The men went about their duties, most of them cheerfully, some sullenly. It was evident that Slater had "stirred" them up. Slater said he would go aft and talk with the captain. He went on the poop deck. Captain Slocum told him that he must be put in irons. Slater said: "No [expletive evidently deleted] man on ship can put me in irons," and started to run forward to the sailors. Captain Slocum shot at him twice as he was running off. The captain then insisted that Slater must go in irons, as he was too dangerous a man to be left free. Slater then went forward, and seeing that he could not take charge of the ship he returned aft and allowed himself to be put in irons. Two pairs of handcuffs were placed on his wrists at that time, and he twisted them off as if they were string. He broke seven pairs of handcuffs . . .

The difficulty of nonfiction is that the reporter is stuck with the documents he finds, however far-fetched. The benefit of nonfiction is that however risibly far-fetched the document, the reporter cannot be blamed for having created it. If you're wondering about the odd outbreaks of calm between the storms aboard the *Northern Light* that night, so am I. The problem with discrediting out of hand Dimmock's account of pistol waving and misfired gunshots is that his version of events was sworn to by his fellow crew members in court in New York, after a postmutiny passage of fifty-three days, with Henry Slater in irons the whole way.

(Victor Slocum has little to say about this final passage aboard the *Northern Light*, other than to assure his readers that his father brought her into New York "spick and span, and in much better condition than when she was towed out through Long Island Sound eighteen months before.")

It was in irons that Slater was discovered on November 22, the day the *Northern Light* docked, and interviewed by the *Police Gazette*. This tabloid republished its story, titled "A Specter from the Sea," four months later, as an extended caption to a photograph of a robust, dark-haired, mustachioed bruiser with fists raised and huge chains shackled to his ankles:

The horrible story of this gallant sailor's sufferings was given in these columns at the time that he arrived in this port, laden with chains and confined in a dark closet in the hold of the vessel. The captain had him arrested on a charge of mutiny, but investigation developed the fact that if justice was to be done complainant and prisoner should change places. For a trifling offense the poor man had been brutally treated and placed in confinement, loaded with over 300 pounds of chain. When found by the officers of the law, who were sent to arrest him, he was a pitiful object. Hunger and cold had reduced him to a skeleton, and the rats had almost torn the clothing from his body. It took two men more than twenty minutes to cut off his shackles.

The portrait shows him with the chains and clothing that were found on him when he arrived in this port. Slater is now but a wreck of his former self. He was at one time one of the most robust sailors that ever trod a deck. Some five years ago, while on board the *Garribaldie,* lying in an English port, he took part in an athletic contest at the Adelphia theatre, London, and took the first prize for heavy lifting . . . He also won a medal for athletic sports at Rio de Janeiro some three years ago, and another at Port Elizabeth, Africa, in September, 1883.

The *Police Gazette*'s account dovetails perfectly with Henry Slater's account, twelve years later, to a reporter for the *Daily Telegraph* of Sydney, Australia. One might almost imagine that he had his copy of the tabloid at hand in Sydney, as an aide-mémoire. Here is Slater's story:

In the year 1883 I signed articles as second mate [*sic*] of the ship *Northern Light,* then under the command of Captain Joshua Slocum, at Port Elizabeth, South Africa. In the course of conversation the captain told me that he had a very mutinous crew, and that as the other officers were afraid of the men he wanted an officer of my stamp to keep them in order. He gave me to understand that I was to be a regular "Bucco," or bully, on board, said Slater.

Shortly after I had come on board, the next morning, I heard Mrs. Slocum, the captain's wife, scream, and running to the gangway found that one of her children had fallen overboard. I jumped over after the child, as also did a man in my watch named Hansen, and succeeded in saving the child and bringing it safely on board. The harbor, I may state, is infested by sharks. Mrs. Slocum was effusive in her thanks, but the captain never mentioned a word about the matter.

All went smoothly until the day before we started on the voyage to New York, whither we were bound. The captain and first mate being ashore I was in charge of the ship. I told the third mate, M'Quaker [*sic*], to do a job with some of the crew forward. Shortly afterwards I heard a row, and going forward, saw M'Quaker unmercifully beating one of the crew. I remonstrated with him, whereupon he answered me in a very insulting manner, and said that my time would come when we got to sea. I ordered him to his cabin, when he began to use most disgusting language, and on his way aft kicked a boy whom he passed, saying at the time that he was one of my favorites. I was so incensed that I gave him a thorough thrashing. The captain and mate came on board a little later, and M'Quaker was for some time closeted with Slocum.

Some days after we had sailed from Port Elizabeth, Captain Slocum came to me and asked me when I "was going to start on the crew," explaining that I had said that I would play the deuce with the men when we got to sea. I intimated that I was not prepared to beat and ill-treat the men for his satisfaction, as I found them good seamen and respectful and obedient. I also warned him that if he ill-treated any of the men I would be a witness against him. He went away muttering to himself. About a fortnight after leaving port the captain came up while I was directing a job on the mizzen mast, and found fault with the work. I pointed out that I was competent to do the work, and had satisfactorily superintended the same work on the fore mast. He had a sheath knife in his hand, and he rushed over and struck at me. I caught his hand, twisted the knife out of his grasp, and threw it over-board. He then went below.

That evening I slipped and fell, fracturing my right ribs, and the next day called the captain and told him that I would have to lay up. He replied that he would have no loafing on his ship, that he would disrate me, and ordered me forward to the forecastle. I told him that he dared not disrate me, when he rushed at me, knocked me down, and kicked me about the face and head. I was carried forward by the other officers, and placed in a berth in the forecastle. The next morning the captain, first and third mates, carpenter, and boatswain dragged me on deck, and the captain spat at me and struck me in the face with a belaying pin. I managed to crawl back to the forecastle, and then fainted. When I woke up in the evening the men held a consultation, and agreed that they would not stand by and see me ill-treated in the manner I had been.

The men began arming themselves and sharpening their knives, but I begged of them not to interfere, as the officers were armed, and I feared that there would be bloodshed. I entreated them not to interfere with the captain and officers, pointing out that they would be severely punished as mutineers if they did, and I would be charged as the ringleader. At first they would not listen, but finally I got them to promise not to interfere, whatever happened, but to take note of everything, taking day and date, so that when we reached port we could have justice meted out to us.

The next morning the captain and officers and carpenter and boatswain came forward, armed with revolvers and cutlasses, and hand-cuffed my hands behind my back. They then threw me down the half-deck, and kept me there all day without food or water. About midnight I wrested my hands free, and crawled on deck, and into the mate's cabin, where I secured a revolver. After deliberating for some time, I threw the revolver over-board and went forward and lay down.

About 8 o'clock the following morning the carpenter came to the forecastle and nailed up one of the doors and the shutter. Then the captain and his officers and petty officers came forward and ordered all the men on deck. The officers then began to fire their revolvers into the forecastle. Fortunately I was not struck by any of the bullets. After a time the mate, Mitchell, called upon me to surrender. He was afraid to enter the forecastle for some time, but at last came in when I told him that I was unarmed. He told me that the trouble would blow over, and that he would see me reinstated as second mate. I got up, and he helped me to the door. When I got out on deck I was seized from behind, knocked down, and two pairs of handcuffs were put on my wrists. I was then dragged aft to the poop, where shackles were put on my ankles. A chain was then placed round my throat, crossed behind my neck, wound around my body under my arms, down through the handcuffs, down through my legs, then up to the back of my neck, and made fast. Then a length of chain was made fast to the shackles on my ankles, and the whole lot of chain riveted together. I had then over 80 lb. of chain on my body.

The captain then told the carpenter to partition off a portion of the lazaret [locker] for my reception. This was . . . about 4 ft. wide and 4 ft. deep. One end was nailed up, and I was dragged up and thrown down the hatch into the lazaret. The captain then ordered the other end to be boarded up. I was then in a space 4 ft. by 4 ft., and 5 ft. long. I am 5 ft. 10 in. in height, so I had not too much room in which to lie down, I could not reach my mouth with my hands on account of the chains. A hole was cut in one of the boards, and one end of the chain attached to my ankle was pulled through and made fast to a stanchion outside my "box."

At first my daily fare was one ship's biscuit and a half pint of water. That did not kill me, so the same amount of biscuit and about three or four tablespoonsful of water was tried. Still I did not die. For the first three weeks in this "box" I suffered the tortures of the damned, my hunger and thirst were intolerable. I begged Captain Slocum to give me water and food; but in vain.

After I had been for about thirty days in the box I heard Mrs. Slocum playing a hymn on the organ [sic]. She played, "Nearer, My God, to Thee," and I joined in, and began to sing.* Suddenly, while I was singing, the chain attached to my ankles was hauled up to the hole, bringing my feet up about three feet from the deck. I was kept in this position for over three days without food or water. At the end of that time the captain came down fully armed to see me. He let my legs down again.

I begged of him to give me some water. He laughed, and said, "Are you very thirsty, old man? Very well, I will give you a good drink if you

---

*Dimmock testifies: "He would make all the noise possible, and sing obscene songs that the captain's wife must hear."

promise to behave yourself." I promised I would not sing again, and he went and got me a big dipper of water. I said, "God bless you, Captain Slocum, for your kindness in bringing me this water." I then began to drink, and found that he had given me a dipper of sea water. I had drunk quite a quantity before I ascertained that the water was salt, and naturally my thirst was increased a hundredfold. The next day I received my usual allowance of water and biscuit.

I began to find the rats troublesome about now. I would often wake up and find them running all over me, and even biting my skin—I had no flesh. I wondered why they came after me, as I was nothing but skin and bone. I soon found out. I frequently fancied about this time that I could smell butter or melted cheese. I found out later on that Captain Slocum used to pour melted butter or cheese on to what remained of my clothes to attract the rats.

After I had been about 40 days in the box, a large rat was running over me, and I succeeded in catching him in my hands. I was in such a desperate state of hunger that I squeezed the life out of the rat, and then ate it. I never, however, managed to get this change of diet again.

My box was never once cleaned out for the period of 53 days during which I was confined therein, nor was I allowed to wash myself. After the first couple of weeks I broke out into a rash, and found that I was covered with vermin. The rats had almost stripped me of my clothing, and were often gnawing at my legs and arms. Captain Slocum would occasionally come down, bringing with him bread and meat or cakes or doughnuts, show them to me, and then deliberately eat them before me. Shortly before we arrived in New York, the captain brought down some carbolic acid to disinfect my box, and sprinkled some on my body and face, drops falling in my mouth and eyes.

On arriving at New York I was arrested and tried for mutiny, and honorably acquitted. Captain Slocum and his two mates were then arrested, and were each severely punished for their cruelty to me. The captain was fined 500 dollars.*

The sequence of events in New York after the *Northern Light* docked in Brooklyn is easier to follow than the story's underlying facts are to know. From the moment Slater was shipped aboard at Port Elizabeth, reversals of fortune became commonplace. On November 22, 1883, a dispatch from New York to the *Milwaukee Sentinel* (an indication of the national interest in shipping news) reported that Slocum had gone immediately upon docking to the U.S. marshal's office to charge Slater with "having fired on one of [his] sailors and an attempt to get up a mutiny." Two

---

Sydney Daily Telegraph, October 9, 1896 (Australian National Library).

deputy marshals accompanied Slocum to the *Northern Light* to remove Slater from the vessel, having been warned by the captain "to look out for Slater, as he was a 'dangerous man.' " They found the prisoner bound in "heavy iron chains" and unable to stand. With assistance from the deputy marshals he was taken before a U.S. commissioner, who remanded him to the infamous Ludlow Street jail. Confined to his cell, Slater "sank to the floor and fainted," but not before asking his keepers "for God's sake to give him something to eat as he was starving." When food was delivered he "revived . . . and he ate ravenously . . . After eating a hearty meal he fainted again and became delirious." The form of delirium was "begging for more biscuit[s]."

Three days later, the *New York Times* reported that Slocum had been charged by Commissioner Shields with "cruelly and inhumanly treating his prisoner . . . [whose] condition had much improved since leaving the vessel." The newspaper also noted that during this busy day in court mate William McQuaker had testified that Slater "had attacked him with a pistol at 11 o'clock [the night after he'd been put in irons], and when he came into the cabin where the witness and ship's boatswain were sleeping he said: 'A word out of you and I'll blow your brains out,' holding a revolver about six inches from [McQuaker's] forehead."

The *Times,* having described the *Northern Light* crew assembled in the courtroom as presenting "a picturesque appearance with their bronzed faces, heavy whiskers, and nautical attire," pictured Slocum as "mild-mannered, of inoffensive appearance," as he listened to "the pitiful story [Slater] told of his sufferings without seeming in the least moved." At the end of the day, the captain was released on $2,500 bail, paid by his partners Benner and Pinckney. Slater's own trial was held over. Less than a week later, after one witness, "a rather thick-witted Swede," according to the *Times*'s court reporter, "glaring at Capt. Slocumb [*sic*] with hatred in his countenance," testified that "the crew often heard Slater, from his pen between the decks, calling for food and water, and shouting in agonized tones that he was dying," the *New York Times* editorial page branded Joshua Slocum a "brute."

Across the country, in the *San Francisco Evening Bulletin* of December 4, 1883, the story appeared with appropriate embellishments, including the brandishing of cutlasses. The *Bulletin* added that when the deputy marshal boarded the *Northern Light* in Brooklyn and peered into the darkness of the ship's dungeon,

Slater cried out, "Are you the officer come to arrest me?" The Marshal said he was. "Thank God," said the prisoner fervently. The miserable man was lying on his back, with one foot hoisted into the air and strapped to the ceiling. Attached to the ankle of his other leg was a heavy iron manacle, to which was fastened an enormous chain weighing about eighty pounds. His only clothing was an undershirt and a sock which covered the foot which was raised in the air. The unfortunate man had been confined in his pen for fifty-three days, and had torn off his clothing while the ship was crossing the equator, when the heat must have been one hundred and forty degrees at least.

William Dimmock's version of this event, however, contradicts this account:

The day before he was released in Brooklyn he broke two pairs of shackles. A weak man couldn't do that. His weakness was all shammed, and the men on the ship were all of one opinion in that respect. He was a perfect sham in every respect. See how quick he got well. When we went down to release him, Slater called for a clean change of clothing, and the mate gave it to him. He then went back into his cabin. He took off his pants and shirt and came out naked. The [ship] was full of reporters and other people, and the cunning of Slater created undeserved sympathy for him. Slater came out trembling, and feigned so much weakness that he reached the deck with apparent difficulty. He had good drawers, pants, stockings, etc, if he wanted to wear them. There was no vermin in his prison except cockroaches, and they were all over the ship. He used to catch them and put them in a pan. When they were taken away from him he would become very angry. He had some reason for wanting to keep them. I can truthfully say that Slater never was injured or brutally treated on the Northern Light. He was punished for his actions, and that justly deserved.

Capt. Slocum is as fine a man as ever I want to have anything to do with. He is a worker himself, and expects everybody else to be. He hates a loafer, and don't want anyone soldiering on him, but he is kind, cheerful and generous to his men. I have read the evidence against the captain in the New York papers, but very little of the testimony favorable to the captain was printed. They were one-sided reports, and I was disgusted with the reading of them.*

*Dimmock's testimony—given to a *New York Telegram* reporter—appeared during the course of Slocum's trial. Slocum kept the undated clipping, and printed it in the chapbook he produced in his defense, more than a decade later, in Sydney.

By this time the public was hungrier for tales of shipmasters' cruelty than for penny-dreadful accounts of crews' mutinous treachery, and especially in San Francisco, the city hosting the world's most notorious crimps. In 1888 a booklet entitled *The Red Record: Ecce! Tyrannus* was published in San Francisco by the Sailors' Union of the Pacific, detailing instances of brutality aboard ship and naming captains previously accused in *The Coast Seaman's Journal*. The booklet's cover was illustrated by a drawing of a disembodied fist gripping a belaying pin dripping with blood.

It would be folly to generalize about the distribution of rights and wrongs between human beings at sea. Nothing other than specific instances can inform judgment, and contesting those in the *Northern Light* drama is like watching one of those Laurel and Hardy revenge comedies in which no offense—a slap in the face or a broken window— can ever go unanswered or unescalated. Thus Slocum's charge was followed by Slater's countercharge, which was followed by the testimony in court on December 8, 1883, by the shipmaster Everett Staples, of the *Charter Oak,* that Slater's discharge papers from his service were forgeries and his service as a mate was a pipe dream. Captain Staples, a Maine sailor of impeccable reputation, declared he was extraordinarily incompetent and idle even as an ordinary seaman, feigning illness as an excuse to escape his duties, and fell into that category known as sea lawyers, concluding that "since he has parted from me I hope that [he] has improved morally, as when I knew him last in my judgment he was a magnificent scoundrel and no seaman."

The locution "sea lawyer" brings us closer to the end of this squalid chapter—but by no means to Henry Slater's obsession with Joshua Slocum. One month after Captain Staples had addressed the court, Slater gave a bizarre interview, swearing to its truth before a notary public, to the editor of the influential *Nautical Gazette*, attesting to the falsehood of his claims against Slocum and claiming he himself had been the victim of a conniving tort lawyer named Isaac Angel. He had been drawn, unwittingly and innocently, into a scheme to extort money from Slocum and his fellow owners of the *Northern Light* by "these designing persons," tossing into his jackpot of villains the deputy marshals who had been sent to arrest him. The papers he'd signed he now repudiated, "for I was confused and sick [in Ludlow Street jail] and knew not what I was signing," claiming as well to have been ignorant that he had in fact sued

Captain Slocum, "an A-One man, a genuine Yankee captain of high reputation."

This new farrago of charges, published on January 13, 1884, by the *New York Sun,* inspired Isaac Angel's $2,000 suit for libel against that newspaper. That complaint failed a year later when the court learned that the reputation of Mr. Angel—who had been indicted in Massachusetts on more than fifty charges of theft, false dealing, and cigar smuggling—was of no material value even before the *Sun* brought him to New York's attention.

Whether Slater's recantation came at a price in dollars, and if so who paid it, is not known. Despite Slocum's vindication, he had been declared a "brute" by the nation's newspaper of record. And while he was busy defending himself against criminal accusations, the *Northern Light* had sailed from New York with a new master. Slocum's controlling partners, having had their sugar pumped overboard and their hemp jettisoned, having paid for the renovations in New London and Port Elizabeth, bought out his interest in her at a painful discount. They would soon sell the great ship, then stripped of her masts and "ignominiously towed" by her nose as a coal barge, as her proud ex-owner explained in *Sailing Alone Around the World.*

This is a good juncture at which to consider what a strange and discouraging impression is left by the biographical treatment of Slocum during these unhappy events. Perhaps it is naive to be amazed that everyone, even a writer of such otherwise good human sense as Walter Teller, accepts that this command marked the high-tide line of Slocum's career. This is akin to endorsing Howard Hughes's delusion that the *Spruce Goose,* owing to its monstrous scale, was the finest airplane ever to (almost) fly. That the *Northern Light* was flawed—its rudder poorly designed, its planks leaking at their seams, its crew a gang of criminals, its cargo chucked into the sea—seems to count for nothing set beside the outward show that she presented to the world: costly and grand, biggest and best-looking. How American, it is tempting to write, how imperial. How vulgar, how sad.

The Aquidneck

EIGHT

Stranding

In this story of a voyage filled with adventures common to the life of a sailor it is only right that I should square myself and explain how it happened that on a subsequent voyage I sailed all alone. It came about in this manner: After the events which I am about to relate, and when I cast about for a hand to join my new ship, the person I wished to have along said, "Joshua, I've had a v'yage," which indeed was the truth. Madame was thinking of the cruise when in a short three years we had experienced many of the vicissitudes of sea life and traversed the round of plagues, such as cholera, smallpox, yellow fever, and the like; the whole ending in mutiny and shipwreck.

—JOSHUA SLOCUM, *The Voyage of the "Liberdade"*

THE MISADVENTURES ABOARD THE *Northern Light* were heartbreaking, literally, for Virginia. How exactly the malady had first shown itself is unrecorded, but her children were unanimous in lamenting their mother's weak heart. To the demands that weather and violent motion put on a woman going deep sea must be added her recent history among would-be mutineers and cutthroats. Victor likened it to "voyaging with a volcano under the hatches," and believed that the "constant alarms at sea had undermined her health." In addition to the shame her husband had suffered, the Slocums' financial distress was acute. Without a home ashore and unsettled after the New York trials, Virginia and the children traveled to Boston to distribute themselves among Joshua's married sisters during the winter of 1884, while her husband sought a new command.

This was a depressing challenge, confirming that the glory days of sail were done. The reasons suggested earlier were exacerbated by the toll taken on America's merchant fleet by the Civil War, and the opening of the Suez Canal in 1869 providing passage for steamships from Europe to the Indian Ocean without rounding the Cape of Good Hope. Nevertheless, as *Slocum* would emphasize a few years later, he despised steamships, remaining stubbornly loyal to those "tramp" sailing vessels that were left to pick up the shipping world's droppings, odd lots of freight destined to far-flung ports in no hurry to receive them.

In this economic climate, Slocum traveled south by train to Baltimore, celebrated for the fast clippers among its fleet. There he offered the winning bid at auction on the *Aquidneck*, a "trim and tidy craft," as he would describe her, 326 tons and 138 feet long. The money came from the last of his savings, an amount put aside when he received his gold pieces from the sale of the *Pato*. Slocum told the story of the *Aquidneck* in several versions, but the details of her purchase appear only in an article published in *Outing: An Illustrated Magazine of Recreation* (November 1902): "The auctioneer, while selling the *Aquidneck,* dwelled upon the lucky side of her character while he harangued; throwing a wink my way . . . he bawled, 'Sailors know what a lucky ship means'; and forthwith I gave the extra bid that fetched the bark."

That extra bid, together with what he'd need to spend to get her ready for sea, tapped out Slocum so completely that he couldn't afford to insure her. Built in Mystic, Connecticut, in 1865, she was a pretty bark, with three masts and a rakish bowsprit. It's a wonder to note Slocum's unflagging enthusiasm for his vessels, even as he now traded down by a factor of five or more from the *Northern Light.* His new boat was beautiful, he boasted, and, "when the wind blew" fast, asked "no favors of steamers."

In early March 1884, the family came aboard the *Aquidneck* in Baltimore with enthusiasm. Many years later Garfield Slocum gave Walter Teller his recollection of the *Aquidneck*'s layout: on deck were pens for sheep, pigs, and chickens, and below a well-equipped workshop for the carpenter and master staterooms; the saloon on board was "a beautiful room" with a "parquetry floor . . . The captain's room had a full size bed . . . and the other rooms a single bunk," and oil lamps swung on gimbals. "There was a long table and in rough weather racks were put on the table, [which] was built around the mizzenmast. Swivel chairs were bolted to the deck around the table." Above them was a stained-glass skylight, and keeping the family company "a canary that sang all day—a beautiful singer. Also a square grand piano was bolted to the deck . . . There was a cabinet with glass doors for carbines, guns and revolvers and ammunition." He remembered his father at that time as generous—lavishing books and toys on his children—but "stern."

Bright memories, closely juxtaposed with ominous rumbles—the canary chirping at revolvers and ammunition—seem always to characterize the Slocums' circumstances. Virginia had needed her respite ashore in Boston, a break from shouting and stabbing and shooting and the clank of irons binding a swine who sang dirty lyrics to her gospel songs. At least the *Aquidneck*'s crew would be smaller in number—undermanned at ten, in addition to the family members—than the *Northern Light* gang.

It began well, with a comfortable and fast passage carrying flour to Pernambuco, on the easternmost bulge of Brazil, near enough the equator to provide a hot and humid climate that was made more comfortable by reliable trade winds. While anchored behind a breakwater as they discharged flour, the family often had picnics ashore in a nearby coconut grove. Pernambuco would be the site of many a Slocum adventure, but during this voyage it was merely a port of call on the *Aquidneck*'s route to Buenos Aires. In mid-July, sailing past the luscious island of Santa Catarina, six hundred miles southwest of Rio and more than a thousand miles northeast of Buenos Aires, Virginia suddenly fell ill and began to deteriorate quickly. Writing to Walter Teller, Garfield remembered that his mother quit her chores (she had been making candy), lost her energy, and put aside the tapestry he had been watching her create; she "left her needle where she stopped" and crawled into her berth. Reflecting years later on their mother's decline, the children agreed that she had seemed energetic and characteristically joyful during picnics a few days earlier. But, as young as they were, they had been mindful that her lack of stamina had lately alarmed their father.

Imagine what it must have been like for her adoring husband to realize that Virginia was suffering, then to continue sailing south—for at least six days—to get help in Buenos Aires. During that passage, he promised his wife that he would try to find freight to be carried to Sydney, so she could see her home and family again. Having reached the Plata River, Slocum had to anchor the *Aquidneck* in the outer roads, a dozen miles from Buenos Aires, owing to the river's shallow delta and unreliably dredged channels. Virginia seemed to recover enough on July 25 to rise from her berth to make butter. That morning Joshua set out in a launch to look for business, having agreed with her on a signal—the blue-and-white flag letter *J*—to be hoisted in the event that she needed him to return from shore. Almost immediately the flag went up, hoisted by Benjamin, then twelve. It was near noon; Joshua returned to the *Aquidneck* immediately and that evening summoned his children to kneel at their mother's bedside, and then she died, at thirty-four.

Her brother, George Walker, believed that she died from the consequences of a miscarriage, but no evidence supports his hunch. The Slocum children agreed that her heart killed her, probably a congenital or rheumatic-fever-induced defect such as valvular stenosis or congestive cardiomyopathy: heart failure. (She had more than once fainted when acutely stressed.) What Joshua knew he did not share. "I never cared to ask father," as Benjamin confided to Walter Teller. That he found Joshua's reticence unassailable is less extraordinary than the breach in that reticence many years after Virginia's death, when father and son were looking together at a photograph, and "tears streamed over [father's] face. Finally he said, 'Your mother had the eyes of an eagle and she . . . saw things I could never see.' "

In this light, it's good to remember that bravura display of ship handling in Hong Kong harbor when Joshua steered the *Amethyst* among a fleet of British warships crowding the anchorage, with Virginia at his side. Whatever she said to him that day, or imparted by body language, he chose precisely the right moment—indeed the only possible moment—to turn the wheel hard over, rounding his full-rigged bark into the wind to carry it to a stop, without over- or underrunning, precisely where there was a vacant spot to drop its anchor. A failure of patience (heading up too soon) or of nerve (delaying) would have brought a scandalous collision. In addition, his composure—witnessed by the world's most celebrated sailors—determined whether Slocum's feat would be regarded as the lucky chance of a daredevil or the deliberate seamanship of a masterful captain.

Judges of Slocum's history must take seriously Benjamin's judgment that his mother knew his father "better than all others. She knew father could sail ships. She also knew more about father than herself. On many occasions mother had proved herself to be very psychic . . . Father learned to understand her powers of intuition and he relied on it fully until she passed on. His ill fortunes gathered rapidly from the time of her death." Later he added: "Father's days were done with the passing of mother. They were pals."

Virginia was buried in the English Cemetery at Buenos Aires. In her Bible Joshua wrote—under the rubric "Family Record"—her name, dates of birth and death, and, on a separate line, "Thy will be done not ours!" This headlong exclamation, stripped of punctuation, leaves a reader unsure whether this was composed in resignation or defiance.

Petey, the canary, quit singing, and Victor records that before the anchor was up after his mother's burial, the bird, having "made glad music for us for seven years in calm and storm . . . fell victim to a strange cat which came aboard." This tidy and sympathetic mystery shows signs of apocrypha, but nevertheless has value as a display of grief's narrative tropism toward allegory.

A few days later Slocum ran the *Aquidneck* hard aground on a sandbar in the Plata River and had to pay dearly to have her rescued. He set out at once to sail for Baltimore, and from Washington, six months after Virginia died, he wrote to his mother-in-law, reporting that his family would have been more secure financially "if I hadnt got crazy and runn my vessel onshore. As it is now I am just swimming out of trouble on borowd money." His fanciful figure of speech—"swimming out of trouble"— reveals how far off course he had strayed.* The figures of speech gather like buzzards around such calamities: Garfield Slocum wrote Walter Teller that when Virginia died, his father "never recovered. He was like a ship with a broken rudder."

Many sailors believe that short of death, stranding (running a vessel aground) is the most awful catastrophe a seaman can experience. Joseph Conrad—in *The Mirror of the Sea*—writes of the experience:

> It is as if an invisible hand had been stealthily uplifted from the bottom to catch hold of her keel as it glides through the water.
>
> More than any other event does stranding bring to the sailor a sense of utter and dismal failure. There are strandings and strandings, but I am safe to say that ninety per cent of them are occasions in which a sailor, without dishonor, may well wish himself dead . . .
>
> "Taking the ground" is the professional expression for a ship that is stranded in gentle circumstances. But the feeling is more as if the ground had taken hold of her. It is for those on her deck a surprising sensation. It

---

*What Slocum meant by "crazy"—despite the seeming transparency of his rare outburst of candor—is unclear but provocative. He might have been confessing that driving the *Aquidneck* aground was a kind of furious suicide, or he might simply have meant that a master and navigator distracted by grief cannot safely navigate a river bristling with snags, shoals, and shifting sandbars.

is as if your feet had been caught in an imponderable snare; you feel the balance of your body threatened, and the steady poise of your mind is destroyed at once . . .

And that is very terrible. After all, the only mission of a seaman's call-ing is to keep ships' keels off the ground. Thus the moment of her strand-ing takes away from him every excuse for his continued existence. To keep ships afloat is his business; it is his trust; it is the effective formula of the bottom of all these vague impulses, dreams, and illusions that go to the making up of a boy's vocation. The grip of the land upon the keel of your ship, even if nothing worse comes of it than the wear and tear of tackle and the loss of time, remains in a seaman's memory an indelibly fixed taste of disaster . . . To be "run ashore" has the littleness, poignancy, and bitterness of human error.

Joshua Slocum in his grief was not one to bore holes in the bottom of his vessel to sink it. His first thought was for his motherless children, and he brought them to Boston to rejoin his sisters while he—with Victor, now fourteen and first mate and as sturdy as a windlass, in his father's boast—made the *Aquidneck*'s trade the shipping of goods to and among countries along the Atlantic coast of South America. As soon as Ben-jamin was safe ashore with his aunt Etta, he declared—a resolution he honored for the rest of his life—never again to go to sea.*

To keep distracted by work, Slocum made three fast back-and-forth passages between Baltimore and Pernambuco. These were eventful. Car-rying machinery and pianos south, the *Aquidneck,* rolling violently, broke the cargo loose in the hold, the damage announced by snapping piano strings, followed figuratively by money fluttering from the master's pocket. And coming back north on the last round-trip during the late fall of 1885, as the *Aquidneck* entered the Gulf Stream, Slocum looked aloft to see that the mainmast rigging had parted. To save the ship it was neces-sary to bring down and cut free other masts and trestles and yards, an unholy mess of wires and canvas, leaving only a few small sails flying. Slocum and son and crew were then hit by a ten-day gale. During its course a young Norwegian ordinary seaman who had shipped aboard at Pernambuco went missing, assumed to have been lost overboard. Dur-

---

*For his part, Victor also made a lifetime choice at this moment by joining his father's calling, "a decision I have never since regretted, for I would rather be a sailor than anything else." Closing this paragraph, perhaps catching a high-flown tone in his phrasing, the son did as his father would have done and brings himself down to sea level with a flat declaration: "Anyway, that is how I became a sailor."

ing the tenth day, a seagoing tug approached the *Aquidneck* off the Delaware coast and offered to tow Slocum to New York for an exorbitant fee. At sea this is usually the moment when a captain, at the crew's urging, says, "Sure, whatever, get us out of here, just get us home." But Slocum dismissed the offer, and the tug skipper—who gave, in Victor's words, "a twirl to his wheel, and an emphatic jingle on his engine room bell"— turned away and was almost over the horizon when he recalculated his prospects and returned, agreeing to tow the *Aquidneck* to Brooklyn for the price of the coal the journey required. Once the ship was tied up to Pierrepoint Stores on the East River, the ghost of young Olaf arose from below, where the terrified Norwegian had hidden himself, alive on a diet of sugar, since the gale began.

While the *Aquidneck* was being repaired and rerigged during the winter, *père et fils* entrained for Boston, where the former met and on February 22, 1886, married his first cousin, Henrietta M. Elliott. "Hettie" was twenty-four at the time, one of seven sisters, a spinner, weaver, dressmaker, and gown fitter who had moved to Boston from Mount Hanley, Slocum's own birthplace in Nova Scotia, from which he'd run away two years before his future wife was born. Photos show a robust woman with a sturdy face and frank expression. Grace Murray Brown described her at the time as "very pretty," and Joshua as "kind and courtly." He was also, in Benjamin's recollection, "sad and very much alone, seeking company and a remedy for his lonely life."* On dry land and beneath the shelter of a sturdy roof, the travels and adventures of a seafaring father and widower of forty-two, conveyed with the estimable narrative powers at his command, must have been seductive to a young woman from the Maritime Provinces. The situation recalls Othello telling the youthful Desdemona the story of his dramatic life, the "battles, sieges, fortunes" he has experienced, the "most disastrous chances" and "hairbreadth 'scapes." "It was my hint to speak," as Othello relates, "of the

*Walter Teller writes in *The Search for Captain Slocum* that "in [Slocum's] search for guidance, he even went to a spiritualist." He is scrupulous to note that this was not "an unusual move in that more credulous age." But on the same page is Teller's report of his own "analysis of Slocum's handwriting," which the biographer had commissioned in hopes of determining the psychological contours of his subject's most private life, such as his excessive "masculine protest," the "frustration" of his "longing for feminine warmth." Specifically, Teller's graphologist, Dr. Meta Steiner, addresses with unintentionally hilarious effrontery the "strong sensuousness" and "extraordinary desire to prove his masculinity" revealed by "the determined pressure of the down stroke of letters" in Slocum's agonized letter to his mother-in-law following Virginia's death.

Cannibals that each other eat / . . . and men whose heads / Do grow beneath their shoulders." Like Desdemona's father, Hettie's parents opposed the marriage, though less dramatically, and for reasons that need no elaboration beyond their hunch that for Slocum, with four children, two of them younger than ten, their daughter was principally attractive as a convenience. (Moreover, her suitor assumed that she would join him at sea.) She disregarded their misgivings and the deal was done. Bedazzled, she couldn't have had a clue what she was in for when she left immediately after the wedding for New York, where six days later she boarded her husband's vessel for a honeymoon voyage carrying case oil to Montevideo.

They sailed right into a monstrous winter tempest of hurricane intensity. It was blowing forty knots when they left, so it wasn't as though the storm took them by storm, its ferocity having been forecast with unusual accuracy and specificity. In fact, even as Slocum set sail, New York was so blustery and cold that ships were torn from their moorings and the Hudson River froze solid. Why, with teenaged Victor, five-year-old Garfield, and his new bride aboard, did Slocum behave so recklessly? Or did hard Atlantic weather seem to him so commonplace that braving its bullying seemed no great shakes? In his story there have been so many gales and buffetings and towering seas—and will be so many more to come—that this three-day blow will be condensed to its singularity, which was the imminent threat of the *Aquidneck* sinking. Running before winds of eighty and ninety knots, the vessel, newly refitted in Brooklyn, began to take huge seas aboard from astern. These waves were not draining through the scuppers as they should, washing along the decks and emptying into the ocean. The bark began to sit lower and lower and move slower and slower, offering a sluggish target for the following seas. Everyone except Garfield and Hettie, confined below and seasick, manned either the pumps or the helm for thirty-six hours, nonstop. Victor remembered it was a "desperate sensation, pumping for all you were worth, and at the same time feeling that the ship was going down under you. It was like pumping the Atlantic Ocean through the vessel."

His father sounded the hold with a rod and discovered six feet of water, rising. To prevent capsize, he readied axes stowed on deck to chop down the *Aquidneck*'s masts. He stocked the lifeboats with food and water and clothes, and was on the point of ordering his crew and family to abandon ship when a kind of outraged refusal seized him, compelling him to find and repair the leak. He had already hung over the sides, searching for sprung planks or uncaulked seams, but then chanced to notice that a rough seal, twelve feet in length, where the deckhouse joined the deck, had been insecurely fastened. Through this joint gallons were streaming into the hold. He and Victor managed to jam ropes and sailcloth into the gap, stopping the leak just as the gale decided to blow itself out.

Every sailor who has experienced hurricane-strength winds at sea marvels above all at the noise of the onslaught, the roar and scream and anger. Hettie later confessed to her husband that during the height of the storm, with the wind shrieking and no human voice audible, she believed herself and Garfield to be the only survivors after the decks had been swept clean of human beings, or perhaps that they'd been abandoned.

They dropped anchor at Montevideo, on the northern shore of the Plata River, on May 5, two months after leaving New York. The days following the horror of the winter gale had been clear, indeed wonderful sailing, with the *Aquidneck* skipping along with a bone in her teeth—as sailors call the benign bow wave that announces a vessel traveling near her maximum hull speed—and porpoises riding the waves. Wet clothes were dried, chanteys were sung. The memory of pain is mercifully brief; if Hettie was staring intently at her hole cards, she stayed in the game nonetheless. And so in Montevideo, after discharging his cargo of case oil, Slocum sailed the *Aquidneck* in ballast nine hundred miles north to Antonina, Brazil. It makes sense to assume that such a canny and well-connected shipmaster would have been alert to international disputes between Argentina and Brazil—including outbreaks of war—but he had determined to provide for his family by trading between the countries. During the early summer of 1886, he carried a cargo of yerba maté back to Buenos Aires, and from there was commissioned to salvage a cargo of Bordeaux from a Spanish ship that had run aground on the Plata and deliver this wine two hundred miles up the Paraná River to Rosario. Hettie now had her first foreshadowing of mutinies to come when her husband had to lock and guard the hold to prevent his sailors from drinking his cargo dry.

At the port of Rosario there began the kind of collisions between fairness and circumstance that keep trial lawyers joyful and drive sane people mad. First, Slocum struck a commonplace business agreement with an Argentine merchant to transport bales of alfalfa from Rosario to Rio de Janeiro, where a Brazilian merchant wished to buy the alfalfa. But it chanced that just when the alfalfa was loaded and the *Aquidneck* was ready to sail in the fall of 1886, a cholera outbreak was decimating parts of Argentina, Rosario among them. Slocum, like all international merchant shipmasters, required clearance from the Brazilian consul to take his freight to Rio—which clearance, putatively owing to Brazil's reasonable fear of Argentina's deadly disease, but also to international spite, was denied. Slocum was required to enter Brazilian quarantine at Ilha Grande, sixty miles west of Rio, to be disinfected before discharging his cargo. While burdensome, this requirement did not delay Slocum's departure from Rosario, and on January 7, 1887, he entered the harbor of Ilha Grande, a lovely island of perfect beaches and pristine rain forests, indeed an ideal destination for a much-delayed honeymoon.

Here port officials ordered him—pointedly, turning the heavy guns of the armored battleship *Aquidiban* at the *Aquidneck*—to leave Brazilian waters, even though his documents were in order.* Denied permission to come ashore to replenish food and water for his crew, he was sent back to Argentina. From Slocum's point of view, he had been grievously wronged: singled out for betrayal, his American flag insulted, his investment of labor and expenses stolen from him, his personal honor affronted.

He now had to decide what to do with the alfalfa. A fellow captain suggested that he dump the bales overboard, and Slocum—bless him!—still had sufficient sly humor to report that this captain's hailing port was Boston, where they knew a thing or two about dumping freight over the side. But he was also stubborn, so he sailed back to Rosario, where he might have returned the hay to its original owner. This he did not do, deciding with characteristic obduracy to wait out the epidemic. On April 9, Brazilian ports reopened and Slocum sailed immediately, arriv-

---

*The officious official who blustered this high-handed order was Admiral Custodio de Mello, a notable foe of Slocum later in these pages.

ing in Rio to discharge his cargo on May 11, 1887, after a brief visit to Ilha Grande for the pleasure of thumbing his nose at "the authorities." He had lost a great deal of money to bad luck. Fifteen years later, writing in "The Voyage of the *Aquidneck,*" the plaintiff still felt freshly wounded: "A thunderbolt striking from a clear sky could not have surprised us more or worked us much greater harm—to be ruined in business or struck by lightning, being equally bad." (No, actually, they are not.)

The crew that sailed aboard the *Aquidneck* to Rio replaced a crew made up mostly of Finns who'd made such alcoholic hullabaloo ashore in Rosario in their "drunken frenzy," as Victor reports, that they'd been jailed by the Argentine police. Their replacements were "a gang much worse . . . When the cholera was at its height the jails were opened and the birds released. We shipped at least four of these who were guilty either of murder or highway robbery. They were all sheep thieves. One of them a burly scoundrel, with an ugly saber cut across his face, was known as 'Dangerous Jack'; while 'Bloody Tommy' was more of a sneak." The shipping agent who shanghaied this motley crew was "Dutch Harry," for whom Slocum developed a wholesome loathing. But after slandering him in *The Voyage of the "Liberdade,"* Slocum thought better of naming him the "vilest crimp" in Rosario, below whom there came one "worse than he, one 'Pete the Greek,'" who cut off the ears of a rival boarding-master . . . and threw them into the river." At any rate, Dutch Harry was hanged soon after.

In *The Voyage of the "Liberdade"* Joshua's prose rolls merrily as he remembers—from the sanctuary of time and distance—this unspeakable bunch "picked up here and there out of the few brothels [that] had not been pulled down during the cholera, and out of the streets or from the fields." With these brigands aboard in Rio, the *Aquidneck* loaded a consignment of pitch, tar, flour, kerosene, wine, and three pianos at Rio's Dom Pedro docks, where a "change of rats" was made, and "fleas, too, skipped about in the hay as happy as larks, and nearly as big." Slocum also suggests that Hettie had a bit of fun ashore. She bought a "tall hat, which I saw nights looming up like a dreadful stack of hay," which he resolved to pitch into the sea.

That was the most benign of the plots being hatched aboard the *Aquidneck,* now en route south to Brazil's Paranaguá River and upriver to

Antonina to load a cargo of yerba maté. It was an index of how difficult it had become to find shipping commissions that Slocum was carrying this cargo free of charge, merely to act as ballast. But he was also indemnified against damage to the freight, assuming that he would exercise prudence. So when the *Aquidneck* was struck by a *pampero*—a vicious offshore wind that arises on the pampas—and knocked on her beam ends and partially dismasted, Slocum was not responsible for the damage to the pianos (fearfully out of tune, as he reported) that he was again carrying.

On July 23, 1887, at anchor in Paranaguá Bay, Slocum was asleep when Hettie was awakened in alarm by the sound of crewmen walking and whispering near the aft end of the *Aquidneck,* an area of the vessel— "abaft the mainmast," as sailors say—strictly off-limits to ordinary seamen, who have shipped "before the mast."

Hettie stirred her husband awake, and he went on deck carrying a loaded .56 carbine. He had earlier that day rebuked Dangerous Jack (James Aiken) and Bloody Tommy (Thomas Maloney) for insubordination, and would have been a fool, so soon after the incidents aboard the *Northern Light,* not to have been mindful that his family's survival depended upon his resolve. On deck, he ordered the mutineers forward, but Maloney jeered at him and Aiken attacked him with a sheath knife. Slocum shot and wounded Dangerous Jack, whereupon Bloody Tommy lunged with his knife and Slocum shot him dead.

Victor writes persuasively of the situation: " 'Dangerous Jack,' ploughed by a .56, I took ashore about midnight, still howling and cursing. 'Bloody Tommy' was left where he fell for the police to inspect the next morning. Face down on deck, and in the rigor of death, he still clutched the same knife he had used killing sheep."

Slocum was arrested and charged with murder and jailed in Antonina for a month until his trial on August 23, at which he pleaded self-defense and was acquitted and released. Three months later, the U.S. consul general in Rio reported to the Department of State in Washington that the Brazilian proceedings had been in every respect thorough and goodwilled, and "the verdict is in my opinion a righteous one." In the meantime, trying to keep family and vessel afloat, Slocum had hired a Spanish shipmaster to take the *Aquidneck*'s cargo to Montevideo, with Victor aboard as first mate, leaving Hettie and Garfield ashore. When he was released from jail in Antonina, the captain traveled alone by steamship to Montevideo to resume command of his ship.

The dismissal of his Spanish replacement provoked another dispute between Slocum and his crew, who insisted that they be paid off and rehired, a demand that found favor with the U.S. consul in Montevideo.*
During this interval the protesting employees seem to have done some sightseeing and gift buying for their families at home. It is interesting that this crew—almost all Brazilian—were sober when they went ashore and sober when they returned, a virtue characteristic among Brazil's sailors of the time. However, virtue did not protect them from exposure to smallpox at the boardinghouse where they slept, and having been enlisted by Slocum they sailed north toward Paranaguá carrying that disease.

The first hint of the nightmare about to descend on the *Aquidneck* was a complaint from one trusted sailor that he was suffering from chills and a fever, but he didn't beg off his duties, merely requested a dose of quinine to ease what he took to be a recurrence of malaria. A couple of days later, he and three crewmates were felled by spinal rigor and Slocum—if not his men—recognized these deadly symptoms as smallpox. He altered course immediately for Maldonado, east of Montevideo along the coast of Uruguay. With a wet easterly storm already blowing hard, the *Aquidneck* raised signals of distress asking for emergency medical help for port officials to see. These went unanswered for thirty-six hours, and when answered it was by a couple of uniformed Uruguayan "yahoos," borne by rowboat to command the shipmaster to leave their port at once, the dead and dying crew's disease being immediately manifest.†

With great difficulty, the healthy crewmen—down now to three, including Victor—got up their anchor and headed downwind back toward Montevideo. The gale stripped off their sails "like autumn leaves," as

---

*This in turn provoked Slocum's bitter description of the American as "one of these small officials . . . better adapted to home life; one of those knowing, perhaps, more than need a cow-boy, but not enough for consul." Given Slocum's obsessive pursuit of what he took to be justice in his many, many complaints about his treatment by government officials at home and abroad, his sarcasm sounds a warning bell.
†In fairness, it should be noted that American ship captains sailing these waters had been known to hoodwink quarantine officers by applying pink tooth powder to the lips and cheeks of deathly pallid crew members.

Slocum wrote, and following what he remembered to have been "the most dismal of all my nights at sea" they managed to hook an anchor to an underground cable under the lee of Flores Island. At dawn, distress signals were again raised, this time answered with the command to sail into the port, which was not possible. Finally a doctor, drunk, was rowed out with some carbolic acid for disinfectant and the suggestion to dump the victims into the sea, though not into his harbor.

And bury them at sea they did, weighed down with stones from the ballast in the hold. Soon another half dozen were added to the three already dead. Such sorrows draw attention to unexpected details, and later, remembering the experience, Slocum recalled that his most painful task was the "gathering up" and destruction of the "trinkets" the crew members had bought a few days earlier in Montevideo for their wives and children: "A hat for the little boy here, a pair of boots for his mamma there." Then another sailor went over the side, and Slocum and his skeleton crew decided that, whatever the difficulty or cost, they "would remain no longer at this terrible place . . . The wind blowing away from the shore, as may it always blow when friend of mine nears that coast." The *Aquidneck,* that "drifting pest house," as Slocum remembered it, made for Montevideo, where the few survivors were hospitalized, all to carry lifelong the awful facial scars left by smallpox. It cost Slocum a thousand dollars to have the *Aquidneck* disinfected, and so—continuing his first voyage after being released from a month in prison on a charge of murder—the shipmaster set sail again with a new crew for Antonina, where Hettie and Garfield, knowing who knows what of Victor and Joshua's fate, awaited. Not far from the mouth of the Plata River, the *Aquidneck* sailed into a dead calm and "we came to a stand." They were at a spot on the ocean that Slocum remembered well: "A spell seemed to hang over us . . . I recognized the place" as being where "a very dear friend had stood by me on deck, looking at this island, some years before. It was the last land that my friend ever saw."

Haunted by the ghost of Virginia, fresh from death and jail and mutiny—what could that have been like for them? How could this continue?

It didn't. Making one last effort, Slocum entered the timber trade again, shipping huge logs from gigantic ironwood trees. During Christmas of 1887, the *Aquidneck* was loaded with lumber at an arm extending into Paranaguá Bay and soon after, with Hettie and the boys aboard, set forth to the Atlantic to deliver her freight. Almost immediately, while still in the bay, "currents and wind caught her foul," as Slocum wrote, and she "stranded broadside on, where open to the sea, a strong swell came in that raked her fore and aft, for three days, the waves dashing over her groaning hull . . . till at last her back was broke—and why not add 'heart' as well!"

Virginia Slocum's grave in Buenos Aires

Joshua Slocum

The Spray

TWO

Sailing Around It

The Liberdade

Joshua, Hettie, Garfield, and Victor aboard the Liberdade

NINE

Salvage

Shipwrecks are *apropos* of nothing.
—STEPHEN CRANE, "The Open Boat"

I had myself carried load on load, but alas! I could not carry a mountain; and was now at the end where my best skill and energy could not avail. What was to be done? What could be done? We had indeed the appearance of shipwrecked people, away, too, from home.
—JOSHUA SLOCUM, *The Voyage of the "Liberdade"*

THE STRANDING AND SEA BATTERING of the uninsured *Aquidneck* cost the Slocums not only all their money but what son Garfield described as "our beautiful home." For the remains of the wreck they were paid $1,000, of which—after the crew was paid off—only a "moiety" remained. Once again Slocum found exactly the right word, "moiety" meaning a portion of a molecule to chemists. The U.S. consul at Antonina offered to return the family to Baltimore or Boston by steamer, but Slocum—at the bitter end of his rope with government officials— refused the offer out of hand and commenced his interminable demand for redress from the government of Brazil for all his woes, using as the instrument of his complaint the offices of the government—yes, the government!—of the United States. How a man so delicately calibrated to recognize irony could have failed to register this instance of it is hard to understand. But it's ever thus with torts, fabricated as they are to confront caricatures of deviltry with caricatures of innocence. Slocum's story will show his appeal for recompense—for the loss of the *Aquidneck*, together with the cost to him in commissions and time due to highhanded Brazilian and Argentine port regulations—slithering along, via diplomatic pouches carrying his elaborate and increasingly theatrical grievances, from the week of the shipwreck until the case was finally dismissed in late 1893, killed by the U.S. Department of State.

Complaining, suing, and writing unsubtle letters was not all that occupied Slocum's passion during these six years. By a grand exercise of imagination that was informed by his shipbuilding experience and energized by his craftiness and defiance, Joshua Slocum performed an extraordinary feat of self-salvage with his five-thousand-mile journey in a homemade thirty-five-foot sailing canoe—his only crew a young wife, a child, and a teenaged boy—from Paranaguá to Washington, D.C.

The provenance of this boat is complicated by inconsistent accounts given by Victor and Joshua, down to whether it was begun after the *Aquidneck* foundered, or before, as a means to transport the heavy timber felled at the edge of Paranaguá's beachfront forests. Father and son both refer to their admiration of the crudely built local native canoes, brightly painted and seaworthy, that were used as lighters to bring rough-sawn ironwood alongside the *Aquidneck*. But the Slocums' rescue vessel was a bigger boat than those and owed more to the shape of a Gloucester fishermen's Cape Ann dory—if it had mated with a Japanese sampan, that had itself mated with a Chinese junk, that had in its bloodline a Puget Sound Makah canoe—than to a coastal workboat.

The sailing canoe was named *Liberdade,* in honor of her launch on May 13, 1888, the day Brazil's Golden Law, freeing her slaves, was passed.[*] Portuguese for "liberty," *Liberdade* is a resonant name for a boat completed within six months of the *Aquidneck*'s wreck, mostly from scraps and planks and instruments scrounged from the remains. At first Slocum might not have realized fully the Thoreauvian experiment that circumstances had enforced on him. "Simplify, simplify!" What other choice was he given? Here he was, shipwrecked, marooned, and with a jack-knife.

They worked near Antonina—at a primitive shipyard whose facilities were donated by a sympathetic owner who had modified the *Aquidneck*—with tools more refined than a pocketknife, but not by much. Joshua and Victor had salvaged from the wreckage jackplanes to smooth the forty-foot rough planks bought from native sawyers. The bottom was built of ironwood, tough and heavy, providing natural ballast for stability. For the deck and topsides, lapstrake cedar was used. Metal fastenings were

---

[*]As Victor Slocum details in his first book, *Castaway Boats* (1938), their vessel's name drew the generosity of "red-hot" abolitionists all along their route. Whether this useful outcome was calculated by the shrewd captain is not recorded. (Anti-abolitionists, let's assume, didn't know Portuguese, or how to read what was written on a boat's transom, or anything else.)

scrounged from the *Aquidneck* or cast anew from melted pieces of copper and brass scrap. Humans have built ships from wood for a long time, and as laborious as the process is, it is also forgiving. This tolerance of error, assuming the error is recognized, inspired confidence in father—who profited from his endeavors as a shipwright on the Columbia River and in the Philippines—and son, his apprentice roustabout, carpenter, and rope maker. Garfield, seven, kibitzed, and Hettie, new to sail making but not to emergencies, sewed canvas.

When they were finished, the Slocums had spent $110 to build the *Liberdade*, and they sailed her around Paranaguá Bay to get a feel for her "and shake things into place," as Joshua wrote. He liked what he felt. On June 24, 1888, they crossed the bar and into the Atlantic: "The old boating trick came back fresh to me, the love of the thing itself gaining on me as the little ship stood out; and my crew with one voice said, 'Go on.' "

Among other admirers of Slocum's prose, Van Wyck Brooks yoked the author of *Sailing Alone Around the World* to Thoreau, describing that book as the "nautical equivalent" of *Walden*. In circumstance and temperament the two writers were at least as dissimilar as they were akin, but from Slocum's phrase "the love of the thing itself" flows an irreducible, nut-hard recognition and radiant sentiment. In his conclusion to *Walden*, Thoreau exhorts his reader to "be a Columbus to whole new continents and worlds within you, opening new channels, not of trade but of thought." If a wash of boosterism and the power of positive thinking sometimes overviolin Thoreau's music, this particular appeal is inspiring, and in much the same way that Slocum invokes his deceptively homely "old boating trick" to rouse his little congregation, only to be answered by the hallelujah chorus of "Go on."

The adventure's first hours were exhilarating. The *Liberdade* clocked 150 miles heading out to sea before turning up the coast to Rio and then sailed into a squall, one of the coast's notorious *pamperos*. Hettie's laboriously stitched suit of sails was shredded, and Slocum turned toward shore under bare poles, managing somehow to reach the safety of Santos, a coffee port depressingly near to where this leg of the journey had begun. What must Hettie have imagined? And considering the situation of Victor and Garfield, it is impossible not to recall Joshua's virtual enslavement to the will of his father back on Brier Island, laboring at boot making even as he longed to be elsewhere.

Slocum doesn't write about his family's state of mind, except to be mindful in his later account of their stoicism and hardiness.* Nor does he mention whether Hettie then repaired the *Liberdade*'s sails, or started over from scratch. But he tells in detail of meeting in Santos with an old friend, one Captain Baker, master of the mail and passenger steamer *Finance,* who was setting out to Rio and offered them not only a tow but also sanctuary aboard his vessel for Hettie and Garfield. Joshua and Victor remained on the *Liberdade,* the former at the helm and the latter huddled in the bow with an ax in his hand ready to cut the tow rope in the event of a catastrophe. And one of those was not unlikely, given that the voyage up to Rio was through high and cresting seas, the *Finance* steaming at an astonishing thirteen knots. The *Liberdade*—on a mechanized Nantucket sleigh ride—was at the exciting end of a hawser ninety fathoms long, almost the length of two football fields. The passage lasted twenty hours, with Joshua at the helm connected with his shivering son in the bow by a length of line tied to his ankle so his father could jerk him awake if the boy dozed off, which he did not. So troubled became the seas that Captain Baker spread oil astern to calm them, having a negligible effect on the safety and comfort of the crew of the *Liberdade* but so liberally befouling the new vessel—"I was smothering in grease and our boat was oiled from keel to truck"—that Captain Slocum protested that he had never intended to be a blubberhunter. On they went—"Away, Rio!" as the chantey goes—on what Slocum called "the most exciting boat-ride of my life." Safe in harbor, with the luxury to muse, he added that he was "bound not to cut the line that towed us so well; and I knew that [Captain] Baker wouldn't let it go, for it was his rope."

The *Liberdade* remained in Rio until July 23, 1888, her crew recovering and preparing for the voyage home. Let's hope that Hettie and her stepsons found pleasure ashore, because Joshua was busy petitioning the U.S. consul to intervene on his behalf as he sought compensation for the injuries he had suffered at Brazil's hands, those wounds he felt so exquisitely. He also required appropriate papers from Brazil to permit him to sail their waters, and this proved complicated. It was suggested that bribes might be useful, but Slocum pretended not to understand, at

---

*In *Castaway Boats,* Victor writes that at Cape Frio his young stepmother considered the storm clouds overhead and the rough seas all around "with misgivings and suddenly burst into a fit of hysterical weeping."

length wearing down the officials, or more likely charming them, until finally "His Excellency, the Minister of Marine" presented him with "a 'Passe Especial' [that] had on it a seal as big as a soup plate."

Apart from a substantial brush with a whale—"giving us a toss and a great scare"—the Slocums enjoyed the kind of cruise, three weeks to Pernambuco and another nineteen days to Barbados, that gives sailing a good name. They were beset by high seas, rain squalls, headwinds, contrary tides, calms, fog, near misses, and close calls. But from the captain's vantage this passage home was removing the shrouds from a work of art that had been hidden in plain sight ever since he first went to sea. He could do this! *He* could! Emancipated from absentee employers, shipping schedules, the unfathomable impulses and malignancies of mutinous crews, the perils of cargoes that couldn't be safely stowed to be carried to ports that teemed with disease . . . if he could sail free of these hazards, finding what sailors name and treasure as an "offing," he had reason to believe that necessity had shown him how to navigate safely and happily through the rest of his days.

From Rio onward the music of Slocum's prose in *The Voyage of the "Liberdade"* brightens, conveying a freshening of spirit and a sense of wonder as his attention focused exclusively on the matter at hand: keeping the *Liberdade* on course, properly trimmed, and dry. Aboard the *Northern Light* or even the *Aquidneck* he would be consumed with paperwork, double-entry bookkeeping, the vicissitudes of the wheat or cured cod markets, the mandates of getting and spending. Here and now he contemplated the whales keeping his family company: "I realized very often the startling sensation alone of a night at the helm, of having a painful stillness broken by these leviathans bursting the surface of the water with a noise like the roar of a great sea, uncomfortably near . . . One night in particular; dark and foggy I remember; Victor called me excitedly, saying that something dreadful ahead and drawing rapidly near had frightened him."

This dark and fog and even dread animated Slocum, reminding him of the not unwelcome reality that, whatever his familiarity with the skills a land creature turned seaman may have brought with him offshore, he remained a stranger in a strange land. Some of these whales were twice the *Liberdade*'s length, and to hear them spouting and snuffling, breaching and sounding—to *smell* them!—was as bracing as it was alarming. Anthropomorphism was not a fallacy of logic in his belief system, or a fanciful translation from one language to another; it was an interpretation as vital as celestial navigation. Thus the roar of surf breaking over coral incites the exclamation "how intensely lonely [the coral] were! No sign of any living thing in sight, except, perhaps, the phosphorescent streaks of a hungry shark, which told of bad company in our wake." A suggestion of the respect Slocum paid as a tribute to big sea creatures was his awe of the destructive power of an "infuriated swordfish," which he—like most sailors of his age—believed was capable of stabbing a hole in the bottom of his boat and skewering its crew from below.

Along the Brazilian coast, en route to Pernambuco, they put ashore at a tiny beachfront village and here, as seldom noted before in his recollections, Slocum began to exploit his leisure to mix socially and talk, often playfully, with the coastal dwellers, who heretofore had been of interest chiefly as crew members or stevedores or shipwrights or shipping agents or consular and customs officers. Not that his new world order would be populated exclusively by benign Swiftian Houyhnhnms; Yahoos aplenty crossed his path. At the *Liberdade*'s next port of call, seeking shelter at the Bay of All Saints, Slocum found the best of Todos Santos's citizens "shiftless" and unholy fishermen "living in wretched poverty, spending their time between waiting for the tide to go out, when it was in, and waiting for it to come in, when it was out." The worst of their neighbors were "rough, half-drunken fellows, who rudely came on board, jostling about, and jabbering." To escape their unwanted attentions, Slocum put immediately to sea, "the character of which I knew better, and could trust to more confidently than a harbor among treacherous natives."

As the *Liberdade* sailed near the equator, "we saw the constellations of both hemispheres, but heading north, we left those of the south at last, with the Southern Cross—most beautiful in all the heavens—to watch over a friend." Joshua's homage to Virginia, intentionally elliptical to a reader unfamiliar with his family's personal history, was also emotionally direct. When Slocum disguises his candor he is sometimes coy about it— think of Melville's so-called "sinister dexterity," with which he hid the subversive motions of his left hand by distractingly unguarded gestures with his right—but when Virginia is the subject, his language is veiled for decorum rather than masked for mischief. And a few sentences later, continuing to memorialize his great loss, he senses himself passed closely at hand one night by "the stately *Aquidneck* . . . sweeping by with crowning staysails set, that fairly brushed the stars." This ghost "left a pang of lonesomeness for a while."

The final sentence of Stephen Crane's "The Open Boat"—his remarkable meditation on the blank indifference of the natural world to human beings—sounds as though he had been reading Slocum (though his short story was published in 1897, while the *Spray* was halfway around the world, somewhere in the Indian Ocean). After four shipwrecked men have endured huge seas and injuries, adrift in a lifeboat that they try to row toward Florida's Atlantic shore, they are driven onto the beach, and the most resilient of them drowns in the surf. The narrator's last sentence provides a moral, such as it is: "When it came night, the waves paced to and fro in the moonlight, and the wind brought the sound of the great sea's voice to the men on shore, and they felt that they could then be interpreters."

As the *Liberdade* neared Barbados, pushed by the trade winds, flying fish launched themselves onto the Slocums' deck, so eager were they to be fried in butter for breakfast. And then the island appeared right where it was meant to be, its fertile hills sloping down to white sandy beaches and the coral reefs offshore showing pale green and brown. So pleasing was the prospect from the sea that the Slocums sailed along the island farther than they needed to before entering Carlisle Bay and anchoring in the harbor at Bridgetown, having averaged better than a hundred miles per day since leaving Pernambuco.

Slocum's sociability cheered him in Barbados, where the family lingered from the end of August until early October 1888. There were reunions with many shipmasters he had met going to and fro on the earth, some encountered recently, including the captain of the steamer *Finance*. Hettie made special friends with Captain Alfred McNutt and wife, Nova Scotians commanding the *Condor*. Her letters to this couple, the last mailed in 1910 and bringing news of her husband's disappearance at sea, reveal a young woman warm and good-tempered, plain-speaking and hungry for friends.*

Five easy days after leaving Bridgetown the Slocums sailed into Mayagüez, along Puerto Rico's west coast, and began to accustom themselves to the good publicity that had been following them at least from Rio de Janeiro. Now officials entertained them and newspapers sought

---

*Three of these chatty and candid letters appear as an appendix in Ann Spencer's *Alone at Sea: The Adventures of Joshua Slocum.*

to interview them. A photographer made an unscheduled appearance at the dock alongside the *Liberdade* while the family was being entertained on a carriage ride into the country nearby. Thinking that a shot of a rough-hewn sailing canoe while unpopulated lacked sufficient human interest, he hired a black man to stand at the vessel's helm, dressing him in an excessively formal costume. The resulting photo, as Slocum tells in *The Voyage of the "Liberdade,"* appeared in journals as far-flung as Paris and Madrid. Word came back that the master was "a fine-looking fellow, but awfully tanned . . . and rigged all ataunto" (a sailor's word for a high-masted and tautly rigged ship, making a fine show).

Perhaps incited by jingoism, Slocum snarled at the Spanish popinjays and their troops whose heels pressed against the necks of the Puerto Rican natives: "the atmosphere of the soldier hung over all," he wrote, "pervading the whole air like a pestilence. Musketed and sabered and uniformed in their bed-ticking suits; hated by the residents and despised by themselves, they doggedly marched, countermarched and wheeled, knowing that they are loathsome in the island, and that their days in the New World are numbered." Could a tenured postcolonial theorist have expressed more energetic disdain?

Mid-October saw them bear away for the Bahamas, sailing to the east of Hispaniola and along the north coast of Cuba, hastening now to discover the North Star high overhead. The weather could be dramatic—waterspouts and electric storms, "peal on peal of nature's artillery . . . accompanied by vivid lightning," Slocum remembered—but it was most often gorgeous. Now they were sailing the waters that keep boat charter businesses in high clover. Giving Nassau a pass—always a good idea, though one that he would neglect to honor, to his distress, years later aboard the *Spray*—the *Liberdade* tucked up under the lee of a reef near a beach at one of the hundreds of cays dotting the Great Bahama Banks en route to Bimini. From there it was a short passage to Florida, but as anyone who has intersected the Gulf Stream in a small vessel knows, this is no casual venture. So the *Liberdade* entered the Gulf Stream and rode it, letting that mighty current push her north and west: "The motion . . . was then far from poetical or pleasant," Slocum writes, but it was fast. With the Gulf Stream's assistance the *Liberdade* recorded 220 nautical miles in twenty-four hours, an average speed greater than nine knots; her captain should be allowed to brag that "this was some getting along for a small canoe."

On October 28, fifty-three days after clearing Paranaguá, the Slocums discovered, in the welcome phrase of explorers, the South Carolina hills behind Cape Roman Light, near the Santee River north of Charleston and south of Georgetown, to which port they took a tow from the steamer *Planter*,* but not before going up the Santee to replenish their stores. *The Voyage of the "Liberdade"* retails these and many other meetings with an unfortunate indulgence of rural dialect, Mark Twain being on Slocum's bookshelf next to Swift and Richard Hakluyt. "Said the farmer, 'And you came all the way from Brazil in that boat! Wife, she won't go to Georgetown in the batto that I built because it rares too much." His prose after he enters American waters exudes a sense of relief, even renewal. He's now alert to the lives of others, sitting with his family around campfires ashore and listening to good-natured lies and no doubt telling of encounters with sharks, swordfish, and mighty leviathans.

Ever a pioneer, Slocum—having entered North Carolina's New River—decided to proceed north along what is now the Atlantic Intracoastal Waterway, more familiarly the Inland Waterway or, descriptive of the route in Slocum's day, "the Ditch," a "maze of sloughs and creeks." To navigate it, he relied daily on local knowledge, encouraging more storytelling and food sharing. He hired as a pilot a man whose grandfather had dug a portion of the waterway, who promised only that "if any man kin take y'thro that ditch, why, I kin . . . I have not hearn tell befo' of a vessel from Brazil sailing through these parts; but then you mout get through, and again you moutent. Well, it's jist here; you mout and you moutent." Given what Slocum had done and had done to him, had suffered and endured, these were dead-cinch odds.

And so they made it through to Beaufort, North Carolina, among the shoals and reeds with shovels at the ready, raising ducks and alarming livestock. This experience was jolly: one night thirty fishermen joined

*News of the *Liberdade*'s feat was afoot soon after the *New York Times*, datelined November 3 from Charleston, reported that the *Planter* had given the Slocums a tow to Georgetown. The steamer's master, identified as Captain Hubbard, told of such cordial exchanges with the Slocums that he had received a photo of the *Liberdade* and a note of thanks from her captain, who added that he had "pledged to be home in time to vote (God willing) for the man I esteem most and whom I have found to be so esteemed in foreign lands. I send my hurrah for the man of the day, the hand of a sea-tossed mariner, Grover Cleveland." This enthusiasm may be taken with a dram of salt water, inasmuch as Slocum would soon be on the government's doorstep, begging its patronage, or at least its intervention in his complaint against Brazil.

them around the campfire, talking over "the adventures of their lives. My pilot, the best speaker, kept the camp in roars. As for myself, always fond of mirth, I got up from the fire sore from laughing." Then it was on to Norfolk, Virginia, where they entered Chesapeake Bay and, on December 27, 1888, sailing before a south wind up the Potomac River, docked in Washington, D.C.

Joshua Slocum was able to boast that he and his family were in tip-top tune, as they had been throughout the voyage. "With all its vicissitudes I still love a life on the broad, free ocean, never regretting the choice of my profession." This avowal by now went without saying. What catches a reader's attention on the final page of *The Voyage of the "Liberdade"* is his more hesitant testimony—in its entirety—on Hettie's behalf: "My wife, brave enough to face the worst storms, as women are sometimes known to do on sea and on land, enjoyed not only the best of health, but had gained a richer complexion."

TEN

Destroyer *and Poverty Point*

The sea—this truth must be confessed—has no generosity. No display of . . . courage, hardihood, endurance, faithfulness has ever been known to touch its irresponsible consciousness of power.
—JOSEPH CONRAD, *The Mirror of the Sea*

W HILE THE *LIBERDADE* WINTERED over in Washington, Mathew Brady took a photograph (lost) of the Slocums, affirming their celebrity. Joshua haunted the State Department, filing claims "in relation to the case of the *Aquidneck*," according to one low-level assistant secretary asked to consider the plaintiff's grievance. This began a predictable cycle of dispatches between Washington and Brazil: to American consular officers in Rio and Antonina, as well as Brazilian customs and quarantine officers, who needed to have the inquiries and their responses translated into and from Portuguese. Slocum was obliged to refine the specifications of his losses—the value of his cargo, of the *Aquidneck,* and of his time—and to articulate the logic of his determination to hold Brazil accountable for them. Revisions were required. Documents were misplaced or misdirected. It was *Bleak House* without the fog.

Come spring, Joshua, Hettie, Garfield, and Victor sailed the *Liberdade* to New York, where the captain's wife was interviewed by the *New York World* on May 19, 1889:

Tales of Capt. Slocum and his wonderful small boat, La Libertad [*sic*], have been told far and wide. *The World* wanted to know what the "Captain's Captain," Mrs. Slocum, had to say about it, and sent a reporter down to the small boat, bobbing and rolling with every ripple of the tide that flowed around the gray stone walls of the Barge Office, close to which La Liberdad [different *sic*] was anchored.

"Can you get in?"

Joshua Slocum (in white suit) with the crew of the Destroyer

The Destroyer

This question was Mrs. Slocum's greeting when her husband introduced the reporter, whom he had just handed on board, and who stood at
the entrance to the low, canvas-covered deckhouse, the only shelter
afforded by the limited accommodations of the boat. The hostess sat in
the wee cabin on a plank running the length and raised about three inches
from the deck. A sitting posture was the only attitude possible unless one
chose to lie down.*

It is impossible not to recollect an interview by the same port city's
Tribune less than seven years earlier, conducted with another "captain"
of this particular captain, then aboard the *Northern Light*. Virginia's circumstances, doing needlepoint while seated in a paneled and pianoed
stateroom, had been in conspicuous contrast to Hettie's. The wives had
in common that they made favorable impressions on their interviewers:

[Hettie] Slocum is young and strong with a full brow; bright hazel eyes, a
remarkably well-formed "nez," a frank smiling mouth, and a chin express-
ing both firmness and tenderness . . . [Her] oval face has acquired a rich
bronze tint from months of exposure to tropical suns and ocean breezes.
Here is the face of a woman who would be capable of the most devoted,
intrepid deeds, done in the quietest and most matter-of-fact way, and
never voluntarily spoken of afterwards.

She wore yesterday a dark blue serge yachting dress, with short skirt
and blouse waist trimmed with rows of white braid, and a blue straw
sailor hat, which she had taken off and was holding in her slender brown
hand.

Mrs. Slocum's voice is low and full-toned, although she says she is from
Boston—that region of thin, high-pitched feminine utterance. Her manner is gentle, and she spoke with some reluctance of her voyage.

"It is an experience I should not care to repeat, although now that it is
mine I feel a certain satisfaction in having gone through it."

"Didn't you grow weary and lonely during the long voyage?"

". . . Yes. When we left Rio . . . crowds of people assembled on the
quays to send us off and they cheered us wildly. It was very exciting.

---

*Harper's Weekly (November 23, 1889) would report that the *Liberdade* was a featured display that
fall at Boston's Maritime Exhibition, as a fine example of American shipbuilding ingenuity. But
whatever her merits, she was a floating pup tent. Slocum continued to show her off in New England waters until he gave her to the Smithsonian, which gave her back, whereupon she was dismantled and stored in some barn or pasture, her whereabouts unknown since 1908. She made a
poor impression on Slocum's young Martha's Vineyard neighbor, Joseph Chase Allen, who
boarded her at anchor at Vineyard Haven: "The predominating color on and about her was
brown, the brown of plug tobacco." He noted also that "her cabin was a hut, of the type seen in
pictures of tropical countries," with a crudely thatched roof of overlapping leaves.

Then, as the land grew dim in the distance and finally faded from sight, it seemed very desolate on the sea."

"Are you going on another voyage, Mrs. Slocum?"

"Oh, I hope not. I haven't been home in over three years, and this was my wedding journey."

Mrs. Slocum said she was going from here to Boston for a visit, adding:

"I shall travel by rail. I have had enough sailing to last me for a long time."

Victor departed New York's Battery Basin aboard the steamship *Finance* to take responsibility for his own career as a seaman. The tally thus far for Joshua Slocum at the age of forty-five: He had lost to death three infant children and his first wife. He had lost to shipwreck two clippers, been charged with cruel imprisonment of one crew member and the murder of another. His second wife, Hettie, in sympathy with that seasick sailor of the *Odyssey*, wished to flee so far inland that local citizens wouldn't recognize the purpose of an oar. He was broke. The age of sail had ended. The captain was, that is, entirely at sea.

He traveled to East Boston to live with his father's sister and tried from there to rescue himself from poverty and dependence on the generosity of kin, difficult for anyone to accept and especially bitter for such a proud man recently at the pinnacle of his career. He hectored the State Department to redress his misadventures in Brazil and wrote *The Voyage of the "Liberdade,"* which he printed at his own expense. Where the funds came from isn't known, nor how many copies were printed, nor how many were sold and by what means. It is certain that his first book brims with virtues, and moreover served as voice training for *Sailing Alone Around the World*. Walter Teller justly describes Slocum's voice as "entirely his own," belonging to "a Yankee skipper and trader accustomed to an exact and pungent use of words . . . He saw a connection between navigation and writing." This is helpful as far as it goes, but fails to account for Slocum's jocularity, his slyness and cunning, the indirect course by which he steers through emotionally perilous waters.

The Voyage of the "Liberdade," subtitled by Slocum *Descriptions of a Voyage "Down to the Sea,"* was reviewed by Joseph B. Gilder, coeditor of *The Critic,* an influential literary magazine, on July 5, 1890. He liked what he read, and that it was self-published and self-edited. No one else seemed to notice the book, leaving Slocum to cover the Boston waterfront looking for work. There were no posts for sailing masters. Garfield Slocum believed that his father was offered a berth as captain by the White Star line, which he rejected, and when Garfield asked why, "He told me, 'I followed the sea in sailing ships since I was fourteen years old. If I accepted this offer, I would have to get used to steamships, and I do not like steamships.' "*

That certainly sounds like the Joshua Slocum we know, and so does his account of quitting a job as carpenter at the McKay shipyard in Boston. He was asked to pay fifty dollars to join a union, an unlikely alliance made unlikelier by its element of compulsion. He remembered that bleak period in an interview years later with a Rhode Island newspaper: "One day, when I was doing a bit of an odd job on a boat and a whole lot of coal and dirt mixed—Cape Horn berries they call the stuff—came down all about my face and neck, I stood up, thought of the difference between my state and when I was master of the Northern Light, and quit the job."

And just at this dismal moment came the encounter that changed everything, a lucky break for literature. Think of Melville's Ishmael walking along a Manhattan sidewalk during "a damp, drizzly November in my soul," finding himself "involuntarily pausing before coffin warehouses, and bringing up the rear of every funeral I meet," such that "it requires a strong moral principle to prevent me from deliberately stepping into the street, and methodically knocking people's hats off—then, I account it high time to get to sea as soon as I can." But let Slocum tell it:

> Mine was not the sort of life to make one long to coil up one's ropes on land, the customs and ways of which I had finally almost forgotten. And so when times for freighters got bad, as at last they did, and I tried to quit the sea, what was there for an old sailor to do? I was born in the breezes, and I had studied the sea as perhaps few men have studied it, neglecting all else . . . One midwinter day of 1892, in Boston, where I had been cast up from old ocean, so to speak, a year or two before, I was cogitating whether I should apply for a command, and again eat my bread and butter on the sea, or go to work at the shipyard, when I met an old acquain-

*In *Sailing Alone Around the World,* a rare outburst of indignation interrupts Slocum's blissful passage in the Indian Ocean when he encounters a steamer "groping her way in the dark and making the night dismal with her own black smoke." Speaking of the steam liner *Olympia* in the mid-Atlantic, he noted that her captain—who had hailed him—was too young to be a match for the sea and that "there were no porpoises skipping along" with the smoke belcher, inasmuch as porpoises "always prefer sailing ships."

tance, a whaling-captain, who said: "Come to Fairhaven and I'll give you a ship. But," he added, "she wants some repairs." The captain's terms, when fully explained, were more than satisfactory to me.

The old acquaintance was Captain Eben Pierce of New Bedford, the city Melville chooses to launch Ishmael's briny narrative. Slocum and Pierce went way back, already friends when the *Pato* paused near Pierce's whale ship, the *James Allen,* for a visit and an exchange of fresh food in the Okhotsk Sea. Pierce had thrived as a whaler, and had added to his fortune by the invention and sale of diabolically effective shotgun-style harpoon weapons, advertised in local newspapers as "Pierce Bomb Lances and Shoulder Guns," the latter selling for forty-five dollars and boasting that "whalemen say the recoil is very light." It has become conventional for writers about the *Spray* to accuse Pierce of having played a mordant prank on Slocum by offering him the command of the corpse of an ancient oyster sloop rotting in a pasture at Fairhaven's Poverty Point, across the water from New Bedford. Slocum probably encouraged this hard judgment by remarking in *Sailing Alone Around the World* that upon seeing the derelict he "found that my friend had something of a joke on me."

Not at all. This was inspired matchmaking, and to encourage Slocum toward embarking on the adventure of a lifetime, the bachelor Pierce offered him free room and board and welcomed visits from Hettie and his children while the new master of the *Spray* set about translating the hulk into a world traveler.* Slocum paid only for the materials needed to rebuild what he himself puts in quotation marks as the "ship." He details, in *Sailing Alone Around the World*, the process of restoring (reimagining, really) a craft combining the qualities of sturdiness, simplicity of sail handling, and protection from the elements that he had learned most to value from his decades as a shipmaster and recent experience as the designer and captain of the *Liberdade.*

The origins of the *Spray* are unclear. Claude Berube, a naval historian, declares on the first page of his recent biography of the early nineteenth-century U.S. Navy captain Charles Stewart that she was built in Philadelphia in 1789. Robert H. Perry—a respected contemporary designer of

---

*At eighty, Eben Pierce was run down in New Bedford by an electric trolley car. "Captain Pierce's right leg was found wedged into the rear brake shoe," reported the *Boston Herald* of May 8, 1902. "One of the last remaining relics of the old whaling days . . . he lived fifteen minutes."

blue-water yachts—has written in *Sail* magazine that she was built in Australia in 1810 to be used for fishing. Perry adds that she was "probably a weird-shaped boat even when she was new," extremely beamy at more than fourteen feet for a waterline length of thirty-two feet. Her length overall was thirty-seven feet with a bowsprit, and she had enormous displacement for a boat her size, almost eighteen tons.

Slocum addresses the interesting question of when exactly a vessel being rebuilt with new materials and specifications ceases to be what it was and becomes something else. It is certain that her original makers had no reason to overbuild her as Slocum did, laying her keel from a pasture white oak, so called for its history of having grown in an open field from an acorn to a solitary survivor, exposed to battering gales in the very meadow at Poverty Point where Slocum felled it and shaped it with his steam box. Such oak, twisted and bent by wind, was prestressed and so tough that the *Spray*'s keel would split a huge coral head in two during a mishap in the Indian Ocean's Cocos Islands, leaving the vessel virtually unmarked.

As Slocum worked, whaling captains would drop by the *Spray* with Eben Pierce for a gam, speculating on whether her shipwright could possibly "make her pay." They agreed that she was stout, venturing in Victor Slocum's memory that she was "fit to smash ice" while hunting for bowheads off the coast of Greenland. Her construction in general was as heavy as her keel, planked with yellow Georgia pine, which was also used for her massive deck beams. Her mast was shaped from live New Hampshire spruce, and as Slocum labored, "something tangible appeared every day" and "the neighbors made the work sociable." The *Spray* had two sheltered cabins, both aft of the mast, and remembering the near sinking of the *Aquidneck* during his honeymoon voyage with Hettie, Slocum took special care to caulk her tight and to fasten her with more than a thousand through bolts.

Hettie, during the period of the *Spray*'s construction, visited on weekends from Boston, where she was living with her family and working again as a gown fitter, in addition to caring for Jessie and Garfield. It's not known where the money came from, but the *Spray* cost Slocum $553.62, about the annual salary of a schoolteacher, and despite working at odd jobs around the shipyards of Fairhaven and New Bedford, he was broke once again. The Panic of 1893, bursting another bubble of railroad stock speculation and creating a run on America's banks, did nothing to encourage the prospects of a dressmaker and gown fitter, and if the *Spray* was afloat, the Slocum family was underwater.

But wait! As ever, there's more! In November 1893 there began in Brazil an uprising against the elected government with which Slocum—through the State Department—had had so much sorry business. This civil war was launched by the same Admiral Custodio de Mello who had six years before barred the *Aquidneck* and her cargo of hay from entering Rio—with the admiral's gunship artillery trained upon Slocum and his family. Now de Mello had seized control of Brazil's navy and was demanding—for reasons that might have made sense at the time—the resignation of Brazil's president, General Floriano Peixoto.

In consequence, Peixoto's government wanted warships with which to confront de Mello's, and toward this end was buying up from arms dealers what was on the market and at the ready. The United States, happy to oblige, offered for sale the *Destroyer,* a bizarre ironclad, torpedo-firing 150-foot steamer that had some of the qualities—not always intended—of a submarine. She had been dreamed up by the designer of the *Monitor* (the *Merrimac's* foe in the 1862 battle of the ironclads at Hampton Roads, Virginia), John Ericsson, who had died in 1889 before she could be battle-tested or even confirmed as seaworthy. Brazil's new armada of curiosities also included the *Nictheroy,* armed with a Zalinski pneumatic cannon—history's biggest BB gun—for the comically off-target aerial bombardment of forts by missiles carrying fifty pounds of dynamite.*

How Slocum came to the attention of the government he was suing and slandering is easy enough to imagine, but why he was recommended as just the fellow to deliver the *Destroyer* from New York to Bahia remains a puzzlement. Perhaps his voyage from Brazil aboard the *Liberdade* had encouraged President Peixoto's esteem. It was also true that going to sea and perhaps to war in such a contraption was a discouraging prospect to sailors of prudence. Insurance companies refused to indemnify members of the crew. Seamen were recruited for the voyage mostly by virtue of their ignorance of the sea, and assured they would

---

*For the inquisitive, an entertaining diversion might be H. W. Wilson's *Ironclads in Action: A Sketch of Naval Warfare from 1855 to 1895* (1896), with an unvarnished account of the limitations, indeed uselessness, of the experimental naval follies our government sold to the innocents of Brazil.

be well paid—during a time of economic depression—and that the sea to the south of the Gulf Stream was "like a lake," as Victor Slocum put it, adding "but what lake [they] failed to say."

Peixoto's agents, who had purchased the *Destroyer* for $100,000, promised Slocum $20,000 to deliver the vessel safely. This would be an unorthodox delivery, as the ship was to be towed the entire distance by the oceangoing tug *Santuit,* because once loaded with ammunition the gunship had no cargo space remaining for coal. (*Ironclads in Action* offers a simpler reason: the warship's engines had broken down, not least among the reasons our navy was happy to sell her.) Slocum must have remembered without affection the tow that the *Liberdade* received six years before from the cinder-spewing and oil-spreading *Finance* into safe haven at Pernambuco. Now, in deference to the reality that the *Destroyer* would follow where the *Santuit* led, on a leash of 1,800 feet, Slocum's title was navigator-in-command, a titular demotion from master that more amused than irritated him.

It was good that he was amused, because his part in Brazil's civil war was from beginning to end a farce, a comedy that nevertheless threatened every day that it endured to turn mortally catastrophic. Joshua Slocum's second book, *The Voyage of the "Destroyer" from New York to Brazil,* like his first book self-published, relates an extraordinary and often hilarious story of the two-month voyage that ended—miraculously—at Bahia on February 13, 1894. In a pamphlet of twenty-five or so pages, Slocum gives a comprehensive inventory of the sea's and mankind's available perils and cruelties, together with nature's mercies and mankind's generosity. Odysseus would appreciate the tale's virtues.

Two days after the *Destroyer* cleared Sandy Hook, the State Department mailed to Hettie's East Boston address its final letter to Slocum regarding his claims against Brazil in the matter of the *Aquidneck.* The archive assembled by Walter Teller of correspondence from, to, and regarding Slocum's losses runs thirty densely printed pages, beginning on October 31, 1887. To summarize his complaints, titled by him at the end of 1888 a "chapter of disasters": he was turned away from Rio at Ilha Grande on the receiving end of the *Aquidiban's* nine-inch guns, Admiral de Mello ordering his turrets trained on not only the Slocum family but also the Stars and Stripes. This resulted in a profitless return to Argentina and a change of crew from seamen to pirates, which led to a mutiny, the shooting of two mutineers, a charge of murder, and a costly and humiliating trial. There followed the horror of the *Aquidneck*'s miserable fate as a "floating pest house," as Slocum called it. "We have sailed on a sea of troubles," he complained. Slocum laid the stranding of the *Aquidneck* to the account of Brazil, pricing his loss at $10,000, through the agency of the same Admiral de Mello that Brazil's President Peixoto meant to blow to smithereens with the *Destroyer*. In the event, our State Department—agreeing with Brazil that (rudeness aside) the danger of spreading cholera to their country by allowing Argentine forage to be off-loaded at Rio outweighed considerations of "mercantile profits"—wrote to the plaintiff that "it is believed that this Government would in a similar case adopt the same measures. This Department therefore does not feel warranted in taking any further action."*

With its navigator-in-command and a crew of thirteen, the *Destroyer* got under way on December 7, 1893, from Red Hook's Erie Basin. It was immediately towed into and destroyed a projecting pier. Designed to terrify the wicked only when used in smooth waters, the vessel was soon storm-tossed in no less an Atlantic winter gale than had nearly sunk the *Aquidneck* during Hettie's honeymoon voyage. While her steam engines were useless for propulsion, they could be fired up to blow the *Destroyer*'s whistle and (thanks be!) operate her pumps. Within twenty-eight hours the ship was filling with so much water—from seas awash on her decks and flooding her torpedo tube—that it was a miracle the hulk didn't sink, though if you wait a bit, she will!

From the comfort of a steamer carrying Slocum home from Brazil to Boston several months later, and then from the cozy shelter of the cabin of the *Spray* at anchor in Fairhaven, the survivor reminisced about the adventure:

> Great quantities of water goes over the ship. She washes heavily, still, going often under the seas, like a great duck, fond of diving. Everything is wet. There is not a dry place in the entire ship! We are most literally sailing under the sea . . . Believe me, the *Destroyer*, to-night, was just about ready to make her last dive under the sea, to go down deeper than ever before.

---

*"Confidentially," as Slocum writes in *The Voyage of the "Destroyer"* (1894), "I was burning to get a rake at Mello and his *Aquideban*. He it was, who in that ship expelled my bark . . . some years ago, under the cowardly pretext that we might have sickness on board . . . I was burning to let him know and palpably feel that this time I had in dynamite instead of hay. It would have been, maybe, too great a joke."

They kept her afloat by firing her pump engines not with coal—which cotton wadding and gunpowder had displaced as cargo—but by pitching on the fire whatever would burn, including cooking oil, tables and chairs from the wardrooms, and huge chunks of smoked pork. A week after taking tow from *Santuit*, Slocum—nearly swept from the *Destroyer's* wheel by cross-seas—exclaims, "We suffer!" The crew behaved heroically despite the presence among them of at least one saboteur working for Admiral de Mello's cause. The storm broke, the seas abated, "and we get in under the lee of a small island for shelter and rest—Ye Gods—a rest!"

He rates this passage through and under the sea as "the hardest voyage that I ever made, without any exception at all." But after a near mutiny that was tame by *Northern Light* and *Aquidneck* standards, with only a sliver of one sailor's liver lost to another sailor's rigging knife (in a dispute over a bottle of rum), the warship reached her intended destination of Bahia, putatively a war zone, on February 13, 1894. Slocum explains how it was:

> Everything was funeral quietness . . . The occasional pop of a champagne cork, at the "Paris" on the hill, might have been heard, but that was all, except the sunset gun . . . The average Brazilian Naval man is an amphibious being, spending his time about equally between hotel and harbor, and is never dangerous.
>
> I was astonished at the quietness of Bahia, there was not even target practice. Indeed the further we got away from stirring New York, the less it looked like war in Brazil . . .

President Peixoto's officers did not welcome the *Destroyer*, bringing as she did a combative atmosphere to the peace heretofore reigning in Bahia.

> As it proved, however, there was no danger in meeting the enemy, nor any cause of alarm. [Peixoto], it is well known, was fitted out with peaceful, harmless people in his ships; Mello's outfit was the same. Both sides as harmless as jay birds! Why should they kill each other? That the *Destroyer*, then, most formidable ship of all, must in some way be disposed of, went without saying. When first she came to Bahia though, and it was reported that this was the long hoped "money ship" to follow the fleet—and pay the bills—the large iron "tank" in which the crew lived fitting in size their expectations of the chest out of which they would all get rich. Many visi-

tors came to see her and called her a very handsome ship, saying many pretty things concerning "her lines," etc. But when to their great disappointment, instead of bank notes teeming forth, they beheld sea-begrimed tars tumbling out of the "tank," and worse still barrels of gunpowder being hoisted out, they said, *"Nao maes,"* we give it up!

Slocum wonderfully captured the seasick warriors' point of view: "Let us each die a natural death. Let us all die friends on deck, since there is no one to help us into the sea, and let us have no more war." In fact, Peixoto's sailors scuttled their own ship, and inasmuch as she was now of no use to combatants of either team, Brazil refused to pay the navigator-in-command a single penny of the $20,000 he had been promised. It's not known who paid for his steamer passage home, but Slocum did get from the experience an excellent yarn from whose sale he hoped to profit. This wouldn't happen, either, since his self-published pamphlet was of such poor physical quality that he was reduced to giving copies away to friends and a few reviewers.

The Boston papers, delighted with Slocum's ridicule of foreign cupidity and vainglorious truculence, applauded *The Voyage of the "Destroyer,"* and especially its final words:

> The revolt began in Rio, somewhere in September, 1893, the date don't matter much. The funny war so far as the navy was concerned finished of itself in March, 1894. No historian can ever say more.
>
> They may tell of hot firing and hot fires but it was by the heat of the sun, and by that child of filth, yellow fever, that most lives were lost. In this way . . . some of the members of our own expedition were taken. Were it not indeed for these darker shades, I could now look back with unalloyed pleasure over the voyage of the *Destroyer;* the voyage of past hardships, now so pleasant to bear. The voyage which gave to the crew, and myself, withal, no end of fun.

But that was not quite the end of it, because the newspapers' approving reviews of Slocum's pamphlet came to the attention of a sputtering popinjay, Lieutenant Carlos A. Rivers, a young soldier of fortune attached to the British Marine Artillery, armed with a huge sword and weighed down with "handsome gold bands for his caps," who had been imposed on the crew of the *Destroyer* as a military adviser and as a sailor "was a good judge of a hotel," in Slocum's words. This fool—self-described as a Hero of the Sudan, as Slocum many, many times reminded his readers—

was fond of challenging crew members to duels, and while attempting to defend his honor as a gentleman against a slight imagined to have come from the *Destroyer*'s cook ("Big Alec of Salem"), he was beaten about the head by that black man's iron skillet.

Now, slandered by reviews of Joshua Slocum's pamphlet, the Hero of the Sudan challenged the master of the *Spray* to a duel. Advised of this dare by the *Boston Sun*'s correspondent, Slocum replied: "There are my wife's feelings to be thought of. I have always been of the opinion that duelists should consult their wives."

Slocum, sitting on the Fairhaven wharf alongside the *Spray*, untangling the knots in a fishing line, was asked by the *Sun* reporter whether he worried that Lieutenant Rivers was "on your track."

"I wouldn't be surprised," the captain responded. "He is rapacious, and a fire eater. When he comes for me I shall wrap myself up in the American flag and dare him to do his worst . . . It is better that I catch fish than fight him. Just say that I am a man with a big fist. Do anything to discourage a duel. Good day."

In fact, Slocum was catching no fish from the *Spray*. Having fired (almost) his final salvo at treacherous Brazil by dud torpedo, unavailing lawsuit, and unselling pamphlet, he thought to wrest some kind of a living by hiring the *Spray* and himself out to charter parties during the summer season of 1894 for the purpose of company picnics and fishing trips, "only to find," as he writes in *Sailing Alone Around the World*, "that I had not the cunning properly to bait a hook. But at last the time arrived to weigh anchor and get to sea in earnest."

And so he did, fitting out at first in Boston, where he attempted to interest several newspapers in underwriting his solo voyage in return for his serial dispatches from ports along the way. Reporters haunted major waterfronts in Slocum's day much as they did police stations, on the hunt for stories to amaze the jaded, and a solo voyage around the world had the right mix of bravado, folly, and potential catastrophe to attract attention. Nor is it difficult to grasp why the adventure appealed to Slocum. At fifty-one he had sailed five times around the world; he was an inspired navigator, a serial survivor of crises, and he had nothing better to do. But what of Hettie? On April 16, 1895, he confided to an interviewer for the *Boston Herald* that he hoped to make enough money from the voyage to buy a little farm and settle down on it with his wife and children, and he did in fact buy Hettie such a farm. Always decorous in public statements about his family, he told a *Boston Globe* reporter that he would sail with Hettie if "my wife changes her mind about staying ashore." He knew better. In *The Search for Captain Slocum,* the most striking contrast between Walter Teller's 1956 and 1971 versions is his judgment of Joshua and Henrietta's marriage. The later account is tentative, perhaps gentled by Teller's longer experience of human mysteries. In 1956 he was more certain of what was what, and his bluntness—however unmerciful—sounds about right:

> The captain's home was not with Hettie, who may have loved him once, but scarcely understood him. She was no Virginia with flashing eyes and brilliant intuitions, the game companion on deck, the reading companion in the cabin. Hettie was doomed to disappoint and to be disappointed . . . On the one hand there was the still young, and by now bewildered, dressmaker. On the other the sea-drawn escapologist at a critical stage of life. She could not have been important to him, though he tried to consider her. Their incompatibility was deeply distressing, but it had its uses.

Teller deleted this passage entirely from his revision, but he continued to believe, and to write in letters collected among his New Bedford papers, that the world could thank Hettie for her husband's voyage, and for *Sailing Alone Around the World,* because his wish to escape her company—the tone-deaf "escapologist" locution—drove him out to sea. "Perhaps the world owes [her] something—that is, if she had been more companionable the Captain might never have sailed alone," Teller wrote to Grace Murray Brown. And Garfield had scribbled in the margin of a letter to Teller that "I could feel a storm coming up between [Joshua and Hettie]."*

---

*In *Nautical Quarterly,* no. 3 (1978), Donald B. Sharp writes of Slocum as a sailing master rather than a solo adventurer, and he takes sharp and fair issue with Teller's dismissal of Hettie—in contrast to Virginia—as uninspiring and inadequate to a great man's needs. "This opinion," writes Sharp,

> does great injustice to Henrietta . . . What seems to be the difference is that the man Henrietta married was not the man Virginia married. Virginia married a ship captain who was prospering during the dying days of sail: Henrietta married a man who found himself unable to earn a living for his wife and family in the age of steam. If they grew distant, it was partly because Slocum had to face Henrietta as a failure of sorts . . . Stumping vainly around the waterfront looking for a job is not the same as sailing your own ship . . .

Whatever his marital considerations, a week before his leave-taking on April 24 he was described by the *Boston Herald* as "a kinky salt," "spry as a kitten and nimble as a monkey." Imagine again his freedoms: from schedules, customs regulations, treaties, towboats, seditious mumbling below decks, caprices of national and international politics, children's welfare . . . His first sentences at sea, bound a mere twenty miles or so northeast for Cape Ann, sing the praises of his solitude:

> I heard the clanking of the dismal bell on Norman's Woe as we went by; and the reef where the schooner *Hesperus* struck I passed close aboard. The "bones" of a wreck tossed up lay bleaching on the shore abreast . . . I made for the cove, a lovely branch of Gloucester's fine harbor, again to look the Spray over and again to weigh the voyage, and my feelings, and all that . . . It was my first experience of coming into port alone, with a craft of any size, and in among shipping. Old fishermen ran down to the wharf for which the Spray was heading apparently intent upon braining herself there . . . I let go the wheel, stepped quickly forward, and downed the jib. The sloop naturally rounded in the wind, and just ranging ahead, laid her cheek against a mooring-pile at the windward corner of the wharf, so quietly, after all, that she would not have broken an egg.

This passage precisely describes a place, an emotion, a circumstance, and an action. Norman's Woe is a rocky reef near Gloucester, and it rang a bell to warn sailors away from it. It was the site of awful shipwrecks, perhaps the worst the wreck of the *Favorite* during the winter blizzard of 1839, washing twenty bodies ashore at Cape Ann and inspiring Longfellow's "Wreck of the *Hesperus*" (1839). But a reader doesn't gasp aloud at a run of efficient exposition. "I heard the clanking of the dismal bell on Norman's Woe as we went by." Coming upon those words when I was first led to Joshua Slocum fifty years ago, expecting to experience a yarn of briny adventures, was all the more breathtaking for being unpromised by the casual hope expressed by my friend, loaning me his copy of *Sailing Alone Around the World,* that I would "enjoy a pretty good story." Goodness!

Joshua Slocum aboard the Spray

ELEVEN

The Great Adventure

The weather was mild on the day of my departure from Gloucester. On the point ahead, as the Spray stood out of the cove, was a lively picture, for the front of a tall factory was a flutter of handkerchiefs and caps. Pretty faces peered out of the windows from the top to the bottom of the building, all smiling bon voyage. Some hailed me to know where away and why alone. Why? When I made as if to stand in, a hundred pairs of arms reached out, and said come, but the shore was dangerous! The sloop worked out of the bay against a light southwest wind, and about noon squared away off Eastern Point, receiving at the same time a hearty salute—the last of many kindnesses to her at Gloucester. The wind freshened off the point, and skipping along smoothly, the Spray was soon off Thatcher's Island lights. Thence shaping her course east, by compass, to go north of Cashes Ledge and the Amen Rocks, I sat and considered the matter all over again, and asked myself once more whether it were best to sail beyond the ledge and rocks at all.

—Sailing Alone Around the World

IT'S THRILLING TO STUMBLE ACROSS a chunk of gold lying in your path, even if you'd gone seeking something like it. Or finding what's wonderfully termed a "passage" in a piece of music or movie you get to impose on a captive audience, at Thanksgiving, say, or on your own birthday. I'm thinking of the playlist I hope visitors at my wake will agree to listen to. Something from a book or play, writing you get to read aloud, maybe hamming it up: Falstaff lying to Prince Hal about his rout of the highwaymen on Gad's Hill ("in *buckram?*") or Nabokov telling about his father's blanket toss in *Speak, Memory.* In hindsight I can't pretend to have been surprised to find gold in those hills, but when I came upon the passage quoted above, and what followed it, I was stunned, and it's simple joy to get to share it. Having meant to read a sea adventure, hoping it would have the Yankee virtues—sly wit, stoicism, descriptive accuracy—that its fans advertised, I stumbled on this run of language, bearing its load so easily, and the emotional burden it discharges so cunningly. Taking my breath away, it made me feel what I can only describe as love.

Well, okay. But *why?* The passage above is packed as tightly as the *Spray*'s hold with the logbook essentials: weather, location, wind direction and force, observed positions and intended course. A reader always knows where he or she is aboard the *Spray*. But behold the "lively picture"! The perspective from Slocum's position is both fixed aboard the *Spray* and in motion with her, jittery and tender as he and his vessel respond to gusts and emotional eddies. The faces at the factory windows, the Sirens beckoning with their arms—*Come in! Come in!*—are vividly seductive, almost shocking in their erotic charge. "Some hailed me to know where away and why alone. Why?" Could the reader's question be shaped more succinctly or prettily? "But the shore was dangerous." This declarative sentence conveys both a simple fact and the most complex autobiographical account of the singular ambitions and limits of the author's personality.

But free of the land, where a less inspired sailor and writer might take a deep breath and enjoy the day, with a fresh wind off Gloucester's point and the *Spray* "skipping along smoothly," Slocum is alert to hazards: "Cashes Ledge and the Amen Rocks"—real obstructions with their actual names, however resonantly admonitory, that can tear the bottom out of a vessel. And asking himself, with stunning cadence, "whether it were best to sail beyond the ledge and rocks at all," he answers: Yes!

No book can continue without interruption such fine concentration and suggestiveness over more than two hundred pages, and *Sailing Alone Around the World* gives way, as it must, to passages responsible for conveying the business of its narrative: names and dates, latitudes and longitudes, capsule histories of islands and colonies, meteorology and geography. But the quality of Slocum's best runs of writing is extraordinary, making it sad but not in the least surprising that his greatest commercial failure during the enterprise that follows was as a writer.

Well, a particular kind of writer, a freelance journalist. With an eye to practicality, making the *Spray* pay, Slocum had changed her hailing port from Fairhaven to Boston, although Fairhaven and New Bedford, home to the world's greatest whaling fleets, might have been at least as well-known between Cape Cod and the Antipodes.* He then set about setting up a syndicate to cover his costs by printing the serial account of his circumnavigation. He enlisted as his agent Eugene Hardy, of Roberts Brothers, a Boston publisher, and Hardy received tentative commitments from the *Boston Globe* and *Louisville Courier-Journal*. The story of his despair as a travel writer, and his putative patrons' serial disappointment with their captain, makes a bitter footnote to *Sailing Alone Around the World*. In brief: the newspapers were irritated that Slocum took his own sweet time getting under way, seeming to loiter as he did in Boston, then Gloucester, and then on Brier Island and in the Bay of Fundy. Weeks went by before the *Spray* left Sable Island astern on July 4, 1895, bound for the Azores and Gibraltar.

Aside from fitting out for his voyage in Nova Scotia, and managing to involve himself in a controversy in Halifax that threatened to provoke a fistfight, Slocum was visiting family members and trying to explain to his agent and editors why the timetable of a small boat being sailed alone around the world could not be as exact as newspapers might wish. There was also the issue of his itinerary, which his syndicate partners wanted to publish as absolute. Slocum's announced intention had been to sail across the Atlantic to Gibraltar, where he would enter the Mediterranean Sea, proceeding through the Suez Canal to the Red Sea, thence to the Indian Ocean and the Cape of Good Hope, running his easting down to Cape Horn and north from the South Atlantic toward home. He believed this voyage would require two years.

It required three years, two months, and two days to sail from home back to home, and after his arrival in Gibraltar, no aspect of his itinerary went unmodified. In fact, he had announced in Fairhaven, before assuring Eugene Hardy of the course laid out above, that he would first take a tow to New York, then proceed down the east coast of South America, double Cape Horn east to west, and then . . . he'd see. For all its hindsight inevitability and rightness—that of all people he would do what he did the best way he found to do it—there was always a wonderfully ad hoc character to his plans.

But early in his voyage, especially, before he learned how generously he would be welcomed and supplied in foreign ports and how success-

---

*Walter Teller reports that Slocum was asked by South Sea Islanders if the "Boston" painted on the *Spray*'s stern was near Fairhaven.

fully he could draw audiences to his lantern-slide lectures, he was desperate for money. He sailed for Gibraltar, he noted again and again, with $1.50 in his pocket.

But by God he sailed! And watched and listened and meditated and in the end conveyed the essence of sailing alone on a small boat, itself a cosmic system whose complications a single person, with humility and experience and alertness, might hope to master. He was, after all, what believers might call the *Spray*'s maker. If her rudderhead twisted away in high seas, or a cabin-to-deck joint parted, he knew whose was the original sin. And this accounts for the lightness in his being as the sun sets behind him and he pushes ahead. "Then I turned my face eastward, and there, apparently at the very end of the bowsprit, was the smiling full moon rising out of the sea. Neptune himself coming over the bows could not have startled me more. 'Good evening, sir,' I cried; 'I'm glad to see you.' "

But later, inevitably, came fog, off fearsome Sable Island. This wasn't the first ever to have settled on Joshua Slocum, but he was impressed by it: "One could almost 'stand on it.' It continued so for a number of days, the wind increasing to a gale. The waves rose high, but I had a good ship. Still, in the dismal fog I felt myself drifting into loneliness, an insect on a straw in the midst of the elements." Slocum's phrasing here is strikingly akin to the narrator of Stephen Crane's "The Open Boat" (1897) musing that "the correspondent . . . watched the waves and wondered why he was there." Slocum would many times come to note what Crane described as nature's flat indifference: "She did not seem cruel, nor beneficent, nor treacherous, nor wise."

But in the face of what Slocum felt like at sea, "an insect on a straw," it is little wonder that there came upon him, when fine weather returned, "the sense of solitude, which I could not shake off. I used my voice often, at first giving some order about the affairs of a ship, for I had been told that from disuse I should lose my speech . . . From my cabin I cried to an imaginary man at the helm, 'How does she head, there?' But getting no reply, I was reminded the more palpably of my condition. My voice sounded hollow on the empty air, and I dropped the practice."

To learn to despise the sound of one's own voice is a sobering event for an autobiographer, and for a shipmaster accustomed to his commands being heard. But it must have been stirring, too, for to find oneself humbled by the sound of one's own voice is not the same thing as to hate the noise the world makes, and to regard oneself as an insect on a straw afloat is not to lose one's wonder at the majesty of a great sea. Perhaps I make too much of Slocum's exactly described epiphany following the gale-driven fog: "The acute pain of solitude experienced at first never returned. I had penetrated a mystery, and, by the way, I had sailed through a fog." The diction unfolds its suggestions: "acute pain" sharp enough to "penetrate" the "mystery" of what lies beyond figurative blindness. Again and again Slocum's attentive cadence refreshes tired phrasing; who could have guessed how much life was left in such an off-hand castoff as "by the way"?

As soon as Slocum touches land on July 20, 1895, nineteen days out from Nova Scotia, the reader realizes how lovingly the transatlantic passage has socialized the solo sailor. Ashore in the Azores at Faial, he's pleased to accept islanders' hospitality and a tour with a young woman and her brother as interpreter. Generous well-wishers press gifts on him before he departs Horta for Gibraltar four days later. His interpreter, Antonio, declares that he wishes to come with Slocum: "Antonio's heart went out to one John Wilson, and he was ready to sail for America by way of the two capes to meet his friend. 'Do you know John Wilson of Boston?' he cried. 'I knew a John Wilson,' I said, 'but not of Boston.' 'He had one daughter and one son,' said Antonio, by way of identifying his friend. If this reaches the right John Wilson, I am told to say that 'Antonio of Pico remembers him.' "

The following night, after gorging on fresh plums and goat cheese given him in Horta, Slocum was overtaken during high seas by agonizing stomach cramps, doubled up in his cabin, writhing on its sole. Through the *Spray*'s companionway, "to my amazement I saw a tall man at the helm." The fellow wore a large red cap, at a rakish angle. With "shaggy black whiskers . . . he would have been taken for a pirate in any part of the world." The sailor declared, "I am the pilot of [Columbus's] *Pinta* come to aid you." (Slocum had recently been reading Washington Irving's 1828 *Life and Voyages of Christopher Columbus*.) The apparition then diagnoses Slocum's disease as *calentura*—tropical heat sickness—and scolds him for his diet. Slocum replies with characteristic irascibility: " 'Avast, there, I have no mind for moralizing!' "

This synthesis of the spiritual and the rational is always available to

Slocum when he distinguishes between penetrable mysteries, such as fog, and impenetrable ones, such as hearing, alone at sea, the voice of a stranger. In most respects his belief in a higher power was in sync with eighteenth-century rationalism, faith in the Great Clockmaker. He invokes the deity much further along in *Sailing Alone Around the World,* as he charts his route across the vastness of the Pacific: "For one whole month my vessel held her course true . . . The Southern Cross I saw every night abeam. The sun every morning came up astern; every evening it went down ahead. I wished for no other compass to guide me, for these were true. If I doubted my reckoning after a long time at sea I verified it by reading the clock aloft made by the Great Architect, and it was right." But during his encounter with the churlish pilot of the *Pinta,* the supernatural seems almost Greek in its very human and quarrelsome manifestation.

Recovering nicely from the gale, and food poisoning, if that was what he suffered, he welcomed his solitude. The reader, recalling Slocum's troubles with the help, will appreciate the conviction with which he reports, "I found no fault with the cook, and it was the rule of the voyage that the cook found no fault with me. There was never a ship's crew so well agreed." And in this happy spirit he passed through the Pillars of Hercules on August 4, 1895, 102 days from Fairhaven and 29 from Cape Sable. At Gibraltar the Royal Navy entertained him like a visiting monarch, paying his port fees, tuning the *Spray*'s rig, celebrating his venture. His welcome was in contrast to the *Boston Globe*'s sour response to his early dispatches, which they found old-fashioned and slow-paced, as prose and as adventure. In the end, they printed only three of his travel letters, his first from Gibraltar (August 21) headlined: "Spook on Spray. Ghost of Columbus's Man Steered the Boat . . . With Frolic Welcome the Brave Tar Greeted the Tempests."

This would not do. Sailing alone around the world was a cakewalk put beside freelancing. Soon Slocum would write Eugene Hardy a bitter letter, complaining that the Boston newspapers, with their pinchfist paydays, had broken their word to him about their interest in his writing. "I suspect that a case of murder or rape would find space for all the particulars, in all the papers." With $1.50 to his name, he accepted a loan of fifty dollars from Gibraltar's captain of the port and repaid it, a year later, with the first money he earned as a lecturer. This, after his warm welcome in Horta, set the pattern for the remainder of his voyage: he was greeted as a hero in foreign ports and ignored or disbelieved at home.

Officers of the Royal Navy warned him strenuously against proceeding through the Mediterranean, owing to the near certainty that pirates would beset him along the coast of North Africa. Trusting their wisdom, Slocum, towed from Gibraltar into the wind, set out on the *Spray*'s newly amended course, back across the Atlantic to Brazil and thence around Cape Horn "the wrong way," east to west.* Dropping tow and picking up a stiff breeze, Slocum was no sooner under way than he saw astern and closing on him fast a little Moroccan craft called a felucca, which he took to be crewed by the very pirates he was being put at such inconvenience to evade. The pages describing the chase make for lively adventure reading, concluding with a great sea overtaking both vessels at the last possible moment and dismasting the bad guys, thus sparing Slocum and the *Spray*.

Following a three-day squall, and within sight of the Canary Islands, he sailed into a dust storm blowing offshore from Africa. Then the *Spray* was in trade winds and sailing pretty past the Cape Verde Islands. During this period, once more suffering the ache of loneliness, he crossed to leeward under the stern of a drogher carrying bullocks from Argentina. "She was, indeed a stale one! And the poor cattle, how they bellowed!" This was the second cattle ship he had passed in these waters; the first didn't answer Slocum's signal, so this time he didn't bother raising a flag:

> The time was when ships passing one another at sea backed their topsails and had a "gam," and on parting fired guns; but those good old days have gone. People have hardly time nowadays to speak even on the broad ocean, where news is news, and as for a salute of guns, they cannot afford the powder. There are no poetry-enshrined freighters on the sea now; it is a prosy life when we have no time to bid one another good morning.

This lament is earned and even-keeled, revealing the sane balance Slocum maintained on this voyage between solitude and society. When he confesses to a sense of alienation it is almost always owing to circumstance rather than to imaginary deprivation. Slocum makes much of how crucial it was that he had rigged the *Spray* to sail herself, leaving him free

---

*The route Slocum finally took was remarkably similar to Ferdinand Magellan's in 1519–21, a likeness probably incidental to Slocum's familiarity with all the waters he traversed. (He was inexperienced in the Mediterranean.) He had also briefly considered crossing from the Atlantic to the Pacific by having the *Spray* hauled by the Panama railway across the isthmus, but the expense was prohibitive, the heat stifling, the cholera and yellow fever prevalent. As W. H. Bunting writes, " 'Isthmus fever' took more lives than did Cape Horn 'snorters.' " He'd take his chances with Magellan, in the dire strait named for him.

to rest below in his cabin, to cook filling meals, and to immerse himself in books that kept him alert to the world's characters and business. Standing unnaturally long watches at the helm staring at the compass binnacle will make any sailor drowsy and eventually hallucinatory. Recent studies of the psychological and physical effects of prolonged solitary confinement have cited long-distance solo sailors as being prey to what one researcher, Emma Richards, described as "soul-destroying loneliness."* Bernard Moitessier, a later solo circumnavigator, became so addicted to self-reliance and privacy that, on the point of completing and winning his solo race around the world, he kept on going around again the other way.

If Slocum were ever to become a misanthropic recluse, his next port of call, Pernambuco, should have given adequate provocation. It's tempting to imagine that the governors of Brazil, even more than the pirates of the Mediterranean, had influenced Slocum's revised itinerary. As he tells his readers:

> I had made many voyages to this and other ports in Brazil. In 1893 I was employed as master to take the famous Ericsson ship *Destroyer* from New York to Brazil to go against the rebel Mello and his party. The *Destroyer,* by the way, carried a submarine cannon of enormous length . . . The Brazilians in their curious war sank her themselves at Bahia. With her sank my hope of recovering wages due me; still, I could but try to recover, for to me it meant a great deal. But now within two years the whirligig of time had brought the Mello party into power, and although it was the legal government which had employed me, the so-called "rebels" felt under less obligation to me than I could have wished.

Slocum's final at-bat in this game of donkey baseball came on November 5, 1895, in Rio, where, "having bestirred myself to meet the highest lord of the admiralty and [various] ministers," to press his case for

---

*See Atul Gawande's "Hellhole" in the *New Yorker* of March 30, 2009, and—more directly relevant—Sir Francis Chichester's *Gipsy Moth Circles the World* (1968), wherein that stoic adventurer confesses that "after three months of solitude I felt that it was all too much; that I could not stand it, and could easily go mad with it. All this is weak nonsense, I know, but that is how I felt when twisting about in my bunk." And this despite keeping in touch with the world by twice-weekly radio dispatches during his nine-month, record-breaking, solo circumnavigation. The downside of communication was made evident to Chichester when he was asked by a reporter, as he approached his homecoming in Plymouth, what he had eaten while rounding Cape Horn. The sailor's reply: "Strongly urge you stop questioning and interviewing me which poisons the romantic attraction of this voyage."

unpaid wages due him, he was told: "Captain, so far as we are concerned you may have the ship." They even offered to show him where she had been sunk and burrowed into mud, her smokestack barely visible.

At last he quit Brazil's field, forever. On November 28 he had been at sea 218 days, was 5,000 miles from Boston, and had traveled 8,500 miles. But sailing south toward Buenos Aires he ran the *Spray* aground on a beach in Uruguay, the result of the classic error of perception that confuses a slight elevation near at hand for a high elevation far away: "The false appearance of the sand-hills under a bright moon had deceived me, and I lamented now that I had trusted to appearances at all." Consider: having sailed alone around the world, this stranding, plus a sharp bump against a coral head in the Indian Ocean, were the only instances when Slocum and his *Spray* "took the ground," as sailors say. This time, a young gaucho approached the *Spray* on horseback, thinking to lasso, corral, and rebrand her, but the captain frightened him away and kedged off his stranded vessel at high tide by using a dory he had shipped aboard to row an anchor through the surf, very nearly drowning when it was overturned, and out to deep water.

He spent Christmas in Montevideo, where agents of the Royal Mail Steamship Company docked and repaired the *Spray* without charge, installed as a gift a fine stove, and added twenty pounds sterling as a lagniappe. If Slocum despised steamships, they in turn seemed to love the *Spray*.* At Montevideo, on one of the rare occasions that Slocum invited company aboard to sail with him, he ventured up the River Plata to Buenos Aires in the company of one "Captain Howard of Cape Cod," described as an "old friend" but not supplied with a first name. Walter Teller believes that Slocum was "surely not" bringing this fellow along "to demonstrate the *Spray's* self-steering qualities," but I'm not so sure. Witnesses to this controversial virtue would become essential to Slocum's credibility after he completed his voyage.

Or it could be that he sailed in company on this short leg of his odyssey because he realized how painful it would be to sail past that spot

---

*That Slocum—like Sir Francis Chichester after him—recoiled from hullabaloo after solitude is shown in his reaction to the *Spray's* welcome in Montevideo, where she "was greeted by steam-whistles till I felt embarrassed and wished that I had arrived unobserved. The voyage so far alone may have seemed to the Uruguayans a feat worthy of some recognition; but there was so much of it yet ahead, and of such an arduous nature, that any demonstration at this point seemed, somehow, like boasting prematurely."

in Buenos Aires's outer roads where Virginia had died, or to visit the English Cemetery where she was buried. Neither the name Virginia nor any reference to his first wife appears in *Sailing Alone Around the World*. Instead Slocum marks his trail by a passage heartbreaking in its cautious navigation around profound emotional obstacles:

> I had not for many years been [in] these regions. I will not say that I expected all fine sailing on the course for Cape Horn direct, but while I worked at the sails and rigging I thought only of onward and forward. It was when I anchored in the lonely places that a feeling of awe crept over me. At the last anchorage on the monotonous and muddy [Plata] river, weak as it may seem, I gave way to my feelings. I resolved then that I would anchor no more north of the Strait of Magellan.

Ah, the Strait of Magellan! Here begins the great adventure within the great adventure of the *Spray*'s circumnavigation within the great adventure of Joshua Slocum's life. He had decided against doubling Cape Stiff the wrong way around, into prevailing winds so powerful that they could have knocked the sticks out of her. Even so, approaching his entrance to the strait off the coast of Patagonia, he was overtaken by a stupendous wave, a monster offspring of some distant hurricane or earthquake. It had been climbing on the backs of other great waves to make a "mighty crest, towering masthead-high above me," roaring as it rolled down on the *Spray* from astern. This was, indeed, what Slocum termed a "culmination," the kind of freak most seamen live a lifetime without meeting. It would have been natural to look back at such a thing bearing down like a locomotive, and freeze, but Slocum jumped up his mast and into the high rigging, freeing sails by the miracle of reflexes conditioned by accumulated years upon great oceans that had translated panic into focused competence. The results of this experience—the *Spray* whole and safe after having been submerged by the wave, shaking "in every timber" and reeling "under the weight of the sea"—was to confirm Slocum's faith in the fundamental wholesomeness of his vessel.

On Valentine's Day, 1896, Slocum came ashore at Sandy Point in the eastern reach of the Strait of Magellan, leaving a bit more than three hundred miles of awful sailing to Cape Pillar, at the Pacific end. Belonging to Chile, Punta Arenas is the world's southernmost city, infamous for its miserable climate and general hostility. European settlers of this coaling station for steamers, with sheep farms along its forbidding coast, managed to pry a living out of the place. But the natives—Patagonian and Fuegian—were another breed, as Slocum advises:

> [They] were as squalid as contact with unscrupulous traders could make them. A large percentage of the business there was traffic in "fire-water." If there was a law against selling the poisonous stuff to the natives, it was not enforced. Fine specimens of the Patagonian race, looking smart in the morning when they came into town, had repented before night of ever having seen a white man, so beastly drunk were they, to say nothing about the peltry of which they had been robbed.

The reputation of these coastal natives was well established long before Slocum arrived among them. Charles Darwin wrote in *The Voyage of the "Beagle"* (1839) with excited contempt about the savages' pathetic helplessness in the face of European powder and shot:

> During our stay at Port Famine, the Fuegians twice came and plagued us. As there were many instruments, clothes, and men on shore, it was thought necessary to frighten them away. The first time a few great guns were fired, when they were far distant. It was most ludicrous to watch through a glass the Indians, as often as the shot struck the water, take up stones, and, as a bold defiance, throw them towards the ship, though about a mile and a half distant! A boat was sent with orders to fire a few musket-shots wide of them. The Fuegians hid themselves behind the trees, and for every discharge of the muskets they fired their arrows; all, however, fell short of the boat, and the officer as he pointed at them laughed. This made the Fuegians frantic with passion, and they shook their mantles in vain rage.*

Slocum had read that book and was using as his principal sailing guide to these waters the U.S. Department of the Navy's second edition of *The West Coast of South America, Including Magellan Strait, Tierra del Fuego and The Outlying Islands,* printed by the Hydrographic Office as a precursor to what seamen today know as *The Coastal Pilot*. Slocum's edition, arranged according to the sequence of typical passages, alerted sailors to circum-

---

*Bruce Chatwin's *In Patagonia* (1977)—an eclectic book of storytelling, anthropology, natural history, political history, and legend—heaps an even greater portion of contempt not on the Fuegians but on Darwin himself, accusing him of lapsing into "that common failing of naturalists: to marvel at the intricate perfection of other creatures and recoil from the squalor of man."

stances and conditions to expect in traversing the most dangerous stretch of water on earth.* ("Westward of Cape Froward the weather is undeniably very bad, and it is probable that no portion of the globe frequented by man experiences, the whole year round, worse weather.") In deliberately dispassionate prose, the coastal guide warns of riptides, fog, sleet, snow, hail, treacherous holding ground for an anchor, and the frequent occurrence of the dread williwaws, furious and unpredictable blasts of wind that sweep down on the mountainous fjords of the Magellan Strait, hurling sturdy vessels over on their beams, uprooting anchors, and howling like fiends. This was the wind that caused Antoine de Saint-Exupéry's single-engine plane to fly backward. Bruce Chatwin tells of a sixteenth-century British sailor caught in the strait during its winter season: his "frostbitten nose fell off when he blew it."

But the otherwise stick-to-the-facts Hydrographic Office reserved some high-voltage prose for the native Fuegians, who generally kept themselves hidden, "but it is extraordinary how rapidly a hundred or more will get together if they see an opportunity for attacking boats, small vessels, or a wrecked party." (In fact, their means of sharing bad news for European and American sailors gave their land and tribe its name, *fuego*, or fire: they used smoke signals.) Summoned—in a frenzy to loot—they swarmed. And that's not all:

> There is none of the graceful gliding of the North American, or of the New Zealand, canoe in these miserable boats. Instead of being propelled by paddles, they are rowed by oars, rudely made of some pieces of board tied on to the end of a pole . . . [The Fuegians] are generally almost naked, the women appearing to care less about clothing than the men.

Or shall we give Charles Darwin the last word? These observations, written by a celebrated man of science and reason, an evangelist of direct observation, would have been familiar to Slocum:

> While going one day on shore near Wollaston Island, we pulled alongside a canoe with six Fuegians. These were the most abject and miserable creatures I anywhere beheld, . . . quite naked, and even one full-grown woman was absolutely so . . . In another harbor not far distant, a woman, who was suckling a recently-born child, came one day alongside the vessel, and

---

*A few of the strait's place-names hint at its nature: Famine Reach, Desolation Bay, Last Hope Inlet, and—my favorite—Useless Bay.

remained there out of mere curiosity, whilst the sleet fell and thawed on her naked bosom, and on the skin of her naked baby! These poor wretches were stunted in their growth, their hideous faces bedaubed with white paint, their skins filthy and greasy, their hair entangled, their voices discordant, and their gestures violent. Viewing such men, one can hardly make one's self believe that they are fellow-creatures, and inhabitants of the same world. It is a common subject of conjecture what pleasure in life some of the lower animals can enjoy: how much more reasonably the same question may be asked with respect to these barbarians! At night, five or six human beings, naked and scarcely protected from the wind and rain of this tempestuous climate, sleep on the wet ground coiled up like animals . . . The different tribes when at war are cannibals . . . When pressed in winter by hunger, they kill and devour their old women before they kill their dogs: the boy, being asked by Mr. Low why they did this, answered, "Doggies catch otters, old women no." This boy described the manner in which they are killed by being held over smoke and thus choked; he imitated their screams as a joke, and described the parts of their bodies which are considered best to eat.

While the *Spray* was moored at Punta Arenas, the port captain, a Chilean naval officer, attempted to persuade Slocum to ship bodyguards to protect him against the treachery of the Fuegians in the strait, where they were said to have recently massacred the crew of a vaguely referenced schooner, in retaliation for which the governor of the region had sent a "party of young bloods"—a lynch mob—"to foray a Fuegian settlement and wipe out what they could of it." Despite Slocum's skepticism about the distribution of rights and wrongs between the natives and their Chilean masters, he was pleased to have on board a Martini-Henry .577/450 lever-action carbine, with an effective range of six hundred yards. And before he set out alone, he received as a gift from Captain Pedro Samblich* a sack of carpet tacks, with the caution, "You must use them discreetly." (The reader's patience will be rewarded.) He was also urged, as his son Victor reports, "to shoot straight and to begin shooting in time."†

On February 19, 1896, the *Spray* cleared Sandy Point and headed westward through the strait. The going was miserable: the labyrinthine chan-

---

*An Austrian, and not to be confused with the "Black Pedro" whom readers will soon meet.
†Rockwell Kent offers countervailing testimony from the point of view of the Firemen, whose territory and way of life had been invaded by foreign meddlers, Christians, in the "ruthless pursuit of their benevolence."

nel acted as a funnel for contrary winds from the Pacific, which might be suddenly broken by williwaws blasting from random directions. Slocum beat against this severe seascape "with hardly so much as a bird in sight," dodging hidden rocks and false channels, and facing a chaotic gauntlet of islands. The next morning he anchored long enough to celebrate his fifty-second birthday with a cup of coffee, and was no sooner under way again, in the neighborhood of Cape Froward, when he spotted "canoes manned by savages" coming in pursuit. It was a supplemental perversity of these hellish waters that while storms and fog kept natives ashore, any easing of conditions set them forth. And so it was that Slocum now heard the insistent cry of "Yammerschooner! Yammerschooner!" from the nearing canoes. This he had been taught to understand as forceful panhandling, and he shouted back, "No!"* He also rigged scarecrows forward and aft to give the appearance of additional crew, a contrivance more reassuring to himself than persuasive to Black Pedro. For leading the charge toward the *Spray* was that very villain, and Slocum fired a shot—designed to miss—in his direction: "However, a miss was as good as a mile for Mr. 'Black Pedro,' as he it was, and no other, a leader in several bloody massacres. He made for the island now, and the others followed him. I knew by his Spanish lingo and by his full beard that he was the villain I have named, a renegade mongrel, and the worst murderer in Tierra del Fuego."

During the *Spray*'s first passage through the Strait of Magellan—there would be another, and far more trying—Slocum dodged natives, and dropped and raised anchor again and again, until on March 3, exhausted by the effort, he reached Port Tamar, with Cape Pillar and the Pacific Ocean in sight to the west. He had now sailed 13,000 miles.

> Here I felt the throb of the great ocean that lay before me. I knew now that I had put a world behind me, and that I was opening out another world ahead. I had passed the haunts of savages. Great piles of granite mountains of bleak and lifeless aspect were now astern; on some of them

---

*Chatwin tells of a missionary among the Fuegians, Thomas Bridges, who compiled before his death in 1898 a dictionary of the natives' language, listing a vocabulary of 32,000 words. Whether or not "yammerschooner" was among them, it is certain that the people to whom Slocum shouted "No!" knew the names, "as complex as Linnaean Latin, of everything that swam or sprouted, crawled or flew" in their neighborhood, had words to describe the least signs of approaching shifts in weather, not to mention the geography of the place in which Slocum, by necessity, was taking such a lively interest.

not even a speck of moss had ever grown. There was an unfinished new-
ness all about the land. On the hill back of Port Tamar a small beacon had
been thrown up, showing that some man had been there. But how could
one tell but that he had died of loneliness and grief? In a bleak land is not
the place to enjoy solitude . . . There was a sort of swan, smaller than a
Muscovy duck, which might have been brought down with the gun, but
in the loneliness of life about the dreary country I found myself in no
mood to make one life less, except in self-defense.

What happened now raises Slocum's voyage from merely extraordinary to miraculous. For once he entered Pacific waters a vicious northwest gale drove him back under bare poles, and with no hope of
reentering the Strait of Magellan, "there seemed nothing to do but to
keep on and go east about, after all."

A pause is required. Even a writer as skilled as Joshua Slocum cannot
possibly convey the reality of duration by the medium of prose. Even if
he were to abandon his reflexive taciturnity, a writer cannot escape ellip-
sis: the *Spray* is moored at Fairhaven on page 10, and 13,000 miles later—
on page 69—he writes that oh, wow, what a pity, he'll have to cross the
Atlantic again! We don't read backward, even though Slocum—beaten
back by wind or tide—sometimes sailed in reverse. There is no chance
for a reader to be given to understand, through a linear and consecutive
medium, the crabwise progress of the *Spray,* or the assault on Slocum's
senses hour after hour, and sometimes day after day, of nature's din, the
sea's aggressiveness, the sometimes awful dampening of a sailor's senses,
not to mention his clothes, food, bunk, and body. Slocum has been
detoured to the extreme latitudes of the southern oceans, adding thousands and thousands of miles to his journey, and this reversal unfolds in
the space of a page, in the brief number of words needed to describe a
shift of wind.

And what a wind! What a battering he took! Heading southeast, with
two long hawsers trailing astern to break the combing seas, the *Spray*
endured "the worst sea that Cape Horn or its wild regions could
afford." Meantime, having cooked himself an Irish stew in conformity
with his custom always to prepare warm meals at sea, "my appetite was
slim . . . (Confidentially, I was seasick!)." The man who added that paren-
thesis to his story was likely to come through okay, and so he did. "Even
while the storm raged at its worst, my ship was wholesome and noble.
My mind as to her seaworthiness was put at ease for aye."

But seaworthiness cannot prevent a thirty-seven-foot sailboat from being crushed by rocks, and that was now nearly the *Spray*'s fate. On the fifth night of the storm—March 8, 1896—Slocum entered the worst patch of the world's worst waters. Darwin had been there half a century earlier, and thus described the Milky Way, a broken strand of barely awash rocks barring the waters south of Cape Horn from the strait: "One sight of such a coast is enough to make a landsman dream for a week about shipwrecks, peril, and death." Slocum sets the scene:

> Night closed in before the sloop reached the land, leaving her feeling the way in pitchy darkness. I saw breakers ahead before long [and] was immediately startled by the tremendous roaring of breakers again ahead and on the lee bow. This puzzled me, for there should have been no broken water where I supposed myself to be. I kept off a good bit . . . but finding broken water also there, threw her head again offshore. In this way, among dangers, I spent the rest of the night. Hail and sleet in the fierce squalls cut my flesh till the blood trickled over my face; but what of that? It was daylight, and the sloop was in the midst of the Milky Way of the sea, which is northwest of Cape Horn, and it was the white breakers of a huge sea over sunken rocks which had threatened to engulf her through the night . . . This was the greatest sea adventure of my life. God knows how my vessel escaped.*

On March 10, Slocum anchored in the strait at St. Nicholas Bay, where he'd drunk his birthday coffee eighteen days before. He would fight his way westward for forty-three days and nights through the same waters he had traversed so painfully starting on Valentine's Day. High on his list of anxieties stood the persistent threat of more "Yammerschooner!" demands. It requires little imagination to conjure an inventory of complaints against interloping white men by their unwelcoming hosts, but I hope the reader's wish is to keep Joshua Slocum alive to endure more interesting dangers than deadly armed robbery at the hands of Black Pedro. Trust him to share this wish, and here—at anchor in wonderfully named Thieves' Bay—he slept below while his gift from Samblich kept watch on deck:

---

*A casual reader might accuse Slocum of carelessness in his use of absolutes, but in fact he was fastidious in his record keeping: the "most dismal of all my nights at sea" (aboard the pestilent *Aquidneck*) is very different from the "most exciting boat-ride of my life" (aboard the *Liberdade*, towed by the *Finance*), and quite distinct from the "hardest voyage that I ever made, without any exception" (aboard the *Destroyer*).

Now, it is well known that one cannot step on a tack without saying something about it. A pretty good Christian will whistle when he steps on the
"commercial end" of a carpet-tack; a savage will howl and claw the air,
and that was just what happened that night about twelve o'clock, while I
was asleep in the cabin, where the savages thought they "had me," sloop
and all, but changed their minds when they stepped on deck . . . I had no
need of a dog; they howled like a pack of hounds. I had hardly use for a
gun. They jumped pell-mell, some into their canoes and some into the
sea, to cool off, I suppose, and there was a deal of free language over it as
they went. I fired several guns when I came on deck, to let the rascals
know that I was home, and then I turned in again, feeling sure I should
not be disturbed any more by people who left in so great a hurry.

This is almost too good to be true, and with his customary diligence
Walter Teller interviewed Slocum's brother-in-law George Walker, who'd
heard the yarn at first hand; the event having had no available witnesses,
Walker was never able to authenticate it, though it "lost none of its interest for that reason." Among his papers, Teller adds a parenthetical note
to himself: "That's just how I feel about the captain's above paragraph."
And just how I feel, too.

After day upon day of uphill sailing, an evolved sense of determination overtook Slocum. In the face of the relentless battering he took, it
would be inaccurate to describe this as resignation. Imagine hauling a
heavy anchor and chain aboard every morning, let alone having to reset
it when it dragged along the kelpy bottom or snagged on a rock. Imagine
raising heavy sails and lowering them, furling and reefing them, patching
and restitching them. Imagine the constant work of repairing broken
spars with the primitive tools he carried.

Rockwell Kent—whose stunning drawings accompany *Voyaging:
Southward from the Strait of Magellan* (1924), his account of sailing these
waters in the wake of the *Spray*—tells of williwaws and foul currents,
ghastly cold and exhaustion. He had known in advance of a "mountain
sea . . . thundering eternally on granite shores," in a region known as
the Sailor's Graveyard, offering a fine chance of "getting wrecked or
drowned or eaten." This provided Tierra del Fuego with "the spirit-
stirring glamour of the terrible." Kent had a friend aboard his small sailboat, and they had finally abandoned their plan to voyage from Punta
Arenas to Cape Pillar after being beaten back time and again by headwinds, when a kind of fury overtook them:

Then with fatigue the glamor of adventure wanes, and loneliness comes over us and the sense that we are destitute of all that sustained our lives. We that have come so far and left so much then know, out of the poignant singleness of our desires, what in the confusion and abundance of life's offerings is best. But no one tells—so intimately close and dear is that desire. And when at last, suddenly in the darkness here, I ask my companion what one thing he desires most out of the whole world, tonight—he starts at the shattered silence, and, slowly emerging from far away to here, covers his thoughts and answers, "A fair wind to carry us through Gabriel Channel."

However, there's an end to everything. "Mate," I said one dreary night as we turned in, "I need a new chapter for my book. Tomorrow we sail no matter what happens." And we did.

Unavailingly, as it fell out. But Victor Slocum, who understood better than anyone except his mother the seaborne character of his father, captures the ferocity that had evolved from his native determination and pugnacity: "Since the gale which drove him south, his attitude toward the entire transit of the strait had changed. It was now: 'If you want to play ball, come on. I am ready for you and I can beat you at your own game.' " Or, as he writes in *Sailing Alone Around the World*, "I now enjoyed gales of wind as never before, and the *Spray* was never long without them during her struggles about Cape Horn. I became in a measure inured to the life, and began to think that one more trip through the strait, if perchance the sloop should be blown off again, would make me the aggressor." Rockwell Kent, for his part, perhaps echoing the wrath of Lear on the heath, writes that "the unrelenting fury of the wind enraged us."

Having salvaged wine and tallow from a ship wrecked at Langara Cove, near Borgia Bay, Slocum filled his water tanks and sailed through a snowstorm to Port Angosto, the jumping-off harbor for Cape Pillar. He tried and failed six times to beat out of the harbor, and a Chilean gunboat offered to tow the *Spray* back through the strait to Punta Arenas, which generosity the captain disdained. After all, why was he in this game, except to play? His ambition was neither commercial nor imperial; he'd already seen the world. He was here in a contest, and good sportsmanship was chief among its rules. A new virtue came to him, a kind of extreme patience: "I made up my mind after six attempts . . . to be in no further haste to sail." So on the seventh try, on April 13, 1896, he made it out of the harbor, took a right turn and sailed into the Pacific after sixty-nine days of struggle, whereupon a huge "fine-weather sea," as he called it, "broke over the sloop fore and aft . . . the last that swept over the *Spray* off Cape Horn. It seemed to wash away old regrets. All my troubles were now astern; summer was ahead; all the world was again before me."

Thirteen days later he made landfall at night, off the islands of Juan Fernández. He spent ten days ashore where Alexander Selkirk, marooned and dwelling in a cave, had inspired Daniel Defoe's *Robinson Crusoe*. Joshua Slocum's choice of destinations during his voyage around the world was often guided by his literary enthusiasms. Along the way one of Slocum's most important ports of call would be Apia, at Samoa, where he met Fanny, recently the widow of his idol, Robert Louis Stevenson. Slocum's abundant library aboard the *Spray*, updated as he traveled by swaps and gifts and new purchases, had been stocked with the help of Mabel Wagnalls, the young and unmarried daughter of the publisher who owned Funk and Wagnalls. Before the captain sailed from Boston, she had brought aboard a box of books and had written in Slocum's log, "The *Spray* will return," a vote of confidence that so moved the author of *Sailing Alone Around the World* that he dedicated his book to her.*

Ashore at Juan Fernández, Slocum was especially beguiled by the island's children, an affection that cheered him his whole way around. He loved teaching kids the names of things, and liked to tease and be teased by them. It is helpful to remember that he grew up caring for many siblings, and had delighted in his own children when he had the means and leisure to care for them. Anybody who has been among children in the South Pacific has experienced how joyful they seem. The little girls dance without self-consciousness, and little boys—knowing the reputation some of their people have among civilized aliens such as vacation among them—might lick their lips and cry "Yum-yum," before they laugh and run (neither fast nor far) away. No wonder Slocum remembered one experience at Juan Fernández as perhaps "the pleasantest on my whole voyage," his final day ashore there, "when the children of the little community, one and all, went out with me to gather" quinces, peaches, and figs for the voyage.

But once under sail again, "with a free wind day after day," he was not

---

Spray's library, at the time he sailed from Boston, included the poems of Burns and Tennyson, Darwin's *Descent of Man*, Boswell's *Life of Samuel Johnson*, Trevelyan's *Life of Macaulay*, a set of Shakespeare, and—perhaps most prophetically—*Don Quixote*.

tempted to put into land for an astonishing seventy-two days. After making his desired northing, up to 12 degrees south of the equator, he ran down his longitude, as sailors say, week after week, riding the trade winds west. The *Spray* sailed herself during this period, while her master read and rested, his ordeal at Cape Horn and in the strait unforgotten.

> My time was all taken up those days—not by standing at the helm; no man, I think, could stand or sit and steer a vessel round the world: I did better than that; for I sat and read my books, mended my clothes, or cooked my meals and ate them in peace. I had already found that it was not good to be alone, and so I made companionship with what there was around me, sometimes with the universe and sometimes with my own insignificant self; but my books were always my friends, let fail all else.

Spray made the Marquesas forty-three days and five thousand miles out from Juan Fernández, finding Nuku Hiva right where that high island, of Melville's *Typee,* was meant to be found. Of all islands along his march, Nuku Hiva—romantic, lush, with abundant food and fresh water—should have seemed attractive to Slocum, but something pushed him forward, the push itself, perhaps. Perhaps this leg was the apogee of his evolution into a creature of the sea, at home on it, as he writes in *Sailing Alone Around the World:* "To know the laws that govern the winds, and to know that you know them, will give you an easy mind on your voyage round the world; otherwise you may tremble at the appearance of every cloud."*

When, in clear weather, he spied lofty Nuku Hiva, within five miles of his dead reckoning position, he boasted, a rare indulgence: "This was wonderful . . . this was extraordinary. All navigators will tell you that from one day to another a ship may lose or gain more than five miles in her sailing-account, and again, in the matter of lunars, even expert lunarians are considered as doing clever work when they average within eight miles of the truth." Rod Scher, whose *Annotated Sailing Alone Around the World* (2009) is more reliable in his sailing judgments than in his pyschologizing, puts this achievement in context:

---

*It's interesting to contrast this offhand passage with the confession of Conor O'Brien, another legendary long-distance sailor: O'Brien was frightened silly by big waves and winds. In the early days at sea "I used to be scared of every puff of wind . . . I really took things ridiculously seriously; even after two years I connect my passage down the Atlantic with nothing else but anxious readings of the barometer and thermometer, and speculations about wind and weather."

Slocum's feat of navigation is akin to magic. With only a few degrees of southerly error, he would have missed the Marquesas by hundreds of miles and, if he were lucky, perhaps fetched the islands of French Polynesia; if the error had been in a northerly direction, he might have encountered *nothing at all* until sighting the Marshall Islands, another 3,000 miles away.

In fact, the early history of the Marquesas was notable for the European explorers who sailed right past without noticing a peak as high as 3,900 feet atop lush green ridges and black, volcanic cliffs, impossible to miss—even given the frequency of clouds—at a distance of twenty miles.

Melville found Nuku Hiva, where he jumped ship in June 1842 after eighteen months aboard New Bedford's *Acushnet,* hunting quite vainly for sperm whales in the South Pacific. The opening passage of his autobiographical first novel, *Typee,* makes a persuasive case for a sailor longing to go ashore after a hard passage at sea:

> Six months at sea! Yes, reader, as I live, six months out of sight of land; cruising after the sperm-whale beneath the scorching sun of the Line, and tossed on the billows of the wide-rolling Pacific—the sky above, the sea around, and nothing else! Weeks and weeks ago our fresh provisions were all exhausted. There is not a sweet potato left; not a single yam . . . Oh! for a refreshing glimpse of one blade of grass—for a snuff at the fragrance of a handful of the loamy earth! Is there nothing fresh around us? Is there no green thing to be seen?

Melville's longing raises the question of Slocum's diet during such prolonged passages between ports as he was now undertaking. Flying fish, in their native latitudes, were a self-serving staple, and he kept aboard quantities of potatoes and salt cod. Biscuits were the sailor's friend, especially when crumbled up or sopped in liquid. He carried an abundance of flour, and fried doughnuts from the tallow he had salvaged in the Strait of Magellan. Coffee and tea, with sugar, helped keep him warm and alert at night. Clifton Johnson—who profiled Slocum for *Outing* magazine in its October 1902 issue—used outtakes from his interview at Martha's Vineyard for a follow-up article in *Good Housekeeping* (February 1903) about the captain's diet and cooking techniques while aboard the *Spray.* He writes that "I repeat what he said in substantially his own words."

Slocum emphasized that he was never short on rations, a casual reassurance in light of the well-known danger of contracting scurvy on any passage approaching sixty days at sea. (Sir Francis Chichester tells of cases that began as few as twelve days alone at sea, announced by depression, loose teeth, and boils, and provoked by an insufficiency of vitamins C and D from fresh fruit and vegetables. Slocum and his crews—during all the voyages that he mastered—were never said to have suffered this ubiquitous malady.) He relished mangoes, but complained that they were so juicy that after eating them he needed a bath.

Many of his supplies he put by in tin cans, which he trusted only himself to seal with solder. He used curry as a staple, for its flavor and qualities as a preservative, a taste he had acquired in South Asia. From firsthand experience in the Okhotsk Sea he had become expert at preparing salt cod, not "these little tom cods, skinned and bleached and tasteless . . . but big fellows, thick as a board and broad as a sole of shoe leather." Potatoes he baked in their skins. In common with coastal Yankees everywhere, he was fiercely proud of his chowder-making powers. Slocum didn't bother trying to catch fish during his voyage, but took potluck from the sea: "Often I'd get up in the morning and find [flying fish] down the forescuttle right alongside the frying pan." That throwaway phrase "get up in the morning" is worthy of attention: he got up from sleeping, that is, while the Spray kept herself company. It has been estimated that a steamer and sailboat on a collision course have at most twenty minutes from the moment they see each other on the horizon—assuming clear weather by day or clear weather by night with bright lights aloft—to avoid crashing. There were passages of thousands of miles during which Slocum never saw another ship in the Pacific. Despite a close call—a "startled snort" and wetting from the flukes of a humpback "plowing the ocean at night while [he] was below"—Slocum trusted whales to see him and get out of his way, and his way avoided reefs. (Sounds easy, doesn't it?)

At noon on July 16, 1896, Slocum anchored at Apia, a harbor at Samoa, after the longest unbroken passage of his voyage. He didn't rush ashore, but rather spread an awning across the Spray's cockpit, where he sat alone listening to voices ashore, particularly to women singing. To understand Slocum fully, one would have to understand him at that moment—not rushing ashore—with his baffling complexity of relief and pride, hunger for society, and disciplined delay of gratification. His mix was not patchwork but constitutional, appetite governed by restraint to an almost heroic degree.

He lingered more than a month at Samoa, where he was befriended by Fanny Stevenson, who came aboard the *Spray* the day after she anchored, together with envoys from the U.S. consul ashore, who invited Slocum to festivities in his honor. From this port onward, the circumnavigator was destined to be celebrated wherever he went, being entertained and flattered by personages—tribal chiefs, explorers, foreign emissaries—who were justly impressed by the ambition and achievement of the master of the *Spray*. Slocum responded well to adulation, and despite his disdain for self-celebration he manages to drop into *Sailing Alone Around the World* the names and résumés of celebrities as various as "Oom Paul" (Uncle Paul) Krüger, the president of Transvaal; and the late Robert Louis Stevenson, whose grave he visited with Fanny on Samoa. Stevenson, forty-four, had died there eighteen months earlier, and his headstone inscription stirred deep emotions in Slocum: "Home is the Sailor, home from the sea, / And the hunter home from the hill."

Fanny, an American, knowing that Slocum idolized her late husband above all writers and travelers, invited him to visit the Stevenson villa, Vailima, where her guest was encouraged to use the writer's desk to compose letters. She then pressed upon her new friend volumes of sailing directions for the Mediterranean, inscribed "To Captain Slocum," with the assurance that her husband "would be pleased that they should be passed on to the sort of seafaring man that he liked above all others." For his part, Slocum wrote of Fanny, who, along with her husband, "had voyaged in all manner of rickety craft among the islands of the Pacific," that "our tastes were similar." Fanny must have made him think of Virginia, as though he needed reminding.

On August 20, 1896, after selling the last of his salvaged tallow to a German trader who would use it for candles and soap, Slocum shipped the *Spray*'s anchor and sailed from Samoa, setting a course north of Fiji; after forty-two days of gales he took refuge halfway around the world from Boston, at Newcastle, New South Wales, and ten days later, October 10, arrived at Sydney Harbor. Many visitors came aboard in Newcastle, and his arrival there was announced by the Australian newspapers, extravagant in their praise. A writer bylined "The Pilot" wrote in the *Sydney Morning Herald* that, among explorers seeking new frontiers,

> Captain Slocum [might have been] placed in a special class of derange-
> ment by himself . . . [But instead he] is feted by British squadrons and
> hailed everywhere as a worthy descendant of an illustrious line of sea-
> kings. And so probably it will be to the end of time; the highest intellectual
> development is not likely ever to lessen the delight which we all naturally
> feel in stirring action—in worthy deeds worthily carried to an end.

Well, it's always folly to predict what "we all" feel or will feel about anything or anyone. Slocum was greeted in Sydney by a police boat "giving me a pluck into anchorage while they gathered data from an old scrap-book of mine, which seemed to interest them."

> Nothing escapes the vigilance of the New South Wales police; their repu-
> tation is known the world over. They made a shrewd guess that I could
> give them some useful information, and they were the first to meet me.
> Someone said they came to arrest me, and—well, let it go at that.

Casual readers of *Sailing Alone Around the World*—scrupulous readers, too—should be forgiven for failing to comprehend that Slocum is alluding here to the continuation of his feud and legal entanglements with none other than Henry A. Slater, arch villain of the *Northern Light's* Grand Guignol. Here is Slocum at his most bewildering: "—well, let it go at that." It is one thing to allude to his visit to Virginia's grave in Buenos Aires, and his tears while anchored at the mouth of the River Plata. Why refer at all now to the Slater fiasco in Sydney? He must be writing out of some sense of fair play, of confessional obligation to readers he is at pains to befriend.

His trouble with Slater continued in Sydney (as it ended in New York) as farce. The course of the feud—but not its truth—is thoroughly documented by newspaper accounts in the collection of the National Library of Australia that give both sides' charges and countercharges.

Slater, after recanting his charge, had left the United States and settled in Sydney, where the ex-convict—at no handicap in a society founded by ex-convicts—became a policeman. Severely indignant about Australia's celebration of Slocum's arrival in Newcastle, he began a raucous campaign against his former master's reputation that reached its apogee in the slanderous article published in the *Sydney Daily Telegraph* the morning before the *Spray* sailed into that port.* A provocation in Slater's first-person account caught Slocum's attention: "I ask the public before

---

*See pp. 104–7 above for a long excerpt from the article in question.

making a god of this man to wait until I am placed face to face with him. I do not make these statements to gain notoriety, or even sympathy, but simply to show my fellow-citizens what kind of man they are dealing with in Captain Joshua Slocum."

The last we heard of Slater—twelve years earlier, in 1884, having recanted in sworn testimony before a New York justice of the peace (and the editor of the *Nautical Gazette*) the very charges he was now elaborating—he was suing the tort lawyer who had fired him up to make false charges. So in 1896 he was either spectacularly forgetful or ferociously angry that his confession hadn't better rewarded him. But Slocum quickly struck back—"disgusted," as he wrote, by Slater's slanders—and shared that "old scrap-book" (indeed!) with the Sydney police and press. Moreover, he had his accuser brought before a magistrate of Sydney's Water Police Court, charging him with making violent threats. He quoted one of Slater's recent public declamations: "This Captain Slocum, God help him when we meet. I'll not be responsible for my actions. This man you are making an angel of, I'll make an angel of him when I get hold of him." One witness for Slocum was his brother-in-law, George Washington Walker, who had sailed aboard the *Washington* during Virginia's honeymoon voyage to Cook Inlet. Another witness, a police detective, testified that Slater had said, addressing a crowd at the General Post Office, "Captain Slocum is a coward. He daren't meet me face to face. But I will force him to meet me."

Testimony in the matter of *Slater* v. *Slocum* was printed on October 12, 1896, in the *Sydney Morning Herald*. Slater directly asked Slocum: "Are you afraid of me?" Slocum replied: "Well, you are a most excitable man, and from the language you have used, you might possibly do me an injury. I certainly am, to a certain extent, afraid of you." Slater, compelled by the court to pay an eighty-pound bond as surety that he would keep the peace for six months, said to his tormentor: "You ought to be at least morally afraid of me."

As always in feuds stirred by daily newspapers, both sides gained adherents. But, overwhelmingly, it was Slocum who was vindicated; his remaining months in Australia and Tasmania brought him new and generous friends, as well as increasing celebrity.

The title of Herman Melville's poem "The Maldive Shark" is perfectly calibrated, objectively naming a geographical location even as it suggests

subterranean malice. In sixteen lines it captures the relentless predator—
"phlegmatical one," "dotard lethargic and dull, pale ravener of horrible
meat"—from the point of view of "sleek little pilot-fish" who alertly
accompany it. They swim unnoticed near the shark's "saw-pit" mouth,
"his charnel of maw." Melville's characters are perhaps the most famous
anthropomorphists in literature, but the author himself manages not to
confuse natural brutality with human malice.

Slocum took the sea's aggression even less personally than Melville, so
it's odd how much potent and totemic evil he conferred on this beast.
Soon after clearing Tierra del Fuego's battering, he killed one, even as he
reflected on his evolving pacificity:

> On the tenth day from Cape Pillar a shark came along, the first of its kind
> on this part of the voyage to get into trouble. I harpooned him and took
> out his ugly jaws. I had not till then felt inclined to take the life of any ani-
> mal, but when John Shark hove in sight my sympathy flew to the winds. It
> is a fact that in Magellan I let pass many ducks that would have made a
> good stew, for I had no mind in the lonesome strait to take the life of any
> living thing.

In the neighborhood of coral reefs "hungry sharks"—aren't they
designed to stay hungry?—would swim near the *Spray*. "I own to a satisfaction in shooting them as one would a tiger. Sharks, after all, are the
tigers of the sea. Nothing is more dreadful to the mind of a sailor, I think,
than a possible encounter with a hungry shark." There is no suggestion
elsewhere in his writing or history that Slocum conferred motive on
nature's malignity, whether in contrary winds, freak waves, tempests,
doldrums, maelstroms, volcanoes, earthquakes, or diseases.

Shortly before Christmas of 1896, while in Melbourne and preparing
to cross the Bass Strait to Tasmania, he combined this loathing with his
entrepreneurial zest in quite a sideshow. Harbor authorities, to Slocum's
irritation, were charging what he considered excessive port fees. Spoiled
by free tows and dockage, not to mention gifts of food and services, he
now "squared the matter" by charging the curious citizens of Melbourne sixpence each for coming aboard the *Spray* for a look around.
Then:

> when this business got dull I caught a shark and charged them sixpence
> each to look at that. The shark was twelve feet six inches in length, and

carried a progeny of twenty-six, not one of them less than two feet in length. A slit of a knife let them out in a canoe full of water, which, changed constantly, kept them alive one whole day. In less than an hour from the time I heard of the ugly brute it was on deck and on exhibition, with rather more than the amount of the *Spray's* tonnage dues already collected.*

On something of a good-idea roll, he then hired an inventive Irish local, a celebrated waterfront-tavern raconteur, to give a carnival barker's spiel about sharks and their cruelties while Slocum busied himself—as employers will—with more pleasurable pursuits ashore.

Slocum spent the winter months of 1897 in Tasmania, twenty-five thousand miles and almost two years from home, whatever "home" might have meant to him. Certainly it crossed his mind to make his home in these waters. He was welcomed with increasing fervor, learning now to lecture about his adventures with lantern slides to paying audiences in Hobart and elsewhere. An anonymous admirer in Hobart put aboard the *Spray* an envelope containing a five-pound note—equivalent to five hundred dollars today—that Slocum promised himself he would pass along to someone needier than himself. This he did, and soon, contributing the money to a local charity in Cooktown, Queensland, the croc-infested bucket-of-blood nexus of the Australian gold rush, where aborigines from New Guinea suffered terribly after being brought there to mine gold.[†]

Another change of itinerary had brought Slocum to Cooktown. He had planned to sail south and west around Australia's Cape Leeuwin, but

*Six years later, on the Massachusetts coast in Marion, Slocum earned a mention in a local newspaper for his heroic slaying of a shark that had terrified bathers at the fashionable Sippican Casino. He caught this one from the float at the beach club, using "a big hook and chunk of pork."
[†]Slocum was always fastidious about repaying debts, however small. In addition to repaying the fifty dollars he'd had to borrow in Gibraltar, and from Durban, South Africa, the twenty dollars that had been advanced to Victor by Roberts Brothers of Boston, he actively honored the reciprocal custom among sailors of putting ashore stores in remote places visited by voyagers in need, whether owing to shipwreck or simple hardship. In Tierra del Fuego he removed a dozen and more letters that had been nailed to trees, most left by sealers and whalers, "with the request that the first homeward-bound ship would carry them along and see to their mailing, which had been the custom of this strange postal service for many years. Some of the letters brought back by our boat were directed to New Bedford, and some to Fairhaven, Massachusetts." For Slocum, so long accustomed to solitude, decency of action was unrelated to being observed.

pack ice drifting up from Antarctica had scotched this plan, instead sending him north around the continent, inside the lagoon of the spectacularly beautiful Great Barrier Reef, 1,200 miles of coral dividing the rocky coast of Queensland from the Coral Sea. As he had followed in Magellan's wake, he now was plowing waters explored in 1770 by Captain James Cook, on the *Endeavor.*

On May 20, 1897, the *Spray* rounded Great Sandy Point and picked up the trade winds, enabling him to sail through the treacherous reef system at night, against the advice of local mariners. Slocum decided it was less taxing to remain vigilant through the night than to anchor and haul anchor again and again. He mentions a few times in the latter half of *Sailing Alone Around the World* how acutely his body continued to feel the aches and strains of his exertions in the Strait of Magellan. After bouncing without consequence off a reef north of Cooktown (within sight of a lightship anchored to warn of the hazard), Slocum arrived on Thursday Island, off the northern tip of Queensland, on June 20, two days before Queen Victoria's Diamond Jubilee. As the only American ashore on the tiny island, he was entertained—and royally—by British authorities at a corroboree performed by hundreds of native warriors and their families from the mainland. "When they do a thing on Thursday Island they do it with a roar," dancing with their weapons, wearing war paint and beating animal bones against drums. And the captain was keen to show his own colors, flying her "noble" Stars and Stripes as high up the *Spray*'s masthead as the flag could be raised.

When departing from Thursday Island on June 24, Slocum was anxious about what lay ahead, across the Indian Ocean at the Cape of Good Hope. Remembering his travails there aboard the *Northern Light,* he refused to confront those waters during the winter. Deliberately stalling his arrival off South Africa, he nevertheless racked up huge distances sailing the trade winds, aiming to pass to the south of Timor and over three thousand miles to the Cocos (or Keeling) Islands southwest of Java, coral specks nine miles square whose history is as confused as their name. En route, the *Spray* sailed through the Arafura Sea,

> where for days she sailed in water milky white and green and purple. It was my good fortune to enter the sea on the last quarter of the moon, the

advantage being that in the dark nights I witnessed the phosphorescent light effect at night in its greatest splendor. The sea, where the sloop disturbed it, seemed all ablaze, so that by its light I could see the smallest articles on deck, and her wake was a path of fire.

Having for twenty-three days sailed west, "true as a hair," along the latitude of 10 degrees, 25 minutes south, charting his progress by dead reckoning and adjusting his course to allow for the upper-air disturbances he'd noticed, he decided on July 17 that his "reckoning was up."

Springing aloft, I saw from half-way up the mast cocoanut-trees standing out of the water ahead. I expected to see this; still, it thrilled me as an electric shock might have done. I slid down the mast, trembling under the strangest sensations; and not able to resist the impulse, I sat on deck and gave way to my emotions. To folks in a parlor on shore this may seem weak indeed, but I am telling the story of a voyage alone.

Slocum spent more than a month on the Cocos Islands. He admired the boat-building skills of the natives and was amused by the history of the atoll, which had been discovered and named in 1609 by the British East India Company's Captain William Keeling. In 1825 the islands were explored by John Clunies-Ross, a Scottish merchant seaman who brought his wife and mother-in-law to live there in paradise. But by the time he arrived, Eden had fallen. A wealthy man of uncertain morals, Alexander Hare, had chosen this place to install a seraglio of forty Malay women in a villa. When Clunies-Ross and his family turned up, in the company of eight Scottish sailors, he was dismayed to discover Hare and ordered his sailors to force him and his ladies across a narrow channel to a neighboring sand spit. Let Slocum tell the story:

From this time on Hare had a hard time of it. He and Ross did not get on well as neighbors. The islands were too small and too near for characters so widely different. Hare had "oceans of money," and might have lived well in London; but he had been governor of a wild colony in Borneo, and could not confine himself to the tame life that prosy civilization affords. And so he hung on to the atoll with his forty women, retreating little by little before Ross and his sturdy crew, till at last he found himself and his harem on the little island known to this day as Prison Island, where, like Bluebeard, he confined his wives in a castle. The channel between the islands was narrow, the water was not deep, and the eight Scotch sailors wore long boots.

On August 22, 1897, Slocum sailed westward, and on September 8 he arrived at Rodrigues Island, where he was mistaken—owing to the locals' misinterpretation of a sermon delivered by the resident missionary—for the Antichrist. One woman took refuge in her hut throughout his week-long visit, and the island's British governor could not persuade her that it was safe to leave. Servants of the crown—gloved hand in gnarled paw—had brought to this benighted and superstitious colony all the benefits of civilization, transforming it (in Slocum's neat phrase) into "a land of napkins and cut glass."

After a three-day sail from Rodrigues, the *Spray* next anchored at the island of Mauritius on September 19. Here, at the height of the best season, Slocum planned to wait out storms off the Cape of Good Hope. Once again his celebrity—perhaps abetted by charm—gained him the advantage of a thorough refitting of his ship. Little wonder he chose this island, described by Mark Twain (with tongue only partly in cheek) in *Following the Equator:* "From one citizen you gather the idea that Mauritius was made first, and then heaven." Slocum lingered here, enjoying the beaches and amusing the children, on one occasion taking seven girls and their chaperone for an overnight sail.* Around this time the *New York Times*—having misunderstood the *Spray's* intended port of call to be Yokohama—reported that "it would appear [Slocum] has given up his attempt to circumnavigate the globe." (The newspaper also added that he had been "attacked by pirates on the coast of Japan in early October of last year, but he managed to escape from them." Where do they get this stuff?) True, he was still eleven thousand miles from home, but having sailed with him this far, readers know such a distance to be for this seaman a mere pleasure cruise.

The bogus account from New York had been preceded on August 24

---

*Bruce Catton, writing in *American Heritage* (April 1959), marveled at Slocum's warm reception:

> He comes in out of the ocean and suddenly he knows everyone and everyone is glad to help him . . . Why? Because he had the knack of making people like him; but more, it would seem because the quest he was on was something that touched everyone . . . because he was not just performing a stunt—he was looking for something which the world thought it had lost, and because he looked for it so bravely and with such simplicity of mind the world discovered that it was still there, and he got it.

I'm not certain about "simplicity of mind," but Catton's profile got it, especially in an earlier paragraph, noting that "he had fun at it."

by the *New Bedford Evening Times,* which headlined its dispatch: "Probably Lost. *Family of Josiah* [sic] *Slocum Relinquish All Hope . . . Believed That
He Was Drowned During a Heavy Storm.*" Reporting that he had been
"intent on circumnavigating the globe in a cockle shell," the newspaper
declared that "Captain Slocum kept those at home posted as to his move-
ments and when weeks and then months passed without word from him
the fear became the belief that he was no more." This article rightly
excited Walter Teller's curiosity, and for his *Search for Captain Slocum* he
asked those of the Slocum children still alive whether they, or Hettie, had
in fact received letters from him during the voyage. The responses were
unsettling. If Hettie had got any letters, she probably burned them. Victor doesn't quote from or refer to letters in his biography. Jessie couldn't
remember. Garfield wrote that he had never had any kind of letter from
his father.

If these are facts, they're also distressing. Whether intended or merely
feckless, Slocum's silence seems perverse, worse than emotionally
stingy, especially in light of his generous correspondence with Joseph
Gilder, the admiring critic of *The Voyage of the "Liberdade"*—a long letter
located by its author as from the "*Spray* tied to a palm-tree at Keeling-
Cocos," and dated four days before the New Bedford newspaper suggested he was probably lost at sea.

At least the *Evening Times*'s "cockle shell" was said to have been circling
the "globe." That the earth was round rather than a flat square was a
matter of heated dispute in the region of Slocum's next port of call, Port
Natal (Durban), South Africa. Following a three-week passage from
Mauritius, weathering gales and an electric storm in the Mozambique
Channel, the *Spray* arrived on November 17, 1897, and remained there for
almost a month, until the beginning of the Cape of Good Hope's summer. During his stay in South Africa, Slocum, using his courtesy pass to
the local railroads, rode to Transvaal to visit President Johannes Paulus
Krüger, notoriously and pugnaciously a believer in a flat earth. The circumnavigator was cut dead by the glowering Boer after avowing that he
was sailing "around," not "in," the world. (The British, with imaginable
glee, lampooned this dispute in the Cape Town *Owl* by the medium of a
cartoon.)

In Durban, he also met Henry Morton Stanley, the journalist-explorer who had discovered the long-missing David Livingstone. Slocum sparred with the great man:

> I hauled close to the wind, to go slow, for Mr. Stanley was a nautical man once himself—on the Nyanza [River], I think,—and of course my desire was to appear in the best light before a man of his experience. He looked me over carefully, and said, "What an example of patience!" "Patience is all that is required," I ventured to reply. He then asked if my vessel had water-tight compartments. I explained that she was all water-tight and all compartment. "What if she should strike a rock?" he asked. "Compartments would not save her if she should hit the rocks lying along her course," said I; adding, "she must be kept away from the rocks."

Slocum kept the *Spray* clear, arriving at Cape Town in January after plowing through huge seas: she "ducked me under water three times for a Christmas box. I got wet and did not like it a bit." After delivering lectures that filled his larder,* Slocum was towed from the harbor on March 26, 1898, and pointed north-northwest for home, his final long leg, " 'off on her alone,' as they say in Australia." By April 11, with a steady southeasterly at his back, he had logged two thousand miles in eleven days on an extraordinary run to St. Helena, that "speck in the sea" so unloved by Napoleon. Slocum was as usual celebrated, and well paid to lecture. To mark the esteem in which he was held, an American friend of the British governor put a goat aboard the *Spray*. It's unknown why such a stern master as Slocum, who had resisted the temptation to sail with pets, permitted this passenger, but he explains what happened:

> [The goat giver] urged that the animal, besides being useful, would be as companionable as a dog. I soon found that my sailing-companion, this sort of dog with horns, had to be tied up entirely. The mistake I made was that I did not chain him to the mast instead of tying him with grass ropes less securely, and this I learned to my cost. Except for the first day, before the beast got his sea-legs on, I had no peace of mind. After that . . . this incarnation of evil threatened to devour everything from flying-jib to stern-davits. He was the worst pirate I met on the whole voyage. He began his depredations by eating my chart of the West Indies, in the cabin, one day, while I was about my work for'ard, thinking that the critter was securely tied on deck . . . Alas! there was not a rope in the sloop

---

*The *Cape Argus* reported that "the placard rarely exhibited in Cape Town, 'House Full,' had to be put up early in the evening . . . [There was] a large attendance of ladies [and] frequent applause rewarding [his] powers of description."

proof against that goat's awful teeth! . . . Next the goat devoured my straw hat . . . This last unkind stroke decided his fate.

It would be no outrage to reason or justice to imagine that this fate meant swimming home to St. Helena. But on April 27, 1898, the sometimes bellicose captain stopped at Ascension Island—a dependency known to the controlling British as a stone frigate, HMS *Ascension,* close to midway between Brazil and Africa—for the purpose of delivering mail from St. Helena and putting ashore the <u>damnable goat</u>, accepted <u>alive and well fed</u> by a local farmer after a suitable bribe. Whatever else transpired on the island, its citizens either neglected to report or didn't know that the United States had declared war on Spain two days earlier.

On May 8 the *Spray* crossed her track, occupying the same patch of ocean that she had occupied on October 2, 1895. Slocum notes the event: "I felt a contentment in knowing that the *Spray* had encircled the globe, and even as an adventure alone I was in no way discouraged as to its utility, and said to myself, 'Let what will happen, the voyage is now on record.' A period was made." What a lovely word, that "period": a moving full stop, let's say, an epic epoch marker, the end of something that can be read both on a chart and in a sentence. By going around toward the goal that was the start, Slocum was in the same place but a different person. Nothing quite compares to a circumnavigation, which might be why Oom Paul so fervently denied that there could be any such thing. Alone, only one person could do it first. To climb a mountain—the highest mountain—is to reach a pinnacle, but it's a linear round-trip; the return, despite its rigor, is an anticlimax. Been there . . .

Six days later the *Spray* intercepted the USS *Oregon,* "rapidly appearing on the horizon, like a citadel," which had steamed sixty-seven days and 12,000 miles from San Francisco to respond to the explosion aboard the *Maine* and join the fight against Spain. (That delay prodded the cutting of the Panama Canal.) The battleship signaled, "Are there any men-of-war about?," showing a Spanish flag to suggest whose these might be. Thus Slocum learned that he was about to sail into contested waters. He signaled back, to a warship a thousand times his size: "Let us keep together for mutual protection"—a joke lost on the *Oregon*'s captain, Charles E. Clark.

Now Slocum cruised through the Caribbean. Anyone who has been aboard a sailboat there in May and June will be jealous of the captain on this leg of his voyage, until remembering the goat's mischief and realizing that Slocum was sailing chartless through reef-strewn waters. He was unable to replace his charts in Grenada or Antigua, where he lectured and got papers from the U.S. consulate to enter his home territory. On June 5 he sailed toward Cape Hatteras but was delayed by calms in the horse latitudes, where the air was so still he read Robert Louis Stevenson by candlelight in the cockpit.

Off Long Island, on June 23, he sailed into "baffling squalls and fretful cobble-seas," followed by an electrical storm and tornado:

> In the Gulf Stream, thus late in June, hailstones were pelting the *Spray*, and lightning was pouring down from the clouds, not in flashes alone, but in almost continuous streams. By slants, however, day and night I worked the sloop in toward the coast, where, on the 25th of June, off Fire Island, she fell into the tornado which, an hour earlier, had swept over New York city with lightning that wrecked buildings and sent trees flying about in splinters; even ships at docks had parted their moorings and smashed into other ships, doing great damage. It was the climax storm of the voyage . . . I had seen one electric storm on the voyage, off the coast of Madagascar, but it was unlike this one. Here the lightning kept on longer, and thunderbolts fell in the sea all about. Up to this time I was bound for New York; but when all was over I rose, made sail, and hove the sloop round from starboard to port tack, to make for a quiet harbor to think the matter over . . .

As storms will, this one passed, having broken the jib stay at the *Spray's* masthead. She limped toward Point Judith on the Rhode Island shore, rounded Beavertail, and crept into the mined harbor of Newport. An hour after midnight on June 27, 1898—after forty-six thousand miles, three years, two months, and two days—his welcome home came in the form of a challenge from the guard ship *Dexter*. "There goes a craft!" the wary navy man shouted. "I threw up a light at once and heard the hail, '*Spray*, ahoy!' It was the voice of a friend, and I knew that a friend would not fire on the *Spray*."

It would be nice to know that Joshua Slocum was right about that, but he was not.

TWELVE

What Came After

Sailor or landsman, there is some kind of Cape Horn for all. Boys! Beware of it; prepare for it in time Graybeards! Thank God it is passed.
—HERMAN MELVILLE, *White-Jacket*

W HEN THE YACHTSMEN OF Newport awoke in their Gilded Age mansions on June 28, 1898, and heard the news of the day, it was not in celebration of Joshua Slocum. They were busy remembering the *Maine,* and when word began drifting around the harbor that an old man of fifty-four was claiming to have sailed his rickety tub around the world alone, many didn't believe him. This set a high standard for the incredulity and outright skepticism that would begrudge Slocum's achievement well past his death. The *Newport Herald* reported on its third page that a "staunch-looking little craft" had "swung lazily into the harbor" early the previous morning. Observing that the *Spray* "was a stranger in these waters," the brief notice said she had "attracted the attention of the early risers," whose desultory curiosity the vessel's "solitary occupant" appeared to ignore. Accustomed to being greeted by the hail of steamboat whistles and the huzzahs of dockside spectators at ports from Montevideo to Melbourne, from the Cocos to Cape Town, Slocum now found himself required to prove the veracity of his voyage by referring doubters to his visa-stamped yacht license. Finally believed, he was then rumored to be a diamond smuggler.

No wonder he got the hell and gone out of Newport. "On July 3, with a fair wind, she waltzed beautifully round the coast and up the Acushnet River to Fairhaven, where I secured her to the cedar spile driven in the bank to hold her when she was launched. I could bring her no nearer home."

A few days later, the *Fairhaven Star* welcomed him back under the

Leaving Fag End and Hettie

headline "AN INTREPID NAVIGATOR: *Capt. Slocum Arrives in Fairhaven from a Voyage Around the World.*"

> The captain came to Fairhaven for a little rest, to put the Spray back in condition, and renew his acquaintance with his many friends in Fairhaven. The hold of the Spray is filled with all kinds of curiosities gathered from various parts of the world. Judging from the books of newspaper clippings in the captain's possession, he is considered an excellent lecturer and has been honored by high officials everywhere. He has a stereopticon and 300 excellent slides, which he uses to illustrate his lectures.
>
> Captain Slocum said he intends to remain around here a few days and will then go cruising with his wife and son. He intends to go to London before long.
>
> Among the mementos brought home by Captain Slocum is a big bamboo stick given him by the widow of Robert Louis Stevenson. The bamboo was grown by the novelist.

He knew what he had done: "To find one's way to lands already discovered is a good thing, and the *Spray* made the discovery that even the worst sea is not so terrible to a well-appointed ship. No king, no country, no treasury at all, was taxed for the voyage of the *Spray,* and she accomplished all that she undertook to do." He was proud that the *Spray* was tight, without leaks, and he insisted from the beginning—again faced with skeptics—that she had steered herself across great expanses of ocean. As to his health and frame of mind, he also spoke plainly and pridefully: "Was the crew well? Was I not? . . . As for aging, why, the dial of my life was turned back till my friends all said, 'Slocum is young again.' "

Who were these friends, and where? Despite Slocum's cavalier suggestion that he would go cruising with his wife, Hettie had not welcomed her husband home. Mabel Wagnalls, who had added to Slocum's library before he sailed in 1895, and who had promised that he would return, traveled to Newport from New York to greet him. Soon, Victor (now twenty-six) and Garfield (fifteen) visited their father in Fairhaven, and after only a few days at home he was already edgy and restless. The war with Spain had not only stolen his headlines, but also stirred his emotions. William Randolph Hearst would have been proud. So wrapped in bunting was the captain, so spoiling for a fight, that the day before Independence Day he fired off a rant of a letter to the *New Bedford*

Evening Standard, shouting hysterical answers with cartoonish bellicosity to many questions that he had not been asked:

> I want to give your people an earache . . . I burn to be of use now of all times. I spent the best of my life in the Philippine islands, China and Japan, but there is some life still in the old man . . . I am not fanatically suffering for a fight, but I am longing to be useful. Does Mr. McKinley want pilots for the Philippines and Guam? If more fighting men were wanted I would be nothing loth . . . But my heart is too full to write. I only blurr the paper. America is all right! . . . I'll fight for it! But it is peace we want, not war! And peace we're going to have, if we have to lick all creation to get it!

Making allowances for Slocum's war fever, this letter announces a distressing exaggeration of his temperamental weaknesses: impulsiveness and hair-trigger belligerence, especially when overexcited by sentimentality. The rigor and discipline and unwavering concentration of reason required by his circumnavigation was now relaxed, and the consequences must have been bewildering to his friends, his family, and himself. He had to have been shocked by the waves of indifference that swamped news of his achievement. He must have been set adrift, without chart or compass, by the *end* of this enterprise. He had, literally, no place to go from here. Crossing his track near the equator had put a period to his sentence, and bringing the *Spray* home to her launching place had redeemed the caretaking he believed had been entrusted to him. He was once again an exhausted man living in the oppressive quarters of a small boat moored to a stake near Poverty Point.

A few churlish critics—with voices loud enough to be heard—sneered at him for using up his fifteen minutes before he actually earned them. Should he not have anticipated skepticism and even hostility? Naysayers accused him of being a show-off or a misanthropic hermit or both. Slocum was a lousy family man. The *Spray* was a tub, clearly incapable of self-steering as well as—to the lunatic fringe of doubters—impossible to keep afloat and in danger of capsizing at any moment, even in Fairhaven harbor. (The specifics of these harangues are addressed later in this chapter.)

How could he have reckoned on such a welcome home? The war was a joker in the deck, but what might he himself have done differently? He was emotionally and physiologically exhausted in the aftermath of three years of exertion and focused purpose. Professional athletes often break down in tears at the end of sixty minutes of play. Should Slocum have guarded against this, perhaps suppressing his ambition in the name of prudence?

A genius at navigation, dead reckoning, calculating lunar tables, and surviving tempests, he was frequently lost on land. Slocum was a slipshod housekeeper below the *Spray*'s deck, and with her cargo of curios—coral, for instance, and giant tridacna conch shells scavenged in the Cocos—she gave off ripe whiffs often associated with low tides. He suffered from arthritic hands and fingers and he had liver spots on his skin, which had been insulted by the sun for over forty years. He was missing some teeth. After all his time alone at sea he had grown careless about his appearance, sometimes leaving his trousers unbuttoned, perhaps heeding nature's calls without Victorian regard for the proprieties.*

At the same time, one does well to remember among whom he had recently and successfully socialized and prospered as a public performer. And it was with an eye to rescuing his fortunes that he turned almost at once to the lecture hall. Within days of arriving at Fairhaven, Slocum gave a performance at the New Bedford city hall. Garfield operated the lantern slide projector while Victor presided over the box office, "with satisfying results," as he remembered. The hall was "jammed to the carlins; the old salts . . . occupying the front seats long before the appointed time." By now the captain was a bravura spellbinder. It's easy to read how well he spun a yarn, and even black-and-white photos—failing to reveal the vivid blue of his eyes—convey ferocious vision and command. It would be fascinating to hear his voice, conditioned as it was with the idioms and inflections of ports around the world, with the sailor's rich idiom close to the lips. Moreover, the podium was a perfect place from which to show off his humility. He liked to make fun of his baldness, remarking that the winds in the Strait of Magellan were strong enough to blow the hair off a dog's

---

*But in a letter from this period, to his editor, Slocum prudishly noted the "indecency" of Roman bath steam rooms popular in New York, adding that "I could never make up my mind to expose my person to the gaze of even my own class."

back, and—rubbing his pate—had also carried away his hat. Audiences enjoyed listening to him, and no wonder.

He landed a few years too late on the lecture circuit to harvest the bonanza fees that had enriched the likes of Mark Twain, Buffalo Bill, Oscar Wilde, and Charles Dickens back in the heyday.* The invitations he'd anticipated to lecture in London were not forthcoming, but during the late summer of 1898, he and Hettie rented a room in New York City, and at the end of October he spoke to a large audience at Carnegie Hall about his ambition—reported as far afield as the Atchison, Kansas *Daily Globe*—to find financing for a large "college ship" that would carry as many as three hundred students for a voyage of two years around the world, "the time to be spent in steady, practical work and the desirable recreation that visits to Oceania and the Orient would supply." Slocum's hope to find a wholesome use for sailing vessels and what was left of their crews, to instruct "young people in the science of nautical astronomy" and biology, was forward-looking. Moreover, to his Carnegie Hall audience he made much of his insistence that women be included among the students, that indeed he "wouldn't have anything to do with the scheme . . . if women could not be included in its benefits."

Although his narratives of adventures aboard the *Liberdade* and the *Destroyer* were commercial failures, Slocum hoped before he left Fairhaven aboard the *Spray* in 1895 that his financial security would be redeemed by what he wrote about his exploit. When a reporter in

---

*Once again, the current was running hard against Slocum. The author of *Eccentricities of Genius: Memories of Famous Men and Women of the Platform and Stage* (1900), Major James Burton Pond, heard Slocum lecture several times, and he gives him a glowing review:

> Captain Slocum is able to write and describe the incidents of the entire voyage and his wonderful experiences in a manner so graphic and simple that it absolutely charms and fascinates his hearers as few ever did or ever could do . . . It is wonderful to listen to the descriptions of some of his hairbreadth escapes and to hear him answer, as quick as a flash, questions of every conceivable sort put to him by expert seafaring auditors. I have listened for hours to these seeming tournaments in navigators' skill, and never yet did the captain hesitate for an instant for a reply that went straight to the mark like a bullet.
>
> Had [his voyage] occurred twenty years ago, it would have meant a fortune for Captain Slocum, and a stimulant for the lyceum such as it is impossible to secure under present conditions. "Because why?" you ask.

Responding to his own question, Pond—himself briefly Slocum's lecture agent—explains that by 1900 the market was oversaturated by lecture agents' clients.

Boston asked him why he was doing this, he immediately answered, "to make money." Even so, that—*pace* Samuel Johnson's "no man but a blockhead ever wrote, except for money"—was not the sole motive for his self-exile to the *Spray's* cabin to compose *Sailing Alone Around the World*. Having begun writing in East Boston, where he once again lodged on the generosity of Hettie's sister, he worked steadily. Soon swept away by his voyage, and referring to the ships' logs he had kept throughout his career, he felt a responsibility to what he realized was a great story.

During his circumnavigation he had corresponded with Richard Watson Gilder, an editor of *Century Illustrated Magazine* who had wired Slocum about writing an article. "I have very decided literary tastes," Slocum had replied, "and could enter into such parts as I am able to do with a great deal of energy."

Slocum was always diffident about early drafts of his work, realizing that he was an uncertain master of spelling and syntax, and believing—as any sane writer would—that he was capable of failures of clarity and proportion. He knew he needed sympathetic and even obtrusive editing, and he not only received it, but was grateful for it. Anyone who has examined the extensive documentation of his editorial exchanges—in papers collected at the New York Public Library's Century Collection, or among the Walter Teller Collection in New Bedford—will realize that his published prose is very much in his own voice. The editorial back-and-forth between writer and editors (notably Clarence Clough Buel at the *Century*) will interest those who practice such collaboration, as it clearly reveals the process: violent swings from anxiety to ambition on the part of the writer, and curiosity tempered by interrogation and skepticism on the part of an editor wishing to check facts and resolve inconsistencies, as well as to break down his author's reticence without embarrassing either him or the publisher. After the final changes had been made, Slocum wrote Buel that while "I do not pose as a professional writer I should not leave a libel on the American Shipmaster," following that sentiment with a condensed account of the entire course of any writer's temperamental swings: "I was considerably interested in the story at the time of telling it and didn't see the enormous sunken ledges that I see now."

The first installment of *Sailing Alone Around the World* appeared in 1899 in the September issue of *Century Illustrated Magazine*, continuing monthly through the following March. The whole was published by the Century Company in April 1900, wonderfully illustrated by George Varian and Thomas Fogarty, whose sketches are used in many of the editions of Slocum's masterwork still in print.*

During the early summer of 1899, Slocum corrected his typescript and galleys here and there along the New England coast, but beginning in July he was using the return address of Cottage City, in the town of Oak Bluffs on Martha's Vineyard. As early as 1897, members of Slocum's Massachusetts family had begun renting modest cottages on the island. Hettie enjoyed being there—how could she not?—and her husband was said by one kinswoman to have been especially impressed by what he found in one of the local graveyards: the names of many shipmasters who had died very old. As far back as his composition of The Voyage of the "Destroyer," Slocum had spoken with perhaps dutiful wistfulness of returning to his earliest experiences as a farmer: "I began to think of the little farm, which so many years ago I promised myself. I say now, I could almost hear the potatoes growing—but not quite."

Now, with the publication of his book, the cultivation of some piece of land was a lively possibility. Even before the first installment appeared he had written to C. C. Buel thanking him for his editorial help: "Best of all, I see my ship coming in under full sail freighted to the load-line." (His figures of speech were not yet, nor would they ever be, clustered around "plows," "silos" or "bushels.")† Following the appearance of the third installment in November 1899, he wrote Buel again: "The Century did well by me . . . No one knows how much I have been paid. When they ask me I say 'double the amount agreed upon'—which is so. They say 'how much is that?'—I say enough to buy me a house . . . All the old women will be sending in sea stories and be looking for [grand]

---

*Walter Teller reports that Century and its successor companies sold 27,700 copies in seventeen printings, and it was in print until 1948. Since 1954, Sheridan House has been an enthusiastic and successful publisher of books by and about Slocum. Sailing Alone Around the World has sold well over 50,000 copies in various editions, and has been translated into a great many languages.

†In 1901, during Slocum's journey to Buffalo, New York, for the Pan-American Exposition, a wiseacre newsman interviewed him somewhere upstate: "NAVIGATOR OF THE SPRAY WEIGHS ANCHOR AND SETS OFF DOWN THE RAGING ERIE CANAL," reads the headline of the undated clip. After the subhead "Hand Which Held the Tiller Is Soon to Hold the Plow," the article continues: "The horse that furnished the motive power to run the sloop down the canal will furnish the power to run a plow on the captain's farm in Martha's Vineyard. The hand that steered the tiller will steer the plow; the voice that refused to allow a woman to accompany him across the Atlantic will say 'gee-up' to the horse when it comes plowin' time." Ah, the perks of celebrity!

houses . . . when they hear of my amazing success." What Slocum in fact bought and named "Fag End" was a Martha's Vineyard farm—later expanded to fifty acres—at West Tisbury.

Even before the book was published, an unbylined writer for the *New York Times* began taking potshots at Slocum's account of his extended runs in the Pacific during which the *Spray* was said to be self-steered. The columnist complained that it was "a sore trial to the temper—and a somewhat severe trial to the credulity—to all who have or pretend a knowledge of matters nautical" that Slocum had not shown proof that "his boat would keep on her course all night" while he read, cooked, or slept below. "The tale is painfully hard to believe," he wrote on November 7, 1899. "We won't say that the Captain has been treating the truth with irreverence." In other words, since the columnist knew this couldn't possibly be true, well, it wasn't.

Livid, Slocum wrote to Buel from New York's United States Hotel: "The Times joker I can stow any time in my waistcoat pocket," and his reply was published by the *Times* on November 11:

> I am honored by a criticism from an old salt . . . It is possible that things occurred on the voyage of the *Spray* inexplicable to some mariners, even of vast experience, and I can only regret not having met them before the articles . . . were written so that I might have taken them on a sail in the *Spray* to demonstrate her prowess. As the matter stands, it is now out of my power to further elucidate . . .
>
> This unpretentious sloop, built by one pair of hands, after circumnavigating the globe, is sound and snug and tight. She does not leak a drop. This would be called a great story by some; nevertheless it is a hard fact.
>
> The story of the voyage is constructed on the same seaworthy lines; that is, it remains waterproof which your navigating officer will discover, I trust, if only he exercise to the end that patience necessary on a voyage around the world.

The newspaper churl was unpersuaded, replying that he was "ready to believe almost anything about a ship or a boat, but belief and readiness to believe are not quite equivalent, and unfortunately Capt. Slocum is not in a demonstrative or explanatory mood."

How—if the *Spray* had not been self-steered, or rigged by her builder to stay on course in steady winds—was Slocum imagined to have crossed oceans? It is pretty well established that boats do not anchor every night midocean. Given the number of days between dated visa stamps in countries far apart, the *Spray* had to have been constantly under way for months at a time. Was the pilot of the *Pinta* stowed away? Did the goat do tricks at the helm as well as devour the charts? If his sloop had *not* been rigged to self-steer, Joshua Slocum did not sail alone around the world.

To give the skeptic his due, the *Spray*'s seaworthiness has never been a settled matter. Readers have heard the opinion of Robert Perry as to her "weird" shape, and though many naval architects and experienced sailors have praised her, a great many others have slandered a design thought to be awkward, even deadly. *In the Wake of the "Spray,"* a labor of love by Kenneth E. Slack, an Australian chemist who devoted years to analyzing disputes about her design and suitability as a blue-water cruiser, doesn't settle arguments over Slocum's craft but does remind readers that almost a thousand replicas of the *Spray* have been built, by professionals and amateurs, of wood, steel, aluminum, fiberglass, and Ferro-cement. Some have been slavish replications and others rough modifications, expressions of her spirit or attempts to copy her lines exactly. (That an exact calculation of those lines has never been agreed upon helped feed the debate.) Some of these inspirations crossed oceans; some sank or capsized.

The vehemence of the dispute, already raging soon after the publication of *Sailing Alone Around the World,* has been its most distinguishing characteristic. The enthusiasts' team was led by Cipriano Andrade, a naval architect who in June 1909 published in *Rudder* magazine a survey of the *Spray*'s lines, dimensions, sail plan, displacement, and probable response to the variety of extreme conditions Slocum experienced during his voyage. He took the figures by which he calculated from a half-model rather than from the hull herself, leading extreme skeptics to discard his considerations as having no practical value. Andrade concluded, "the curve of stability shows that *Spray* was theoretically uncapsizable," and that her theoretical hull speed was an impressive eight knots. (She made, for a known fact, noon-to-noon runs exceeding an average speed of eight knots, though during most of them she got a lift from one current or another, such as the Gulf Stream.) As to self-steering, Andrade—"after a thorough analysis of the *Spray*'s lines"—found her to have "a theoretically perfect balance. Her balance is marvelous—almost uncanny."* He con-

---

*He is adamant: "I attacked her with proportional dividers, planimeter, rota-meter, Simpson's rule, Froude's coefficients, Dixon Kemp's formulae, series, curves, differentials . . ." All these, whatever they might be, are good enough for me.

cluded his analysis "with a feeling of profound admiration and respect. She is not only an able boat, but a beautiful boat; using the term 'beautiful' as defined by Charles Elliot Norton, 'that form most perfectly adapted to perform its allotted work.' "

The most unyielding of the *Spray*'s, and Slocum's, detractors was Howard I. Chapelle, curator of maritime history at the Smithsonian Institution. In a letter to Donald Holm for the latter's book about famous circumnavigators, he took a double-bitt ax to both captain and boat:

> Slocum's letters are like those of a 4th grader and rather backward at that. He was 60 percent fine seaman, 10 percent liar, and 30 percent showman, I would say. Had a lot of guts. He was going nowhere in no hurry so I suppose he sailed as the boat wanted to go . . . Poor Andrade was victimized by the old fraud [one Charles Mower, who had submitted approximate lines to Andrade] . . . Now we have no reliable plans as a basis for analysis. But the whole story of the wonderful abilities of Spray is now highly questionable.

For the purposes of this account, it's enough to refer readers to *Sailing Alone Around the World*'s appendix, subtitled "Lines and Sail-plan of the *Spray*," and to note that the most hotly debated aspect of her design was her "stiffness," the quality of resisting heel—or tilt—with winds blowing more or less at right angles to her sails. It is agreed that her great beam afforded considerable initial stability. What is argued is what might happen when that was overcome: Would she heel or capsize?* Because this is only an academic question—the *Spray* never capsized, unless you choose to believe that a capsize in 1908 killed her master—let's let the brave little boat be.

---

*Writing in *Rudder* magazine many years after Andrade's encomium to the *Spray*, another naval architect took a contrary view. Focusing principally on her beamy similarity to catboats and racing scows, designed of course for inland waters, John G. Hanna was uncompromising in his dismay:

> Since the Suicide Squad has been for many years building exact copies of *Spray* and will continue doing so for many years more unless restrained, perhaps I can save a life or two by explaining, as simply as possible, the basic reason . . . why *Spray* is the worst possible boat for anyone, and especially anyone lacking the experience and resourcefulness of Slocum, to take off soundings . . . Everyone who has handled [catboats] knows that, though they are extremely stiff initially, if they are ever heeled beyond a critical point, they flop right over as inevitably as a soup plate, which they resemble . . . A big lurching cross sea that would scarcely disturb a properly designed hull can—especially if it coincides, as it often does, with an extra-savage puff of a squall—flip over a *Spray* hull just as you would a poker chip.

But the *New York Times* was not finished deriding Slocum's claims in his *Century Illustrated Magazine* serial. He had mentioned his visit to "Robinson Crusoe's" cave at Juan Fernández as his first stop in the Pacific. A letter to the newspaper's editor on November 18, 1899, asked whether "it could be possible that the cultured editor of The Century, as well as the traveled author, Capt. Slocum, have never read Crusoe, which repeatedly states the scene of the story is laid on the Island of Tobago, thirty miles west of Trinidad, in the West Indies, and where the native residents also point out the very cave of Master Robinson?" Poor Slocum! Juan Fernández boasted (truthfully) of being the site of Alexander Selkirk's cave; this corporeal Alexander Selkirk inspired Daniel Defoe to write a tale that he—in company with many novelists—did not wish to have diminished as a mere rewrite of the day's news. Thus he insisted that *his* castaway story was set in an entirely different ocean than Selkirk's. Slocum shot back, his letter published November 28:

> My esteemed critic in your Saturday Review clearly misunderstands my purpose in rehearsing the experiences of a voyage around the world. Many things in this age must necessarily go untouched. It is true that in my own poor narrative I had quite overlooked the hole in the ground on the Island of Tobago. I visited that spot when a lad on my first voyage to the West Indies. It was very disappointing. The cave referred to in my narrative was found cozy and comfortable.
>
> No one needs to be told that Defoe founded *Robinson Crusoe* on the self-imposed exile of Alexander Selkirk on the Island of Juan Fernandez. Nothing is more natural than the giving of his hero's name to the lookout, bay, and cave that bear it. In speaking of Crusoe's Cave, I but adopted the popular nomenclature, feeling under no obligation to argue for or against its literal correctness.
>
> When your various editors and correspondents have done with me, Sir, it is evident that I shall stand exposed as a sailing master who knows nothing of navigation and a traveler wholly ignorant of the world.

An admirer in Slocum's later years, Thomas Fleming Day, noted that he felt this derision keenly and spoke of it often. Of course he did. Astronauts might laugh at those who are convinced that the moon landing was a contrivance of Walter Cronkite and staged in a CBS studio, but the doubt of those who refuse to believe or honor any achievement they cannot imagine having accomplished themselves provokes a chill, even a repulsion. Much of the criticism of Slocum's dares and successes bears an unbecoming meanness, and if he didn't take it personally himself, his friends certainly did.

— And there were new friends and admirers aplenty. Most reviewers of *Sailing Alone Around the World* were ecstatic. In England, Arthur Ransome, the celebrated children's book writer, declared that "boys who do not like this book ought to be drowned at once," even as Sir Edwin Arnold, a journalist and poet, went rather too far: "I do not hesitate to call it the most extraordinary book ever published." Slocum was hardly uninterested in his critical reception, keeping track as well as clipping for his scrapbook. He was shrewd enough to realize that a preface submitted by Mabel Wagnalls was so adoring that it would do him more harm than good, and conspired with Century to keep it out of the book.

Lecture invitations spiked for a time. At the end of 1900, Slocum was one of eight speakers in New York's Aldine Club at a notably excessive dinner in honor of Mark Twain, which many of New York's luminaries attended—including Doubledays, Putnams, and Scribners from the publishing world. The *New York Times* reported on December 15 that Mr. Clemens

> was framed in by a pilothouse, from the corners of which were suspended colored lights and the cornice of which bore the name of Alonzo Child, the name of one of the steamboats which Mr. Clemens used to pilot on the Mississippi River. The walls were festooned with hanging moss, and here and there were suspended oranges, gourds, and other Southern growths, while catfish were sailing about in aquariums.

This same spirit of postwar extravaganza inspired the Pan-American Exposition, which ran from May to November 1901. Slocum traveled up the Hudson River, with Hettie and Garfield aboard, towing the *Spray* with a small motorized lifeboat steered by his son. They stowed her masts on deck at Troy and followed the Erie Canal to the 350-acre fairgrounds in Buffalo, tying up on a lake named Gala Water. Slocum had hoped in vain to be invited to the previous year's Paris Exposition Universelle, which celebrated the new century no more bumptiously than Buffalo's display of invention, empire, and enterprise. World fairs have earned a reputation for price-gouging their visitors, but Buffalo set new standards, overcharging for trolley rides to the site, permits to take snapshots, and tickets for entrance to the exhibits and sideshows, among which the *Spray* was included along with daily faux-bullfights at the Mexico pavilion and "Chiquita the Doll Lady" and a prophetic (and hilariously fanciful) "Trip to the Moon" attraction. Indian tribes whooped, Buffalo Bill strutted, John Philip Sousa played, wild animals behaved tamely, Eskimos in front of fake igloos wore actual fur.

The souvenir guide encouraged tourists to climb aboard the *Spray* and "shake hands with the gallant captain, a man of stout heart and steady nerve, a veteran of the salt seas, and a man of mighty soul and character." Slocum answered questions—let's hope that they weren't about the location of Robinson Crusoe's cave or how he endured steering 46,000 miles without rest—and sold his books, leftover copies of *The Voyage of the "Liberdade"* for a dollar (twenty dollars in today's money) and *Sailing Alone Around the World* for twice that sum. For two bits he sold a souvenir booklet, a compendium of blurbs extolling both him and his voyage, to which he attached a small square of the very sail blown out the night he negotiated the Milky Way back into the Strait of Magellan. He told about Moorish pirates and carpet tacks. He was a huckster, and he knew it. When he left the sideshow, long after Hettie and Garfield had gone home by railroad, he told a reporter, "I got two-thirds of the money owed me by the Exposition Company. I met fine people, was treated well, and considering everything, am satisfied."*

So he bought Fag End, which he sometimes jokingly called Rudder Ranch, and declared himself ready to settle in with Hettie and start farming. But Garfield knew otherwise. He wrote that his father—who "was a mystery to me and will be to my dying day"—and Hettie "did not pull on the same rope. Hettie was cool to me. Father acted as though he wanted to be left alone." Slocum sat for a long profile written by Clifton Johnson for *Outing* magazine (October 1902) that featured photographs of the captain in his garden—appearing most uncomfortable—turning soil with a hoe. He chose hops as a crop, but nothing much came of it. He quarreled with his brother Ornan, who ran a shoe store on the island. In notes for his profile among Walter Teller's papers, Johnson observed privately that Slocum "has a temper and explodes like a firecracker when affronted." He also observed his charm, his relish at acting out incidents, his "knowing" winks and head wags and "keen" eyes, his "lithe" energy.

---

*Among the fine people who boarded the *Spray* was President William McKinley, later assassinated on the fairgrounds by an anarchist.

Grace Murray Brown, who saw much of Slocum at this time, wrote Teller that to Hettie the captain was always "kind and courtly." In July 1952 Teller interviewed Henrietta, then Mrs. Ulysses E. Mayhew, who'd been widowed again in 1939 by the death of her second husband, a prominent Martha's Vineyard merchant. Teller described in his notes "fine features, with an aristocratic look about her." She was known to have thrown many letters and papers "into the stove," and her memory was imperfect—she was ninety when she died later that year—but she confided that she called her first husband " 'Josh,' or 'Captain' if I thought he needed the honor," and that he "spoke his mind, that it did not hurt his feelings to let you know what he was thinking."

Among his fellow islanders he was naturally controversial. Grace Murray Brown noticed, from the exquisitely perceptive perspective of a teenager, "how some found him affable and friendly while others saw him as eccentric . . . It is the little man who hugs the shore who would not render homage even to the Almighty if he were an off-islander." And in fact Slocum *was* an off-islander, so often away from home aboard the *Spray* that the *Vineyard Gazette* referred to his arrivals in their comings-and-goings pages as "visits." Garfield later wrote, "I could feel a storm coming up between them," that he had heard "hush-hush talk" from his sister, Jessie, that their father and stepmother "had separated."

How "hush-hush" could such a circumstance be? Slocum was desperately restless. He'd written to the Century Company that he meant to take the *Spray* on a voyage of exploration to Iceland, or perhaps to sell her in order to finance his purchase of a submarine. He wrote the Smithsonian Institution in February 1901 requesting that if and when a "flying ship" were launched, "I could have a second mates position on it to soar." He had to an acute degree what Baudelaire termed in "Crowds" a hatred of home. When snow flew in New England, he regarded the *Spray* as his "winter overcoat"; unable to fly above or dive below the sea, and perhaps unenthusiastic about Iceland's climate, he took off for the Caribbean.

From 1903 until 1908, Slocum lived mostly aboard the *Spray,* sailing south in the winters. He cruised summers along the New England coast as far east as Maine, but mostly near Martha's Vineyard. He was particularly hospitable to youngsters who showed an interest in sailboats. Charlotte Richmond wrote to Teller that as an adolescent in Marion she had many times rowed out to the *Spray*'s anchorage at her mother's request, bringing food supplies. "In time I grew to regard him almost as a good uncle, a teller of wonderful tales" and a generous gift giver.

A young gentleman-sailor, H. S. Smith, who would later write a remembrance of Slocum, gave Teller his impression of boarding the sloop with friends in New Bedford during this period:

> Captain Slocum struck us all as looking like the typical beachcomber. He wore a battered old felt hat—originally black but bleached out irregularly from sun and rain—a collarless shirt open at the neck, a vest, unbuttoned trousers that would disgrace a clam-digger . . . He seemed in perfectly good spirits and when he spoke his language was that of a cultured gentleman . . .
>
> *Spray* was dirty. Not just a little dirty but very dirty. Again, that is nothing against her. All vessels lying alongside a wharf get dirty . . . But my companions . . . all remarked "I would hate to sail that old trap across Long Island Sound if a stiff wind was blowing." . . . Slocum, at the time we saw him, was much run down physically, and perhaps mentally. He was exceedingly lazy and indifferent to his surroundings.

At the beginning of April 1906, having spent the winter in the Caribbean islands, Slocum sailed from Grand Cayman to Key West and Beaufort, North Carolina, and on Wednesday, May 23, he tied the *Spray* to the dock of the Riverton (New Jersey) Yacht Club, directly across the Delaware River from Philadelphia. He had been invited to give a talk at the club the following evening; on Friday he invited the curious to come aboard. Among his many visitors was Elsie Wright, a twelve-year-old, who had stopped by after school with a young male friend. At the end of the day, done with hosting, Slocum crossed the river to Philadelphia, where he ate dinner at the home of Leslie W. Miller, a friend from Martha's Vineyard and the principal of the School of Industrial Art, who a few years earlier had sat for a portrait by Thomas Eakins. After dinner Slocum asked young Percy Chase Miller to play the piano, which he did. Slocum seemed relaxed. At nine that night he returned to Riverton and was arrested as he descended from a trolley, charged with raping Elsie Wright. The following morning, after a hearing before a town recorder, he was committed to the county jail without bail.

The story of his arrest appeared immediately in newspapers in Boston and New York, and in the weekly *Riverton New Era*, datelined May 26 and headlined "CAPT. SLOCUM IN TROUBLE: *Accused of Maltreating a Girl on His*

Famous Yacht, the 'Spray.' " It told a woeful story, beginning with a reminder that Slocum, "formerly a commander of clippers," had "been in trouble several times for alleged ill-treatment of his crews" and "has for several years . . . been living off the glory and the story of sailing alone around the world." Then the reporter got down to business:

> When Elsie got home [Friday afternoon] she told her parents [Mr. and Mrs. Charles D. Wright] and they called in Dr. C. S. Mills, who said she was not much injured, but was suffering from shock. Capt. Slocum . . . was arrested on his return [from Philadelphia] last night as he stepped off a trolley car. Captain Slocum asked that nothing should be said about his arrest. He said tonight in his defense that he was suffering from a mental aberration.

Other newspapers mocked Slocum's feeble explanation for whatever trespass he might have committed. He was quoted by officers of the court as having referred to a "mental lapse" that might have been caused by an old concussion he suffered in Australia when he'd been hit in the head by a weighted heaving line thrown from a wharf. He was portrayed by a local newspaper as being "indignant at his arrest" and of having "ridiculed the charge against him and when being taken to the jail said he would be vindicated." The *Riverton New Era* the following week observed that Slocum "was a good hand at spinning a yarn."

Six days after Slocum's arrest, bail was set at $1,000, which he could not pay, so he spent forty-two days in the Mt. Holly jail. Walter Teller, who thoroughly researched this episode, suggests decorously that "the aging traveler would seem to have been at a disadvantage in obtaining full consideration of the law." Who wants to unravel all the strands of this frayed and tangled line? Whatever happened during Elsie Wright's minutes aboard the tight quarters of the *Spray*, it surely wasn't rape, as her physician and parents agreed. Indeed, Charles Wright wrote a letter to the *Riverton New Era*, which he asked the editor to publish, saying that the newspaper's previous article had exaggerated the facts and that he and his wife were

> greatly relieved to learn by questioning the child, also by Dr. C. S. Mills' examination, that there was no attempt at rape for the child is not physically injured although greatly agitated by the indecent action and exposure of the person on the part of this creature now posing in the limelight of cheap notoriety. We regret exceedingly the necessity of publicity for

the child's sake but feel assured that the exposure of such a fiend will be regarded as a service rendered the public.

This letter—with its confounding emphasis on "exposure," not to mention its confusion about what "limelight" can be enjoyed in a jail cell—comes from the heart. Evidently no one asked aloud the question: What happened? Clearly, *something* did that upset Elsie Wright extremely. Whether Slocum meant for it to happen, or didn't even realize that it had, we will never know. If he ever gave a running account of exactly what occurred during their encounter, we don't have it. But one would hope—despite newspaper and courthouse decorums—that we could at least know what his accusers *believe* happened. Did he expose himself, or did Elsie otherwise see his penis? Was his fly undone, intentionally or carelessly? Did he say something obscene to her? Did she misinterpret as obscene or malignant some innocent thing he'd said? Did he touch her—on the hand, on the knee—indecently or glancingly? Anyone will remember from childhood the sometimes bewildering experience of being in the close company of old people. Children are often repelled by adoring grandparents, let alone strangers. I can imagine a young girl recoiling from a grizzled, bald, and bewhiskered old man with wrinkles, liver spots, an arthritic claw of a hand, bad breath, a few missing teeth. An unwelcome kiss on the cheek could have a potent effect on a child, who might well have been aboard the *Spray* only because she had been urged by her parents to visit. Whatever happened was done in daylight on deck or below in the cabin of a cramped little boat to which all comers had been welcomed. We don't know where Elsie's companion was during the incident, or what he witnessed or believed he had, or even whether he testified or was asked to.

Slocum chose to have his case settled by a judge, without a jury, and pleaded New Jersey's equivalent of nolo contendere. The Wrights' representative in court asked Judge Joseph H. Gaskill for leniency, believing that Slocum "has no recollection of the crime," which by now was said to be merely a "great indiscretion." The judge, declaring that he was "very sorry to be obliged to administer reproof to a man of your experience and years" and that there had been "no attempt made to injure the person of the girl," freed Slocum, barring him from ever again visiting Riverton "either by rail or water."

In the aftermath, Grace Murray Brown assured Walter Teller that "we who knew the Captain had found him affectionate to a degree with young things just as I know my own dad was. We never heard of any dalliance with the fair sex." But she also remembered hearing hushed talk from family members in Boston about her cousin, and recalled the "yellow journalism matter" as something that was "purported to have happened to the Roosevelt boys on board the Spray."

Grace had conflated two proximate events. Joshua Slocum sailed the *Spray* directly from his Riverton banishment to Oyster Bay, Long Island, more specifically to Theodore Roosevelt's Sagamore Hill, the summerhouse of the president of the United States and his family. Honest to goodness, who could make up such a life? Slocum was carrying rare orchids from the West Indies when he put into Riverton. All but one had died while he was in jail, and this he wanted to give to President Roosevelt. When he sailed into Oyster Bay, he intended merely to send the orchid ashore by messenger, with a note attached. In the event, waiting for the *Spray* dockside was Archibald Roosevelt, the president's fifth child and a sailing enthusiast who had recognized Slocum's sloop entering the harbor. Archie shook Slocum's hand and invited him to Sagamore Hill to meet his father and join the family for dinner, an invitation that the twelve-year-old was (I assume) authorized to extend. The meeting must have gone well, because on August 6, 1906, exactly a month after Slocum sailed from Riverton, President Roosevelt wrote to Henry Cabot Lodge that "Archie is off for a week's cruise with Captain Joshua Slocum—that man who takes his little boat, without any crew but himself, all around the world."

In an age of registered sex offenders, this beggars belief. But even a century ago, how could it have come to pass? If Roosevelt hadn't been aware when it happened that Slocum had been charged with rape, he must have known by the time he sent his son on a cruise alone with the captain. (The story had appeared in many newspapers, including those in New York, Philadelphia, and Henry Cabot Lodge's hometown of Boston.) Security could not have been a matter of indifference to a president who took office owing to the assassination of William McKinley. So what motivated him to entrust his son to him? I rule out indifference, and doubt bravado. He must have believed—for whatever reason—that Slocum had not done what he had been charged with doing.

The cruise, to Newport, was a success, and boy and man became friends during their five days and nights together. Slocum taught him to navigate, and told a New Bedford newspaper that "Archie is one of the cleverest boys I have ever known . . . I like him because he always does what I tell him to . . . He knows how to set the sails at their proper balance and to lash the helm so that it skims along by itself. That is a trick which excites admiration wherever I go, and which few sailors understand. Archie learned the trick . . ."

 Archie studied, "beyond my calculation," as he wrote Teller, Slocum's "sheets of calculations for the lunar observations he had made single-handedly," a great feat "which is supposed to require three people to work out." He learned to hawk curios when the *Spray* docked at ports along Long Island and in Block Island Sound. President Roosevelt wrote a gracious letter of thanks when the adventure was over, and Slocum decided that he wanted Archie to have the *Liberdade*, wherever she might have been just then. He traveled sometime in late 1906 to Archie's boarding school, Groton, where he met the Reverend Endicott Peabody, the notoriously stiff headmaster. The president's son recollected that Peabody—no friend of a Great Clockmaker religion—bristled at the captain's ad hoc reply to an examination of his theological position. Nevertheless, Slocum was welcomed at the White House early in 1907.*

Now Slocum and the *Spray* were both running down. Archie remembered that the sloop was "the most incredibly dirty craft I have ever seen." Writing in the *Rudder* magazine in 1968, W. H. Smith reports without fondness that "Captain Slocum probably was the worst ship's husband I have encountered and I wasn't a bit surprised when the *Spray* went missing . . . about four years later . . . [Her] planking was in poor shape. No two planks appeared to be of the same shape, size, or thickness, or even of the same kind of wood . . . The shape she was in would give the horrors to anyone who went to sea."

Nonetheless, during the winter of 1907, the *Spray* took Slocum to lec-

---

*At this meeting he exchanged with the president an often quoted but to me mystifying bit of jocularity. Roosevelt said, "Captain, our adventures have been a little different." Slocum replied, "That is true, Mr. President, but I see you got here first." I confess not understanding where is "here."

ture in Miami, where an audience member judged him to be "a very capable man; and a lonely, unhappy man." Slocum then crossed to the Bahamas, where he visited a professional yacht captain from Martha's Vineyard and gave a talk at Nassau's Colonial Hotel, a black-tie event that earned him $460. Slocum and some of his audience adjourned to the grill—according to Ernest Dean, the yacht captain—where Slocum spun yarns and his companions became bawdy, "hilarious and liberal," in Dean's memory.

Along the waterfront in Nassau occurred the final known controversy of Slocum's life, and it was at once violent and mysterious. Dean encountered the captain on a sponge fishermen's dock, amid "four or five natives," one of them holding a cloth to his bloody mouth. Excited and angry, Slocum explained that he had been splicing rigging on the *Spray*'s deck when the men—"ginned up some"—began denigrating the sloop, and one of them said, "loud enough for anyone to hear, 'Any mon that says he sailed around the world in that thing is a goddom liar.' I looked up in time to see which one said it, made a pier head leap, and with a couple of side-winders, unshipped his jaw."

Slocum was not destined to end his days as a wharf rat. He dreamed of being the first through the Panama Canal, but was lost at sea seven years too early for that to have happened. Thomas Fleming Day, a young friend of his and the editor of the *Rudder*, later wrote a tribute:*

> Captain Slocum was what we may call an uncommon man. He was extremely intelligent, and in his love of roaming and adventure reminded me of the celebrated Moorish traveler, Ibn Batuta, who wandered from Cape Spartel to the Yellow Sea, making friends with white, black and yellow; always observing, making men and manners his study, and living by the gifts of those whose ears he riddled with his tales of travel and adventure. Slocum, like Batuta, was a friendmaker, and everywhere he went the best of the land welcomed him, bid him to the board, and gave attention, while in his inimitable way he spun yarns of his voyages . . . Even old ["Oom Paul"] Krüger handed him a cup of coffee. From port to port he voyaged everywhere welcomed and entertained, and it was not until he reached this country . . . that a welcome was refused and his efforts belittled and ridiculed. The American newspapers, when they deigned to notice his voyage, made fun of his boat and

*Thomas Fleming Day, "On Capt. Joshua Slocum," in *The Rudder Treasury: A Companion for Lovers of Small Boats*, edited by Tom Davin (Sheridan House, 2003).

himself, and several more than intimated the story of his single-handed world-circling voyage was a lie.

It was not until 1924, three years before Charles Lindbergh crossed the Atlantic alone to Paris, that Joshua Slocum was declared legally dead. In fact he was last seen alive sixteen years earlier, on November 14, 1908,* setting sail alone from Martha's Vineyard to explore Venezuela's Orinoco River and the headwaters of the Amazon, and then down that great river to the ocean. The exact circumstances of his death—the latitude and longitude, the day and time, the weather conditions—are not known. The nature of his end is manifest: lost at sea.

There are many ways to go missing at sea, alone at sixty-four on a small sailing vessel, and no end of speculation about what went wrong sometime after he embarked from Vineyard Haven. Heart attack or stroke can't be ruled out, or any other of the body's natural failures. A broken hip, even a broken leg, can kill a solo sailor. Pissing into the sea from a heeling deck is a commonplace vulnerability of sailors, especially when groggy at night.

Listing only those misadventures we know him to have endured during his half century as a seaman and master mariner, he might have been broached or pooped or pitch-poled by a freak wave, swept overboard by a breaking sea, driven aground off Cape Hatteras or Cape Fear. Perhaps he was dismasted by a winter gale. The *Spray*'s tired planks might have sprung a leak so extreme that it sent him to the bottom. He might have struck a submerged log, or a whale might have stove him in. His worst fear at sea was to be struck by lightning or holed by a swordfish. We can safely discount the possibility that he was murdered by mutineers, and falling prey to pirates is improbable. A favorite theory has him run down and sunk in the shipping lanes, perhaps shrouded in fog, by one of the loathed steamships that put paid to his final years as a merchant seaman.

This speculation—that he was crushed by an iron hull, maybe as an untrustworthy lookout dozed on duty, that in effect he was murdered

---

*Probably because Slocum was declared dead as of 1909 by Martha's Vineyard's Dukes County Court, Walter Teller assumed that 1909 was the last date on which he was seen alive. In fact, further research by Ann Spencer, for her biography *Alone at Sea*, persuasively argues that Slocum was last seen departing from Martha's Vineyard in November 1908. Teller, fastidious as he was about dates, seems to have become a prisoner of what he believed he knew, and in his notes and files, as well as his books, he systematically altered the date of recorded recollections of last sightings from 1908 to 1909.

by modernity—is seductive for its poetic justice. This in turn is attractive for its congruence with Joshua Slocum's poetic sensibility, his art and achievement as a writer.

I want Thomas Fleming Day, his fellow sailor, to have the final words of this memorial:

> Slocum's story is a remarkable one; I do not mean as the story of a voyage but as a piece of writing. It is absolutely devoid of any disfigurements betraying effort, and flows from page to page like a wind-favored tide. It is worthy to be placed beside any narrative writing in our language . . . Posterity will give this book a place, and your great-grandchildren will be advised to read Slocum's Voyage, as a specimen of clean, pure narrative . . . Peace to Captain Slocum wherever he may sleep, for he deserves at least one whispered tribute of prayer from every sailorman for what he did to rob the sea of its bad name; and for such a man, who loved every cranny of her dear old blue heart, who for years made her windswept stretches his home and highway, what is more fitting than an ocean burial?

ACKNOWLEDGMENTS

Stowing aboard Captain Slocum's vessels, sharing at a distance his adventures and mischances, has been one of my happier experiences. I was encouraged in this enterprise by Binky Urban and Sonny Mehta. Gary Fisketjon did everything within his considerable power to make what I wrote coherent, uncluttered, and obedient to logic. He is an inspired untangler of knots and, man alive, do I thank him! My brother, as acknowledged elsewhere, was reading Joshua Slocum while I was writing about him, and our conversations—sparked by Toby's ungovernable curiosity, his eagerness to be astounded by audacity—spurred me at a crucial moment to finish my story and share it. My friends Maile Meloy and Ian Maxtone-Graham took my early pages literally to sea with them, and it was stimulating to get them back salt-stained and bleached by sun, rich with questions and demands.

Walter Teller's *Search for Captain Slocum*—written during the early 1950s long before the Internet, search engines, online newspaper archives, and e-mail—was an exhaustive undertaking. Imagine trying to collect accurate shipping records from Hong Kong, Manila, the Okhotsk Sea, Sydney, Cape Town, Punta Arenas, and so on. He did heroic work, notable for its liberal goodwill and common sense. Teller's extensive collection of papers—correspondence, notes, clippings, and photos—are in the care of the New Bedford Whaling Museum, who kindly permitted me access to their treasures, through which Laura Pereira patiently guided me.

The National Library of Australia, in Sydney, provided me with the privately printed pamphlet supplied by Slocum to support his version of the mutinies aboard the *Northern Light*. I am grateful as well to Jennifer Pearce and Joel Slocum for help and encouragement. Adrian Studer shot (in color) the photograph I've used of the *Ambassador*, stranded in the Strait of Magellan; looking at is has made vivid how terrifying was Slocum's passage through those waters.

A generous fellowship at the American Academy in Berlin gave me the luxury of colleagues with whom to discuss the perils and achievements of Captain Slocum, as well as time to write.

My wife, Priscilla, as again and again, listened and read and read and listened.

BIBLIOGRAPHY OF SOURCES CITED

In addition to books and essays specified below, I have made use of daily journalism from New York, Boston, San Francisco, Sydney, Cape Town, and elsewhere, identified within the body of the text. This list usually cites the latest available editions, a few of which may have slightly altered titles.

Apollonio, Spencer, ed. *The Last of the Cape Horners: Firsthand Accounts from the Final Days of the Commercial Tall Ships.* Brassey's, 2000.

Bunting, W. H. *Live Yankees: The Sewalls and Their Ships.* Tilbury House, 2009.

Catton, Bruce. "Mariner's Quest." *American Heritage* 10, no. 3 (1959).

Chatwin, Bruce. *In Patagonia.* Summit, 1977.

Chichester, Francis. *Along the Clipper Way.* Coward McCann, 1967.

———. *"Gipsy Moth" Circles the World.* Coward-McCann, 1968.

Conrad, Joseph. *The Mirror of the Sea* and *A Personal Record.* Oxford University Press, USA, 1999.

Crane, Stephen. *The Open Boat and Other Stories.* William Heinemann, 1898.

Dana, Richard Henry, Jr. *Richard Henry Dana Jr.: Two Years Before the Mast and Other Voyages.* Library of America, 2005.

Darwin, Charles. *The Voyage of the "Beagle."* Modern Library, 2001.

Domville-Fife, Charles W. *Square-Rigger Days: Autobiographies of Sail.* Pen and Sword Books Naval Institute Press, 2007.

Druett, Joan. *Hen Frigates: Passion and Peril, Nineteenth-Century Women at Sea.* Touchstone, 1999.

Foulke, Robert D. "Life in the Dying World of Sail, 1870–1910." *The Journal of British Studies* 3, no. 1 (1963): 105–36.

Guzzwell, John, Joshua Slocum, and Vito Dumas. *Great Voyages in Small Boats: Solo Circumnavigations.* J. De Graff, 1976.

Holm, Donald. *The Circumnavigators.* Prentice-Hall, 1974.

Hugo, David T. "Nova Scotia to Martha's Vineyard: Notes on Captain Joshua Slocum." *The Dukes County Intelligencer* 11, no. 1 (1969).

Johnson, Clifton. "Captain Joshua Slocum: The Man Who Sailed Alone Around the World in a Thirty-seven-Foot Boat." In *Tales of Old New England,* edited by Frank Oppel. Castle, 1987.

Kemp, Peter, and Richard Ormond. *The Great Age of Sail: Treasures from the National Maritime Museum.* San Diego Museum of Art, 1992.

Kent, Rockwell. *Voyaging: Southward from the Strait of Magellan.* Wesleyan University Press, 2000.

Lopes, Myra A. *Captain Joshua Slocum: A Centennial Tribute.* RPI, 1994.

Melville, Herman. *Typee, Omoo, Mardi.* Library of America, 1982.

———. *Redburn, White-Jacket, Moby-Dick.* Library of America, 1983.

Moitessier, Bernard. *The Long Way.* Sheridan House, 2003.

Morison, Samuel Eliot. *The Maritime History of Massachusetts, 1783–1860.* Northeastern University Press, 1961.

Robinson, John, and George Francis Dow. *Sailing Ships of New England: 1607–1907.* Skyhorse Publishing, 2007.

Rowe, William Hutchinson. *The Maritime History of Maine: Three Centuries of Shipbuilding and Seafaring.* W. W. Norton, 1948.

Slack, Kenneth E. *In the Wake of the "Spray."* Rutgers University Press, 1966.

Slocum, Joshua. "The Voyage of the *Aquidneck.*" *Outing.* November 1902.

———. *The Voyages of Joshua Slocum.* Anniversary ed., edited by Walter Magnes Teller. Sheridan House, 1995.

———. *Sailing Alone Around the World* and *The Voyage of the "Liberdade."* Edited by Anthony Brandt. National Geographic, 2004.

Slocum, Joshua. *The Annotated "Sailing Alone Around the World."* Annotated by Rod Scher. Sheridan House, 2009.

Slocum, Victor. "The Fishermen of Gloucester." In *Tales of Old New England,* edited by Frank Oppel. Castle, 1987.

———. *Capt. Joshua Slocum: The Adventures of America's Best Known Sailor.* Sheridan House, 1993.

———. *Castaway Boats.* Sheridan House, 2001.

Snow, Edward Rowe, and Jeremy D'Entremont. *Women of the Sea.* Snow centennial ed. Commonwealth Editions, 2004.

Spectre, Peter H. "A Postcard in Time." *Maine Boats, Homes & Harbors.* February/March 2009.

Spencer, Ann. *Alone at Sea: The Adventures of Joshua Slocum.* Firefly Books, 1999.

Teller, Walter Magnes. *The Search for Captain Slocum: A Biography.* Charles Scribner's Sons, 1956.

———. *Joshua Slocum.* Rutgers University Press, 1971.

Teller, Walter, ed. *Five Sea Captains. Amasa Delano, Edmund Fanning, Richard Cleveland, George Coggeshall, Joshua Slocum. Their Own Accounts of Voyages Under Sail.* Atheneum, 1960.

U.S. Hydrographic Office, Bureau of Navigation. *The West Coast of South America, Including: Magellan Strait, Tierra Del Fuego and the Outlying Islands.* 2nd ed. Government Printing Office, 1896.

Villiers, Alan. *The Way of a Ship.* Charles Scribner's Sons, 1970.

Wilson, Derek. *The Circumnavigators: A History.* Carroll & Graf, 2004.

Wilson, H. W. *Ironclads in Action: A Sketch of Naval Warfare from 1855 to 1895, with Some Account of the Development of the Battleship in England.* Little, Brown and Company, 1896.

frontispiece: Courtesy of the New Bedford Whaling Museum
x (top): Courtesy of the New Bedford Whaling Museum
x (bottom): Courtesy of Sheridan House
2: Courtesy of Adrian Studer
6: Courtesy of Sheridan House
14 (top): Courtesy of the Maine Maritime Museum
14 (bottom): Courtesy of the Maine Maritime Museum
32: Courtesy of the New Bedford Whaling Museum
46: public domain
60 (top): Courtesy of Sheridan House
60 (bottom): Courtesy of Sheridan House
76: Courtesy of the Library of Congress
86: Courtesy of the New Bedford Whaling Museum
112: Courtesy of Sheridan House
127: Courtesy of the New Bedford Whaling Museum
128 (top): Courtesy of Sheridan House
128 (bottom): Courtesy of the New Bedford Whaling Museum
130 (top): Courtesy of the New Bedford Whaling Museum
130 (bottom): Courtesy of the New Bedford Whaling Museum
142 (top): Courtesy of Sheridan House
142 (bottom): Courtesy of the New Bedford Whaling Museum
156: Courtesy of the New Bedford Whaling Museum
192: Courtesy of the New Bedford Whaling Museum

A NOTE ABOUT THE AUTHOR

Geoffrey Wolff is the author of five works of nonfiction and six novels. In 1994 he received the Award in Literature from the American Academy of Arts and Letters. He lives in Bath, Maine.

A NOTE ON THE TYPE

This book was set in Monotype Dante, a typeface designed by Giovanni Mardersteig (1892–1977). Modeled on the Aldine type used for Pietro Cardinal Bembo's treatise *De Aetna* in 1495, Dante is a modern interpretation of the venerable face.

Composed by North Market Street Graphics
Lancaster, Pennsylvania

Printed and bound by Berryville Graphics
Berryville, Virginia

Designed by M. Kristen Bearse